My Medical-Legal Back Pages

A Physician's Journey Through a Marital,
Medical and Legal Maelstrom

Bryce Sterling

ARCHWAY
PUBLISHING

Archway Publishing books may be ordered through booksellers or by contacting:

Archway Publishing
1663 Liberty Drive
Bloomington, IN 47403
www.archwaypublishing.com
1 (888) 242-5904

Because of the dynamic nature of the Internet, any web addresses or links contained in this book may have changed since publication and may no longer be valid. The views expressed in this work are solely those of the author and do not necessarily reflect the views of the publisher, and the publisher hereby disclaims any responsibility for them.

Any people depicted in stock imagery provided by Getty Images are models, and such images are being used for illustrative purposes only. Certain stock imagery © Getty Images.

ISBN: 978-1-4808-5975-3 (sc)
ISBN: 978-1-4808-5976-0 (e)

Library of Congress Control Number: 2018902243

Print information available on the last page.

Archway Publishing rev. date: 03/06/2018

My Back Pages

There is no other way to say it. This is not a nice book. It is mostly about lawyers and doctors. Few people on this earth despise lawyers as much as I, admittedly a washed-up and disgruntled former orthopedic surgeon. Based on my experiences, I can confidently state that in my opinion, members of the legal profession are *rarely* being held accountable to any standard of professional competence, ethics, or truthfulness, either publicly or by their peer organizations.

Admittedly, a growing segment of the population hates doctors too. Indeed, I too have almost as much scorn for my some of my colleagues as I do for members of the legal profession. Part of the public's hatred for doctors is justified but also misplaced, as doctors have become subservient to ever-increasing bureaucratic and medical corporate control. Health-care costs are going through the roof. Doctors are constantly reminded of how many people die as a result of medical mistakes each year. Equally concerning but seldom mentioned are the number of patients who survive from medical mishaps, only to have to suffer physically and emotionally for the rest of their lives.

Lawyers don't cause direct physical injury or death but certainly can inflict life-long emotional and financial distress. For over twenty-five years, I have held off chronicling the events in my medical career: medical school, residency, marriage, divorce, lawyers, judges, doctors, medical boards, psychiatrists, psychologists, accountants, hospital administrators, medical recruiters, malpractice-insurance carriers. I have dealt with them all.

My stormy, twenty-nine-year orthopedic career has ended, and I am living in a single-bedroom apartment at the other end of a large state while I struggle to see what forced retirement from my former medical profession offers. I have managed to hold on to my state license for now. I had held a tenuous position providing wound care to scattered nursing home facilities until recently when I was terminated without cause.

I would like to be practicing orthopedics, but now realize my medical career has ended. I notified my former professional organization, the American Academy of Orthopedic Surgeons (AAOS), that I had to terminate my membership due to inability to continue practicing orthopedics—too much malpractice and history of licensure suspension. They emailed back asking if I would consider becoming an emeritus member. I said no. Continued contact with my former profession only causes the emotional wounds to fester.

With my orthopedic and medical career ended once and for all, it's time to tell my story. The events are not late; they are not outdated. My story is simply now complete. *My Back Pages* is a song written by Bob Dylan from the '60s and is best performed by Roger McGuinn of the band called The Byrds. I am not trying to unravel any meaning to the words of the song. I just really like the song, and the title was perfect. No dedicated research has been done for this book. It is based on my memory, observations, and opinions, some of which will invariably be disputed or "clarified" by legal "experts." I have no legal training. Several acquaintances, including a hospital administrator, an accountant, a physician, and two lawyers have even suggested I write this book.

No incident, conversation, or quote has been created for embellishment, only those I clearly remember. Other comments I have qualified as hearsay, opinion, or suspicion. I still have all the depositions, video recordings, financial records, appraisals, licensure-board actions, court rulings, and hospital records. It is a massive archive. The notable exception will be the absence of any documentation of my divorce attorneys' work product as far as the necessary, thorough property settlement calculations they claimed to have prepared for trial. They were unable, unwilling, or claimed exemption because of the attorney-client work-product rule to produce any hard answers to my accusations. They were able to rely on the legal system to give them a pass.

I had initially intended to write this book as nonfiction, using the real names and locations, but the publisher advised no, even though the truth, well-documented, and much of it already public knowledge through the press, media, court records, and the medical National Practitioner Data Bank (NPDB), should afford an absolute defense against any claims of libel, except, of course, when it is against attorneys. Only the elusive work-product exception mentioned above might theoretically apply.

I have learned not to expect any sympathy from the public or readers. Quite the contrary, a lot of people are quick to call me a malcontent, a brooder, one who refuses to look in the mirror to see the cause of my problems, refuses to accept responsibility for my acts, and is even a conspiracy nut. Maybe so. I have tried to include some seemingly irrelevant personal history to get a more balanced view of where I am coming from, not all of it good, and why my opinions are as they are. Indeed, a lot of my opinions are quite blunt, and I have spared no one, neither lawyers or doctors, in my attempts to objectively relate these events, but as I like to say, "The facts speak for themselves." If you like it in legalese, *res ipsa loquitur*.

The Legal System in Medicine vs. Law

The legal system has been set up so that when a lawsuit (complaint) is filed against a physician, he is presumed to have committed malpractice until proven otherwise. In contrast, trying to sue a lawyer for legal malpractice is a null hypothesis. If there are no standards for legal practice, then a charge of legal malpractice cannot exist. Before you read further or, worse, are actually faced with a situation where you have to retain a lawyer, remember: lawyers for all practical purposes are held to no standards of legal representation, knowledge of case law, statutes, or even local rules of their court. You are completely at their mercy.

You may talk to friends who say your lawyer is good, but you cannot ever rely on that recommendation. My attorneys were supposed to be good, but clearly, they were not when it came time for them to represent me. I encountered a continuous stream of legal malpractice, incompetence, and deception, lawyer after lawyer, and it was not that I just have bad karma. One-half of readers will go through or have been through a divorce, so this is not some peripheral subject.

The legal profession has insulated themselves from any standard of legal care (i.e., representation of their clients, in contrast to the long-established medical standard of care,) to which they subject the medical profession. Lawyers seldom get sued and rarely disciplined by their professional society for blatant substandard legal representation, and I think maybe in only one or two states—at least it was that way twenty years ago—can the public actually attend state-bar disciplinary hearings. Even the state newspaper wrote an article on June 25, 1994, about the problem of lawyers not being disciplined and their misdeeds being hidden from public view.

The lawyers' acts are casually dismissed with the time-worn observation that "you just didn't have a good lawyer." Rarely can a wronged client even get another attorney to pursue an action against another attorney and certainly not on a contingency basis whereby the client pays his lawyer by sharing a percentage of the award only if the attorney wins his case, in contrast to the medical-malpractice custom. A few lawyers may be all too willing to take your money up front as they file a legal malpractice suit. But eventually, they will drop you when it gets down to crunch time. It happened to me.

Legal malpractice in my mind includes not just negligence but a violation of ethical standards. However, ethical standards in the practice of law are very elusive because there is an operative level of lying, misrepresentation, and fraudulent billing allowed. The public has little recourse. There is no public forum to effectively address these issues, and so the problem persists. Lawyers carry on with their careers, protected from any public exposure of legal incompetence, ignorance, malfeasance, or fraud.

If you have to deal with a lawyer, there are good chances that you could be dealing with a borderline sociopath: one who has no concerns about you as a person or your feelings, one who cannot empathize. They have no concerns that they are stealing from you, lying to you, or looking after their own financial interests first and foremost. I am convinced that law school even goes so far as to desensitize lawyers from feeling any concern about collecting their fees before addressing their clients' concerns.

More ominously, I suspect certain people go into law simply because they have no real sense of purpose in life. They have nothing productive or value added to offer. One-half of graduating lawyers never practice law, a

Bryce Sterling

continuation of the pattern of not really knowing what they want to do, and many wind up in politics—not doctors, engineers, farmers or useful members of society. It is society that winds up supporting these lawyers who are higher up what I call the "parasitic pyramid," whose base is comprised of masses of illegal immigrants or those who abuse social security, student loans, or other government handouts.

Of course, there is bank fraud, military industrial complex, education system, and other forms of corporate welfare at the apex. Lawyers fall somewhere in between unless they climb the ladder to become prominent politicians. Those politicians who wind up in the upper echelons of power in Washington, DC, the "K Street clan" as I like to call them, have arrived not necessarily because of merit, but because they can be controlled.

My cynical theory is lawyers who have little true direction in life are more easily compromised and, therefore, more easily controlled. I certainly cannot prove it, but I suspect that control in Washington, DC, requires more than just petty corruption, bribery, or traditional forms of blackmail. It requires something much darker: pedophilia, but much more horrific than Bill Clinton's "Lolita Express" flights to Epstein's private underage sex island, Anthony Weiner's sexting, or House Speaker Hastert's sexual misconduct. This drama is still unfolding.

When a client approaches an attorney, the first thing that goes through an attorney's mind is "How much money can I make from this case?" In contrast, I would like to think that when a doctor sees a patient, he might first think, "Oh my God, this guy has a really badly broken ankle," and think about whether and how it can be fixed before looking at the dollar signs.

During my entire orthopedic career, I never paid attention to or knew how much I received for a procedure, office visit, or follow-up. Part of this ignorance admittedly was due to the confusing billing requirements and reimbursement rates offered by insurance companies, Medicare, Medicaid, and so on, but as long as I was making a good living, I didn't think about it, especially when starting out in practice. I often was unaware of who would be able to pay and who would not, especially if I saw the patient in the emergency room. Doctors did not advertise our services in formalized terms as pro bono work like lawyers. We just saw the patients and quietly rendered care with no fanfare. Admittedly, some specialties like dermatology or ophthalmology might look at patients as numbers: "How many cataracts or skin biopsies do I have lined up today?" and crunch the numbers. One wound care doctor kept a running total, both daily and year to date, of his billings and compensation as he made rounds.

Medical-malpractice defense attorneys fall into a different category. They are paid by the hour by the medical-malpractice insurance company. The med-mal insurance companies employ defense attorneys with good track records, meaning those who successfully defend malpractice cases at trial or who negotiate less costly settlements. Don't ever let a medical-malpractice defense attorney give you the impression that he doesn't like this system of medical-malpractice lawsuits (torts). Defense lawyers have a huge financial interest in perpetuating the status quo.

Once you settle a case, it is even more difficult to seek redress of your attorney's incompetence, malpractice, fraudulent billing, or insufficient preparation for trial. By convincing you to settle, your lawyers are off the hook. Attorneys and the courts constantly propound the benefits of settling cases as opposed to trial. They rely on the oh-so-convenient argument that the courts (judges), much less a jury, are totally unpredictable, and therefore, you should always try to settle a case.

The reality is, lawyers can rip you off sufficiently in pretrial preparation by billing you for undocumented ghost hours, such as preparation for trial and review of the file. They don't have to rely solely on documentable hours they actually spend in court, taking depositions, or trying a case. Attorneys may intentionally *not* charge you blended rates but instead bill you full freight for work done by their secretary or paralegal at a fraction of the cost.

The same goes on in medicine, to be fair. Patients understandably get upset when a doctor bills for a full doctor rate when the patient was not seen by the doctor, but rather by a nurse.

Some attorneys charge increased rates if they have to appear at trial. That is confirmation, indeed, that at trial, a lawyer suddenly has to earn his keep. On the basis of this statement, I would have to admit that plaintiff trial attorneys are the lions of the legal profession. They have to be ready to try a case and win if they are to get paid. If they lose the case, they lose all the time and money spent on trial preparation, paying expert witnesses, court costs, and so on.

However, if they develop a reputation as a formidable plaintiff's attorney, then a defendant may be more inclined to settle. The next case may then become an easier kill for the plaintiff trial attorney.

But again, to earn that reputation, a trial attorney has had to first prove himself or be lucky and have a hell of a can't-lose case. If the latter, the injured party shouldn't be having to fork over such a large share of the contingency fee (33 percent is the usual minimum) in the first place. I guess I should also mention that a similar argument can be made for a good defense lawyer who gets a reputation for putting up a staunch defense. A plaintiff may be more likely to settle.

I suspect a lot of nuisance medical-malpractice lawsuits are filed by inexperienced attorneys out of the yellow pages. In contrast to the lay public's impression that lawyers are eager to file a lawsuit at the drop of a hat, after seeing what a hassle it can be and a money loser, attorneys think twice about filing their second frivolous lawsuit. The first thing my medical-malpractice defense attorneys focused upon was whether a plaintiff's attorney was from a seasoned firm who had a history of taking only medical-malpractice cases that they were very confident of receiving a substantial return.

Typically, a plaintiff's lawyer will review a case, referring it to a nurse or doctor to see if it has any merit. If it does, he will typically take the case on contingency, meaning his client, the injured patient, pays nothing if the lawyer loses the case. If the lawyer wins, then the lawyer is usually guaranteed a minimum of 33 percent of the award. Sometimes, in more complex cases, additional fees will be negotiated and the attorney may get 40 percent or even more, especially if the case goes to trial, where the attorney actually has to demonstrate his legal prowess.

Just because a jury verdict comes in at $5 million in favor of the plaintiff doesn't mean that it's a done deal. There is a chance the award may be overturned or reduced on appeal. The parties may then renegotiate the judgment amount. Sometimes this appeal may be argued on the basis of a court instruction error and remanded (sent back) for retrial. Sometimes it is not a reversible error, meaning that the result would have been the same and, therefore, the case decision still stands.

Based on my layman's observations, there seems to be a strategy by some lawyers to string along a lot of cases hoping that a few will eventually settle. I saw this when I was in a courtroom on a pretrial hearing in front of the judge who was to rule on my medical license suspension appeal. The lady sitting next to me was finally called up in front of the judge with the opposing counsel, a fat, old, ruddy-nosed, alcoholic-looking lawyer way past his prime. The defendant was an amusement park. After about twenty minutes of back-and-forth in subdued conversation, the female attorney final blurted out in exasperation, "No, Your Honor, he is asking for a continuance (postponement). I am asking for dismissal."

When she sat back down next to me, I kidded her. "What's wrong, some guy slip on a banana peel and wants to sue?"

"Worse," she said. "The roller coaster got stuck at the top of the tracks at the amusement park, and the riders are now suing for emotional distress." Apparently, these thrill seekers had to be evacuated down the steps. We didn't discuss the particulars further, but it appeared to me that this guy had no intention of ever trying the case but was just holding on to see if anything would fall out of the tree. He appeared to me to be employing a variation of the well-known strategy of suing everyone in a single case (called *shaking the tree*) in anticipation of someone finally agreeing to settle, but instead, he may have filed many such lawsuits anticipating that a sufficient number would settle to keep other cases financed. Sue everyone, stall, and see if anyone steps forward to settle rather than deal with the time, hassle, and expense of continued litigation.

Lawyers will also want to know in which jurisdiction (court, city, state, county, etc.) a case is filed and who the judge is. Class action lawsuits have had a strange habit of winding up in some unusual plaintiff-friendly jurisdictions in the past. In my last malpractice case in 2016, my insurance company settled the case without even informing me. My attorney informed me only after the fact that nearly $500,000 had suddenly been paid out. At first thought, one might assume, "Wow! That doctor really must have really screwed up for the insurance company to pay up like that on the spot."

But my particular case was to be adjudicated by a female judge in a small town in the Deep South. She already had a reputation as a *very* plaintiff-friendly judge. Her husband was a plaintiff's attorney. She was black; my patient was female and black. I was a white, male orthopedic surgeon. My contract with the hospital had ended because of declining volume. I was a lame-duck surgeon leaving town. There was no jury. It was a bench trial, meaning the judge alone makes the decision of liability and award. The plaintiff's attorney had expended a disproportionate time on my deposition cataloging my malpractice history and licensure board suspension for this judge to give the impression that I was a terrible doctor, but not so much on the particulars of the case other than her client lost her leg. Now, what kind of justice was I going to get?

The case involved intramedullary nailing of a broken tibia (leg) in a forty-nine-year-old female with some mild diabetes who fell while intoxicated. It was a procedure I had done for decades. Two months later, it got infected and eventually required amputation. More on that case later. I'll just note that I never had the chance to review the reports from my expert or the plaintiff's expert. My attorney never provided me with these or the sum and substance of those opinions.

Many lawyers can't handle a trial. It is like having a nonoperative internist suddenly having to perform surgery. Actually, an internist could not advertise himself as a surgeon since medicine has well-delineated specialties and sub-specialties. Attorneys do not. Their term is "concentration or focus in a particular area of law." Your attorney may make it sound like he or she is ready for trial and has all the tools to vigorously and zealously represent your interests, but in reality, that may be pure baloney.

Some lawyers settle cases that clearly should be tried, and I can assure you the legal community is quite aware of attorneys who are afraid to try cases. These "chicken-hawk" (chickens when facing a court room, hawks when they pounce on their hapless clients) attorneys are the ones who depend on selling their clients the unpredictability of the courts to influence them to settle cases when they should be tried. I am not even talking about a trial in front of a jury, which can be fickle or swayed by the emotional tugging of heartstrings. I am talking about a divorce case where there is no jury, only a judge or commissioner. No courtroom theatrics to sway a jury. The courts love it too when an attorney can convince his client to settle. Anything to avoid having to hear a case. It is therefore a self-reinforcing process. A lawyer who persuades his client to settle a case, even if clearly a terrible and costly recommendation, is encouraged and protected by the system.

In my divorce case, I strongly suspect my ex-wife Mindy's attorney would have made inquiries about my attorney's style and learned that she (Elaine Skyler) would almost never try a case. He could therefore shop around and "pay" an expert who would be willing to wildly inflate the value of the marital estate for Mindy's benefit. He would never be challenged if the case did not go to trial. Indeed, Skyler constantly reminded me how distinguished, knowledgeable, and eloquent Mindy's hired gun expert was, but turned right around and undermined our own expert retained by my first attorney Nathan Salazar. In retrospect, Skyler never had any intention of trying my case if she could help it.

When I complained about her handling of my divorce and intimated a lawsuit, Skyler suddenly represented herself more aggressively and in a more threatening manner than she had ever done for me: "But be aware, Bryce. We will avail ourselves of any and all measures to protect the reputation of this firm." Her first act in my lawsuit against her for legal malpractice was a motion to seal the case from the public eyes.

In contrast, she never moved to have my divorce case sealed. The state's largest newspaper had no qualms about going through mine and nine other doctors' divorce court records in various courts throughout the state, printing our pictures and stating our incomes in an article about (greedy) doctors, implying they were part of the reason for the state-Medicaid-funding shortfall in the early nineties.

Courts also promote the narrative that cases should always be settled whenever possible. Baloney. That's because judges have busy dockets, and a case that is settled is a case that is done. They may even bully an attorney who has a very strong case into settling just because the judge doesn't want to hear it.

At trial, attorneys are on record, just as a doctor is on record every time he enters something on a patient's chart. Lawyers will sometimes deceive their clients, if necessary, into a settlement if they are not prepared for trial. Your attorney may be looking after his or her interests, not your interests, when he or she recommends a settlement. The attorney may be trying to hide their lack of preparation, knowledge, or ability to try your case. If you go back and try to find any work product or preparation for trial, guess what? There may be very little.

The message from the courts and time-honored "sage" legal counsel, therefore, may be to settle a case whenever possible, but my experience was quite the opposite: *never settle*. Once you settle, you effectively waive whatever few rights you may have to contest your lawyer's legal malpractice, incompetence, fraudulent billing, or court errors through appeals. All the records of pretrial discovery, court motions, rulings, are legally extinguished—as if they'd never existed. You cannot go back and get a trial.

An attorney who bills you for ghost hours—work that was never performed is committing fraud. But once you settle, you can never go back and prove your attorney did not prepare for your case. The case gets thrown out on summary judgment in favor of the defendant lawyer.

In contrast, in medicine, if the doctor gets sued and has no charted record or documented justification for his treatment or recommendations, he is automatically presumed guilty of medical malpractice. *If you didn't document it, you didn't do it.*

Medical-Malpractice Actions vs. Divorce Actions

I would imagine medical-malpractice cases are more likely to be appealed than divorces—because they can. Commonly, an instructional error to the jury committed by the judge, for example improperly allowing testimony or evidence, may be a reversible error, meaning the case can go back for retrial with new court instructions to the jury.

Sometimes, rather than going through an appeals process, the parties, seeing the writing on the wall as a result of the jury reaction during trial, may settle a case in the middle of the trial during a recess. Sometimes cases get settled during appeals, after a verdict and judgment have already been reached in the (originating) trial court. Sometimes the parties enter into a pretrial high-low agreement whereby the plaintiff and defendant agree on a range of the verdict, all the way from an acquittal, whereby the plaintiff would get nothing, to a catastrophically high award far exceeding even the plaintiff's expectations. In such a high-low arrangement, the defendant may agree to pay a minimum award to the plaintiff, even if the jury finds in favor of the defendant doctor. The plaintiff is thus guaranteed to recover some or all of his costs. Similarly, in the event of a catastrophically high award, the doctor is protected from a ruinous verdict that far exceeds his malpractice limits.

In a divorce, it's a completely different story simply because courts just don't like to retry divorce cases or waste time trying to reverse a decision or remand (send) it back to trial. It is usually not within the appeals court's discretion to question or disturb any expert's opinion or appraisal that was adopted by the trial court.

Courts' reluctance to relitigate domestic relations cases occurs even when statutes may have been clearly ignored. Technically, in situations where appeals courts determine the trial court clearly made a mistake by not adhering to the statutes, the trial court is concluded to have abused its discretion, but that is a very high standard to prove as a basis for an appeal in a divorce case. This laxity in courts' enforcement of dissolution of marriage (divorce) statutes is great cover for divorce attorneys. They can simply blame the courts for anything.

Except in cases where the parties don't have a pot to piss in where the attorneys often advertise a pre-negotiated rate for a simple uncontested divorce, most attorneys will ask for payment up front (a retainer fee), bill by the hour, or both. Some may be honest about their billings. Others are not. Either way, the old saying in divorces is that both parties (husband and wife) think that they are going to split the marital pot (estate) into two pots. There are two pots all right, but one is shared between the ex-husband and ex-wife, and the other belongs exclusively to the attorneys.

I learned early through personal experience the irrelevance of the legal system through its random, capricious, and arbitrary adjudication. Starting from the lowly small-town divorce court, the sewer line backs up all the way through the legal system to the US Department of Justice and the Supreme Court of the United States. In most cases, the laws may seem to work—except when they don't. My first divorce attorney, Salazar, told me at the start of my divorce, "It takes time for the process to work, but it eventually works." No, it does not work. Not for some.

As part of informed consent, I always told my patients there was a 1–3 percent chance your total hip will dislocate after surgery. If you are the lucky 97 percent like mine where it did not, great. But if you are the 1–3 percent where it did, then for you, the rate is 100 percent.

The problem is, you don't know if the legal system is going to work for you. You don't know if the statutes will be applied and adhered to. If there is a certain rate or incidence of failure in a system, then there comes a point you cannot rely on it. If I know the retractable landing gear in the airplane I fly is going to deploy only 90 percent of the time during landing, I cannot fly that airplane. I need it to work 99.99 percent of the time.

The judicial-legal professional rot goes right to the top. So far it appears that the Clintons will not get indicted, nor will other high-profile government figures: former FBI director James Comey, Democratic National Committee's Debbie Wasserman Shultz, NSA director Susan Rice, US Attorney General Loretta Lynch, Department of Justice (DOJ) Eric Holder ("Fast and Furious"), Lois Lerner (IRS tea party intimidation.) Banking executives who are involved in massive banking fraud get off scot-free while the shareholders pay the fines. Rigging of the precious metals markets, London Interbank Overnight Rate (LIBOR), "robo-signing" of home mortgages, securities fraud, drug money laundering by HSBC bank and various other blatant crimes are barely investigated. No one even gets indicted. These are treated as simply matters, not investigations.

By the federal DOJ guidelines, if a crime may have been committed, the DOJ is required to authorize an investigation by the authorities such as the FBI. The FBI then investigates and reports its findings to the DOJ. The FBI can't take it upon itself to decide not to investigate. The DOJ can't dodge its obligation to investigate a crime, for example, banking fraud, because doing so would destabilize the banking system. Quite incredibly, when asked whose opinions (that DOJ prosecution would destabilize the banking system) the DOJ relied upon when it decided *not* to prosecute bank fraud, it was those very same criminal banks' opinions. These criminal banking elements essentially told FBI and the DOJ, "Don't prosecute us, because it will destabilize the banking system."

There are opinions by the Supreme Court, like Obamacare, that stretch the interpretation of the Constitution to the limit by redefining an unconstitutional requirement that a party purchase something like health insurance as a tax (even the proponents of Obamacare hadn't made the tax argument as I recall). Rulings are determined not by mainstream adjudication but rather through fringe opinions. There are flagrant violations, for example, when the US Court of Appeals overturned Trump's executive order temporarily banning immigration from select high-risk terrorist countries. Whether or not you agree with Trump's order, it was *clearly* within his constitutional authority.

Divorce lawyers are the bottom feeders of the legal profession. In my opinion, they have less expertise than lawyers in other fields of law. Courts are especially interested in disposing of the domestic relations cases as quickly as possible. These cases are the dregs of the civil legal docket. The knowledge requirement/complexity is probably the least of any area of law.

After reviewing my case, applicable statutes, case law, talking to various attorneys, doing research in the state university law library, and so on, I felt I had a better command of domestic relations law than the judge, commissioner, or my attorneys. Am I so smart or a lawyer wannabe? No. It is that based on my experiences, too many lawyers are outright incompetent, assuming they are not already dishonest or sociopathic. Certainly, the standards for getting accepted to many law schools (obviously we are not talking Yale or Harvard here) are far below those for getting into medical school. But then again as a disclaimer, I have only dealt with divorce, medical-malpractice lawyers, and, oh yeah, a little shit lawyer on the state medical board. Maybe my sampling pool of lawyers is skewed.

After talking to a prominent law firm about my divorce attorney's handling of my case, the attorney asked half kiddingly if I wanted to work for his firm. He recognized that I had zeroed in on the issues of my attorneys' negligence. When I talked to another attorney of a big legal firm in the state about suing my divorce attorneys, it took her thirty minutes on the phone before she realized I was a doctor, not an attorney.

Ordinarily, if I talked to someone for more than five minutes about my specialty, I could recognize that person was not in the medical profession. This attorney finally informed me that the decision to sue another lawyer would first have to be passed through the other partners of her firm. This was, in my opinion, a polite way of saying that her firm was not going to let members of the lay public breach the attorney inner circle.

Domestic relations in law is like medical oncology (cancer). The patient ultimately dies. Many doctors don't want to deal with it. The same goes for divorce law. Many divorce cases are fit for Jerry Springer shows. Instead of listening to the case, the commissioners or judges are looking at their watches to see when they can leave. They have seen them all. It is the criminal defense law equivalent of cleaning the stables: representing low life career street criminals. Courts are granted such wide discretion in their rulings in divorce law—wider, I think, than in any other area of law—that it would seem lawyers couldn't possibly be held to any standard of legal representation.

The courts' rulings can be so off the wall that it would appear impossible to hold an attorney accountable for substandard representation, but only up to a point, and that occurs when you have that unique, textbook, pure definition, statutorily applicable case like mine, where there was absolutely no leeway in deviating from the most basic, fundamental, time-honored statutes. In other words, as it will be seen, my attorneys and the judge must have been incredibly incompetent if any and all other disinterested, neutral party lawyers immediately and unanimously recognized their errors.

When asked during the usual pretrial interrogatories process to produce the names of the lawyers who would testify on their behalf at trial and the substance of their opinions, my divorce attorneys refused, could not, or did not identify any. Nathan Salazar responded only with, "Objection. Relevance."

Lower (trial) court rulings are also difficult to reverse because appeals courts don't want to get bogged down with the extra case load, especially if the disputes are over issues of temporary matters, such as divorce cases involving temporary alimony (*pendent lite maintenance*). It's temporary, right? It can't have any long-lasting effect, right? The appeals courts would have to disturb the trial (lower) court's opinion, and that is something they just don't want to be bothered with, especially under temporary orders before trial-in-chief of the whole matter.

Finally, courts don't want to open the floodgates of dissatisfied parties to lawsuits against their attorneys. It would swamp their dockets.

Many of the least capable lawyers gravitate toward domestic relations. They can't hack it in other any other areas of law from which they could earn a living. There aren't enough wills or house sale deeds to keep a lawyer in business, especially since these can be processed in assembly line fashion by pre-printed forms. There is the option of being a commissioner, who screens cases and makes a recommendation to the judge, who usually then rubber stamps the recommendation. I have found commissioners and magistrates (magistrates are not lawyers but are paralegals who act as judges and hear cases rather than the judge) to be the most incompetent people in the entire legal system. They should not be allowed anywhere near an adjudication process.

Lawyers sometimes aspire to the position of judge because they cannot hack it in a regular law practice. Some judges are appointed by their peers. Others, like the one I had for my divorce, are elected by the lay public. That is the biggest travesty of all. Since when can the voting public have any idea of the competence of an attorney who is running for the bench? Judge Lattimer, the judge who presided over my divorce case, even publicly admitted in the town newspaper after his reelection, "I really needed this job." He couldn't make it in a regular law practice.

I remember buying drums from a music shop in town and the older sales guy was saying that if his divorce had been in front of this judge, he would have gotten received better divorce terms. "I would have done better if I had Judge Lattimer. He was my buddy." This is your voter electing someone not because he is a competent judge, but because he was his buddy.

I tried to take out an ad in the local newspaper before the judicial election stating why this Judge Lattimer should *not* be reelected, even stating my name, court case number, and outlining the specifics of the incompetence of the judge. The newspaper would not print it. The paper returned my five hundred dollars.

Instead, an ad appeared in that newspaper a week later in support of this judge asking, "What reason would a doctor and a business man have in seeing this judge not reelected? Judge Dwayne Lattimer accepts no campaign contributions." The fact is, this judge may not have accepted contributions or influence money, but that did not change the fact that he was flat-out incompetent or did not keep a check on his commissioner.

The Beginning

The short story is, my career started slowly. I was led into a marriage trap and got caught. My career then crashed and burned, mostly because of a single event that occurred during this tumultuous period, and finally just fizzled out altogether to be swept away and forgotten. Few people are going to be interested in my personal struggles. I am just one doctor. This story just isn't the stuff for a movie, contrary to what friends have suggested.

Let me start out by stating that, yes, I have an anger problem, maybe even a full-fledged pathological anger syndrome, to the point that I can't let this old bone go, but I have never been formally diagnosed with any specific disorder relating to this. My anger has definitely gotten worse, especially during the last two years as a medical event twenty-six years ago has come home to roost.

The problem is very simple. When you are a doctor, you can never "just put it behind you", or "think positively", or "move on with your life". Your record is constantly and relentlessly revisited on every license, hospital or malpractice insurance application, or renewal, for your entire career! I am tired of hearing that time-worn advice given by people who have no clue what they are talking about and who have never had to walk in my shoes. The following events are in my past, they're in my present, and they would be in my future as long as I tried to slug it out in the medical profession. A recent comment from my senior college wrestler teammate captain who advised me to move on with my life:

> I'll offer one bit of advice/observation, that only one of your
> good friends would do. The vast majority of people never have

the opportunity or experience of living a five-star life or make the type of money that you once did and it's a subject that you refer to in every conversation that we have had. I think you got screwed in ———— but at some point you need to put that behind you and wall it off so it doesn't ruin the rest of your life. You are too good of a person, with too much to give and too much life to live. Find things that you enjoy, that you can put your heart into and enjoy the rest of what I hope will be a long happy life. You don't want to end up at 90, looking back and regretting half of your life.

Did I mention an anger problem? Well, actually, I do have one, or in polite terms a bad temper. It was the only habit I picked up from my father, now deceased. As time passes, I hate him more. Passively, as a role model, I guess I learned from him a few good things about not drinking or smoking. He didn't party, philander, or cuss except *himmel,* or "dammit." He would just fold his tongue, and we knew he was angry. He always wore a three-piece suit, even around the house. He didn't need to. He never did any work. He just liked to give everyone the impression he was a distinguished doctor. He wrote/signed everything with his name and the MD suffix, and he had MD plates. He always tried to give the impression that he was so busy.

He loved to spank my two brothers and me, but he spared my youngest brother as he got older. I got the brunt of the physical punishment as the number-two son. At one point, we three oldest were on a three-times-a-day spanking schedule for one offense. There was some pathologic element to this, I am sure.

At one time when he was around sixty, he reportedly followed a nurse for miles in his car and finally pepper sprayed her. I don't know why, I don't know what happened, but it seems that he too had a tendency to brood and act rashly or spontaneously.

Another time, while riding his bicycle wearing a crazy race car space helmet (before helmets became a requirement), two young men in a van deliberately ran him off the road into the ditch as they laughed at him. One of the two turned out to be a law student at his university. My father got the license plate, and he arrived at the owner's house with the police. Using legal tactics, the homeowner challenged my father to identify which one was the actual driver. He couldn't for sure. My father said he was going to wait until that student was about to graduate before reporting him to the dean of the law school. I don't know what happened after that.

Back to my anger, I carried it to another level: I would smash and destroy inanimate objects (computers, especially) out of frustration when they wouldn't work, or when I did not understand how to get them working properly. I rationalized that once the thing was destroyed, then I could finally move on without wasting more time on an aggravating or fruitless endeavor. (but not inanimate like divorce?) But never was my anger directed against people, especially my family. Okay, so there was this cop I ran into during my orthopedic residency in the 1980s. I digress, but only for an interesting set of coincidences.

I had been on call as a resident at a city hospital all weekend. I was very tired, and I had to drive home for a moonlighting shift at my hometown hospital twenty-five miles away. This policeman parked in the median suddenly stormed out of his patrol car and gave me the angriest, most menacing look as he flagged me to pull over. His motion was violent, as if he intended to attack me.

His unprofessional demeanor immediately struck a nerve. I was speeding, at least forty-five in the thirty-five, maybe fifty, but not reckless or anything like that.

I back talked to him, claiming I had been harassed earlier by a trooper for a few miles over the speed limit last month (I had) and now was being harassed by him, even though I was in my scrubs and white jacket on the way to the emergency room. He said, "I don't believe it."

"Well, don't expect me to cooperate with you in the emergency room." He got more upset, ordered me out of the car, and tried to turn me around to handcuff me. I sensed this guy was unstable. I said, "No handcuffs," withdrew my wrist and faced him. That really got him pissed. He then jumped me and tried to throw a headlock on me, and I threw him off like a rag doll.

Stunned, he got up and tried to kick me in the groin. He missed. As he stepped back, I told him defiantly, "Don't try that again." I told him to go call up his buddies. I was not going to be arrested by him, and I got back in my car with my window still open as he frantically and repeatedly tried to slap the cuffs on my left wrist. He was totally out of control. When his back up arrived (three squad cars), he composed himself briefly and said, "No problem, guys, just some doctor."

Back at the police station, everyone was stone silent as the clerk asked, "What do you want him booked for, Marty?"

"Resisting and harassment," he yelled, huffing and puffing. Then, of course, they asked me if I was a real doctor. This cop scolded me to take off my belt, take off my shoelaces. I called my wife, Mindy, now visibly seven months pregnant, to post bail. When she arrived, it added even more embarrassment to the situation. She even giggled a bit. "You got arrested?"

So what happened afterward? This cop's wife worked in the office of one of the orthopedic surgeons at my hospital. She called the chairman of my orthopedics department to inform him about her husband's encounter with me. The fact was, my chairman hated cops as he had been harassed by them too, and publicly congratulated me during a conference for having stood up to this guy. (Thanks, Rick.)

Privately, this orthopedic surgeon sat me down and informed me. "Bryce, let me tell you about Marty Montgomery. Marty loves a fight. His wife works in my office, and she said Marty had never encountered a person like you before." I suspect that this attending orthopedist probably clued her in that I could have hurt her husband (I was regional collegiate wrestling champion in college, winner and runner-up of several bodybuilding contests, bench press 330, broke the handle off the bolt cutter trying to cut two Luque rods together, etc.), but that I was tired and in a hurry and so on as an explanation for my behavior.

As I talked to more people, I confirmed my initial instincts that this cop was indeed a bully. Even one of the nurses in the recovery room described how he had jammed a flashlight into her face when he'd pulled her over. In hindsight, getting back in the car was the smartest thing I could have done, not only because I would have gone to prison for assaulting, and probably seriously injuring this guy, but mostly because this cop had prided himself on never needing back up. In the emergency room, one of the docs told me that Marty was, in fact, being teased by his fellow officers. "What's wrong Marty, a tired old doc too much for you these days?"

Bryce Sterling

He falsified his report, saying that I had repeatedly called him an SOB, threatened to kill him, and so on.

I later had a casual conversation with the owner of Larry's Gym across the street from the hospital where I moonlighted. I regularly worked out there. Larry said he and Marty had started out as unarmed security guards and that Marty was crazy, was even packing a shotgun in the back of his car and chasing speeders who were not on the property but merely driving by. He mentioned that Marty had been taken off the local police force after having seriously injured a man during one of his arrests. He'd gotten on the force at this other city after delivering some evidence in a case or making some kind of deal. Very vague, but according to Larry, he had started on the local city police force and later wound up in this other neighboring city.

When I took an aviation ground school course in this neighboring city, I sat next to a very affable guy in his mid-forties with a shaved head. He offered to treat me to lunch during our break. We got to talking, and he said he was a retired police officer. I told him what happened to me a few months earlier. He said, "Martin Montgomery"

"What? How did you know?" I asked.

"Because I had to train him," he confessed. "I just could not get him to settle down."

The news had spread across the state. Later, in my second job, a doctor whose father was a retired cop from the other side of the state had learned of the incident through the grapevine.

The charges of harassment and resisting were dropped. I paid the speeding fine. Marty was very cordial to me in that courthouse. "No hard feelings," he said as he shook my hand, "but just watch the speed," seemingly trying to preserve his dignity after he knew more about me. He was taken off the active patrol and placed in an investigator position, which apparently was a form of demotion for him, as he could no longer get overtime.

Basically, the police should try to defuse situations, not acting in a way to escalate them. If Marty had just professionally and officially waved me over, then I would not have overreacted as I did. I recognize that my reaction is telling about my personality. I mentioned his bullying and abusive behavior history to the mayor, who replied that since the case was settled, she could not, or would not, comment on it.

So, Ms. Mayor, if the case had still been open, you could then comment on it? Complete BS.

This guy Marty was a thug. As his trainer explained to me during our lunch, "One-third of cops are nice guys, one-third just do their jobs, and another third, well, they have some issues."

But strangely, except for the Marty Montgomery incident, my anger never spread to people. My youngest brother so astutely observed and explained to my wife. "Just let Bryce throw his tantrum and smash a few things. He gets over it in a few seconds. It's nothing personal. He never hits anyone. He's no threat."

How ironic that in the suburban grade school, I was the toughest kid in my class even though the youngest by nearly a year. At sixth grade, I started my prep school in the city and lost contact with my childhood friends. From sixth grade onward, I started slipping physically and became the runt in my class. No question, it had a profound effect on my psyche. It turned me more toward academics. I graduated each year with honors, until I started catching up physically my senior year, at which point I suddenly dropped off the honor roll and flunked my first and only class in my life. Ever. Whether in grade school, high school, college, medical school. It was the last trimester: Gerald Stevenson's physics. Talk about senioritis. I regret having slacked off.

It was a different crowd at prep school. Privilege and money, plus the isolation brought on by the commute and not being part of my prep school crowd or my old home friends on the weekends.

My parents, both doctors, never showed any pretense of wealth, fancy cars, fancy homes, and such, especially my mother, an anesthesiologist. No jewelry. No fancy clothes. No socialization, no parties. Very few guests to the house. My mother was just a soft-spoken, humble, hard worker. She was always doing for everyone else, never for herself. My three brothers and I lived in a small post–WWII ranch house/bungalow built in the suburbs in 1959 before the area became ritzy in the '80s and '90s. I never dated in high school, never went to a prom, dance, or social function. I stumbled through awkwardly through one or two dates in college my senior year.

My babysitter, or more like my nanny, Margaret, a big, fat, boisterous but good-natured German lady with a heavy German accent, deep traditional work ethic, and the mother of ten kids always remarked how wonderful my mother was: hardworking, unselfish, and deserving of more in life than my father.

Her daughter, Helga, was a very sharp, pleasant, radiant, hardworking billing clerk who did all my mother's billing for her private anesthesiology practice out of our basement office. She was superb. Helga was so efficient that she actually worked fewer hours as my mother got busier. She ultimately handled the whole billing department for one of the hospitals in the city. She and Margaret liked me more than my own mother did, I suspect.

I still remember the first day I woke up and met Margaret in the kitchen and, without even saying hello to her (our family upbringing was void of expression of emotion, love, hugs, or greetings), announced that I had to go feed my pet turtle that was sitting in the washtub in the garage. She complimented me for thinking of my turtle before even thinking about my own breakfast. Now that I think of it, my work ethic or sense of duty and sacrifice came partly from Margaret and Helga as well as my mother. It really felt good to receive a compliment from Margaret that morning.

Once I started private school in sixth grade with forty-five-minute commutes each way, my childhood temper really improved. I even won an award my senior year for the most personal development and was described as a person who "had made friends both young and old."

I went on to be an honors student, twelve sport varsity letterman, although eight of those were in cross-country and track where I was hardly a star, even if elected captain my senior year. The other sport, wrestling, I toiled in obscurity, not winning a single match my entire first three years grades, ninth through eleventh. Finally, my senior year, I started winning a few, even a 1971 Christmas tournament. I was a very late physical bloomer, and the fact that I was already a year younger than most of my classmates increased the discrepancy. Looking back at my high school graduation picture, I was still nearly a head shorter than many of them.

My prep school did not have a good wrestling program, or rather, tradition, as that kind of prep school was not conducive to fielding a wrestling team. Hockey (several pro players) and basketball (one pro) were the big ones. We wrestlers toiled in obscurity. The wrestling program was finally dropped. I still think very highly of my coach, whom we affectionately called "Jungle." He was also my sophomore math teacher. He was a fantastic coach, an exacting math teacher, and the purest straight shooter I have ever known. I miss him and still think of him. He and my English teacher, who helped as a sort of substitute father, influenced me the most during my high school years.

I deeply respected Jungle. He was tough, fair, and certainly deserved more than life gave him. Since I did not win a match my first three years in high school, not one, I felt badly for him. I remember his one comment about himself in particular: "I've lived with a lot of losing." He died of a brain tumor around age fifty. During college Christmas breaks, I came back to visit him and the team for wrestling practice. Incredibly, he was later suspended at the school for a semester because he reportedly struck a football player—a sort of disciplinary strike. In my opinion, it was probably the best thing that could have happened to the kid, and if Jungle did hit him, it was justified. But alas, that kid was probably a whiner and his parents overprotective.

Jungle was the kind of teacher that my school really, really needed. It was somewhat of a rich-boys school, and some of those kids needed some good, old-fashioned hard knocks. You never saw that kind of discipline needed for the few students who grew up in the south side of the city: tough, Irish Catholics from the working-class neighborhoods. The school faculty and administration, except for my English teacher, abandoned Jungle, just as my medical profession later abandoned me. There is a difference in sticking up for someone for selfish gain or political correctness versus sticking up for someone out of principle and loyalty.

My only real athletic achievement, or any achievement for that matter in college, came in wrestling, and very slowly at that. I tried out for freshman football where I was third-string left guard, and that was at a lowly Division III academic institution. Yeah, it was a good way to mingle the jock crowd, but I really had no business trying out for football after having spent four seasons in cross-country. But I was getting too heavy to run and certainly was not the caliber of runner that could make the cross-country team, so I hung on to wrestling, a walk-on, completely ignored by the coaching staff, and recruited only by the senior captain mentioned earlier. I still have that letter, and we still keep in contact as per his advice above.

I spent a lot of hours in the weight room for strengthening and on the track for aerobic conditioning. I had few skills, but it was raw strength and endurance that sustained me. I even traveled a fair distance to wrestle a future Olympic gold medalist but it was not very helpful, as he was into the Greco-Roman style, forty to fifty pounds heavier, and a pure counter wrestler. I won the regional championship my senior year, which was my ultimate (but misguided) raison d'être, it seemed, for attending college.

It was a strangely eerie and uneasy time at college graduation. Many of my classmates had planned well in advance for careers in law, medicine, grad school, business school, working for their father's business, and so on.

I suddenly said to myself, "Now what?" I certainly did not entertain law. I had graduated with a bachelor of arts degree in biology and had sort of taken all the required premed courses but had done nothing with them. After stewing around for the rest of the summer following graduation, I finally got a job at a food distribution company in a suburb close to where I'd grown up, owned by the father of one of students from my prep school. I lasted there several months, working the night shift. I was part-time, but at one point, was putting in sixty hours a week.

During a great snowstorm, I was one of the few who could get to the warehouse. I camped out on the dogfood bales and was told to work as much as I felt like doing round the clock. I would sleep a few hours and then get up and start selecting and loading the trucks. Occasionally, the biggest rats I had ever seen would sneak out from under the pallets and gnaw a few bites off the food bags. The songs that I remember listening to during that time are "Muskrat Love" and "The Wreck of the Edmund Fitzgerald." I was eventually terminated because I finally refused to continue working more than forty hours as a part-timer unless they made me full time—with the increased benefits it would cost them.

I volunteered at a city hospital cancer research center for a few months, but I didn't like that. They tried to recruit me for their respiratory therapy program. I drifted toward a medical career, sort of. I sat for my medical college aptitude test (MCAT), now eight months since I had graduated. I was very surprised with ninetieth percentile scores in science/math. I applied to about ten medical schools, and I took a comparative anatomy class at the university, getting an easy A. (But I wasn't taking a full load of courses, so it really didn't mean much.)

I don't think it had been two weeks after having submitted ten medical school applications, including my father's alma mater, when ten rejection notices bounced right back. I hadn't even made it through the prescreening. My mediocre grades (B-minus average) at college were killing me.

In a way, the uncertainty of everything back then was revisited at the end of my career, when my professional record finally caught up with me to the point that I was unemployable as an orthopedist or even a primary care physician.

My classmate from high school, a very solid, likeable, honest, hardworking straight-arrow type whom both my father and I agreed would make an excellent doctor, had failed to get into medical school and was attending St. George's Medical School in Grenada. I had decided on his recommendation to apply there too. I remember showing up for the interview in NYC at the UN on St. Patrick's Day 1977 in the midst of all the parades. The interviewer sat down in her slit skirt in a very flirtatious way. It really wasn't much of an interview, but I was accepted.

I then traveled to my father's medical school to talk to the admissions director, a very fat, lethargic pulmonologist who had a slow, deep, Southern drawl. He said he "wouldn't touch a foreign medical school with a ten-foot pole." If I tried the graduate school route, he informed me that I had better set it on fire.

I walked out of the admissions office very dejected, and struck up a conversation with another graduate student in the foyer. He said he was going through the graduate anatomy program and then applying for medical school. As a graduate student, you took the entire first year of medical school classes with the medical students, and then spent your second year doing a research project and getting a master's degree. Once you had your master's, you could apply for the second year of medical school. A certain number, about six or seven, of the class of 145 or so, dropped out or flunked out of first-year medical school each year and as a graduate student one could apply for that second-year vacancy. (Those med students who failed were allowed to repeat the first year.) I went *immediately* up to ninth floor to the anatomy department and talked with the chairman of the department. I applied and took the Graduate Record Exam (GRE), and before I knew it, I had been accepted.

During the first year, I learned that there likely were not going to be very many openings in the second-year medical school class and there was a growing number of graduate students vying for those spots, so there was some uneasy competition. There was an open dislike of grad students by the medical students. We were looked upon as predators, waiting for a medical student to flunk out just so we could take his or her place. I did not like being viewed like that. Grim reality, I guess. I worked very hard, got good grades, and completed my thesis. I even slept in the lab until I was discovered by the nerdy program director.

"Misssssterrrr Sterling. Your address is listed as 202 W. Tenth Street. You can't live here. I had been told that you were sleeping in the lab, and I said to myself, 'Well no, that's ridiculous and couldn't be true,' but then I said to myself, 'Well, I had better go take a look and see if it is true,' and it is true." It was so funny and yet so embarrassing.

I sweated it out as I awaited the medical school decision. We were a very strong group. I think nearly all of us were within the top 10 percent of the first-year medical school class. In some subjects, we individually were nearly top ranked. One of us was number one in gross anatomy. I was number two in neurosciences, and I received honors in gross anatomy and physiology, and later in the clinical years, surgery and internal medicine. Another member of our graduate school class did not get in again, and he had to wait out yet another year. When he finally got in, he graduated at the top of his class and went into neurosurgery.

In retrospect, I would say it was very humbling, if not humiliating, for me to have to wait out that graduate school year. I could have gotten in, I think, had my father talked to the assistant director of admissions, his classmate, Ronnie Easley. Pulling a favor ("You only got in only because your daddy got you in") goes deeply against my philosophy of merit-based admission, but I was still well more qualified than over three-quarters of the class. The caliber of students coming out my undergraduate premed class was superior, but this medical school was not familiar with my college. I was the final one in my entire undergraduate premed class to get accepted into medical school, although it had taken me an extra two years.

One night after the Monday morning massacre when I received all ten of my medical school rejection notices, I overheard my father on the phone repeatedly saying, "But, Ronnie, he didn't demonstrate that he was seriously interested in going to medical school … But, Ronnie … Yes, I know he can easily do the work … But, Ronnie … I have no concerns that he could not do the work. It is just that he didn't demonstrate real interest in going to medical school … I know … But Ronnie …"

Clearly, his classmate had called him and couldn't believe that my father had not alerted him that I had applied. Ronnie's own son was accepted to that year's class. Based on the fact that my father never published, never practiced, never became board certified, and vegetated at the state university's pathology department as a fully tenured associate professor his entire career, and whose teaching duties steadily declined from initially teaching pathology to the residents to finally watered-down biology for English majors, calling him a hypocrite was quite the understatement.

I did well through medical school, probably would have been AOA (Alpha Omega Alpha—the medical-school honor society) had I been a little more focused in what specialty I was interested in, and had not been spending time entering bodybuilding contests. I even actually won a few. I just couldn't get that gym- after-class mind-set out of my existence.

I met my ex-wife Mindy in my senior year of medical school during my surgery rotation. She was doing her general surgery internship, having graduated number two in her class. She would later drop out of surgery and switch to anesthesiology, and from there after our divorce into academia where she wouldn't have to do much work.

We dated through the remainder of my senior year, and I switched my specialty from emergency room medicine to orthopedics. Part was Mindy's recommendation. "You will have a stable practice and make lots of money." The other was the strong recommendations of the interns and residents when I did an elective orthopedic rotation my senior year. Something like, "Man, Bryce, you're a natural for orthopedics. You fit the mold to a 'T'. You should be going into orthopedics."

I switched to orthopedics. It was one of the most competitive residencies. By then, it was getting late, and there were only two residencies still open in the country. I was too late, I recall, to file for the match. I accepted one of the two positions early decision after talking with the chairman, Dr. Rick James. He was a collegiate wrestling fan, and he liked that I had wrestled. That's what we talked about for most of the interview.

Meanwhile, it had taken the anesthesiology department chairman only two minutes to review Mindy's resume and accept her on the spot. He put a call in to Dr. James to see if he would take me in the orthopedics program in a two-for-one. It was done. She entered an excellent program. Mine, not so much. It finally was put on probation my fifth year. I missed the best rotation my senior year due to a doctors' strike (malpractice-insurance issues). Then I got stuck with an extra rotation at the rehab center. Chart keeping and dictation, no orthopedics.

Some of my fellow residents were really nice guys. A couple were assholes, especially Josh Nicoles. I got burned by him one night when a kid came in with a femur fracture and I called the attending (the doctor in charge). He told me to put a Steinman pin through the femur bone above the knee to put the kid in traction, but he said also to get Josh, my more senior resident, to help.

I called Josh and told him what the attending wanted. "No, no, no! You don't put the pin in the femur, you put it in the tibia." Josh took the drill from me and put the pin in the tibia despite my reminding him what the attending wanted.

Sure enough, a few days later in the hall, the attending pointed at me and said, "You. Come here. What did I tell you that night when that kid came in?"

I replied, "You had asked for femoral skeletal traction."

Before I could say anything more, he said, "When I ask for femoral traction, that's what I expect. And why didn't you get Josh to help you like I told you if you didn't know what you were doing?"

I replied, "I called him, and he insisted upon tibial traction, despite your order."

"Well, you take that up with Josh then." Josh and the attending were Jewish and buddy-buddy. When I approached Josh and told him I really got in trouble for his insistence, he just blew it off—no admission of error, no apology.

However, during a discussion at a conference about some political situation with the residency program, he made sure to announce publicly that I didn't know what I was talking about.

Then there was Dr. "Enterprise," who approached every surgical intern and asked if he would be willing to trade call. That meant taking his night first and then never, ever bothering to return anyone's call when it came time to reciprocate. I guess there were too many conflicts with his Jewish holidays. Other than that initial request, he never spoke to me again during our entire internship or residency.

When I was assigned call, two residents, both a year ahead of me and one who had gone to undergraduate college with me, would always assign me the extra day if there was one left over in the schedule. When it was my turn to do the schedule, it was unbelievable how quickly they snatched the schedule from me and started counting the number of days I had assigned to them—on the spot—to be sure I hadn't done the same thing to them.

I have always said I would hate to have to go to war and fight in the trenches alongside doctors. One look to either side, and they would be gone. There are no men in medicine. The only exception to this notion was a cover story, in Newsweek magazine, called "Hero MD," and I was very impressed. It was about a young urologist in Iraq or Afghanistan who risked his life rescuing wounded soldiers right in the middle of enemy crossfire.

As far as I am concerned, if I were sitting on a medical school admissions committee, any applicant who had started out as an E-1 and ground it all the way through boot camp and then competitively completed the premed curriculum would automatically get admitted. In contrast, most doctors who have military experience have used the military only to pay for their training. They enter the armed services with undergraduate degrees and are automatically officers, meaning no boot camp. These don't count in my book.

Mindy and I did well during our five years of residency. We married in her hometown around four months into our residency, and we had the reception at a state representative's house. He was later convicted of accepting bribes.

Mindy gave me the impression of her intent to continue her medical career after residency. She completed two (actually, three if you count pain management) fellowships while waiting for me to complete my longer and delayed residency. She worked right up to our son Sean's birth and, in fact, had been called down to help out for a heart bypass case when she informed them that she couldn't because she was in labor. After the birth, she took off three months and returned to start training in an obstetrical anesthesia fellowship. She had done so well with the open-heart surgery fellowship that the director waived the makeup time.

After the birth of Sean, my sister-in-law helped out with babysitting while my younger brother completed his engineering master's degree at a nearby engineering school.

July 1, 1987, was the last day of my residency. The truck was literally loaded up and ready for me to drive to my new practice near Mindy's hometown. Mindy found out she was pregnant with our daughter Sherri. Instead of the usual sincere joy, saying "Bryce, I am pregnant. We are going to have another baby!" she simply said the word "Yessss!" several times, as if she had won the pot at a poker game. In retrospect, this was not the expression of a joyful mother. It was a victory celebration. Her timing and plan had worked perfectly.

Since she was pregnant, she could argue that she should not bother starting up work until after she delivered. Indeed, she had already dodged the issue by reassuring me that she should wait until I got settled in before starting, implying that her getting a job would be no problem. The latter certainly was true because she already had standing written offers from both the local surgical center and the hospital.

Now that she was pregnant, it was very credible for her to justify staying home for nine months during the pregnancy to avoid interruption at work, and after delivery, stretching the wait another six months. By that time, she figured she could persuade me that she should not have ever have to work again and instead should stay at home and become a full-time mother. This was no exaggeration. She would literally drop out of her medical career- forever if she could, before it had even started. That had been her plan all along. I had just walked into her trap.

I may be accused of being a chauvinist or insensitive to women's issues, but I am against letting a disproportionate number of women into medical school. They simply do not want to work. Many go to medical school only to look for a husband, and wind up taking a spot from one who is seriously interested in a medical career. It really never occurred to me that Mindy had never intended to work from the day she entered nursing/medical school. Both my parents were doctors, and my three brothers were engineers. We were a professional family. We all worked. Mindy's parents both worked.

Once we arrived to start my practice, Mindy's deception rapidly unfolded. I knew I was not as well trained as I would have liked, and I was having more than the usual insecurities of starting out in practice. Mindy had a progressive maternal, marital, and professional meltdown. Even some of her classmates from high school started hinting to me that she had never intended to work from the day she'd entered nursing school, and from there, medical school, and so were not surprised. She had bragged she was going to find a rich doctor to support her and hide behind her professional façade so that no one could accuse her of being a gold digger. She is the type that even today, if I accused her of this, she would laugh and smirk at me for having been such a chump whom she had snookered. She is that evil, manipulative, and treacherous.

The events that occurred leading up to, during, and after my divorce rekindled my anger. Objectively, I could say my temper was easily manageable as long as I was not faced with an overly stressful or perceived grossly unfair situation.

First Visit to Attorney Guy Johnston to Set Up Trust for Children

My partner at my new practice raved about his attorney, Guy Johnston. He told me, "When you are in trouble, it is always good to have Johnston in your corner." My partner had been telling me about his plans to set up a trust for his kids through Johnston's firm, especially in view of how successful our orthopedic practice had been going, and the anticipated revenue from our business venture in a new rehabilitation hospital. An irrevocable trust would place assets into the children's hands and shield them from a lawsuit, whereas a revocable trust would not. The problem is, of course, if your kid turns out to be irresponsible, then an irrevocable trust only enables him further.

Sayed "Ahz" Ahmar, a local orthopedic surgeon, had arrived in town well before my two partners and me. He initiated this rehab center venture jointly with a national rehab corporation. Upon completion of the building, the corporation learned that Ahz had some past issues—mostly with malpractice, I was told—and needed the rest of us to support (salvage) the project.

My two orthopedic partners and I, and a general surgeon in town, muscled into this venture like a pack of hyenas snatching a fresh kill from a lion. We had this high-priced lawyer who negotiated this contract. Later, I requested from her a recommendation for a fairly aggressive female lawyer as a second opinion for my divorce. This lawyer made the fateful recommendation of Elaine Skyler.

I gave this general surgeon the secret nickname "Piggy" because he appeared obsessed with making money, seemingly doing cases solely so he could make money and, in my case, even screwing me over with a paltry offer of $100,000 a year as his employee as an orthopedic surgeon at my initial interview. He didn't cut his other three partners into my employment or the rehab facility deals. Then he proposed that I surrender my 10 percent share of the rehab to him. I refused.

Here I was in orthopedics, a specialty closely aligned with rehab, and he, a general surgeon, knew nothing about rehab. The nerve! The corporation kept half of the operation, 10 percent for Piggy, 10 percent for me, 10 percent for each my two partners, and 10 percent for Dr. Ahmar, while Dr. Ahmar would keep 100 percent ownership of the building.

My partners had been generous enough to cut me in 10 percent of the share, even though I had just walked into town, although they paid me only $88,000 the first year, but then paid me another $12,000, not even mentioning it as a bonus, since my production easily exceeded that (but was well below theirs), and I became full partner after just one year. After that, we split the income three ways evenly, which was unheard of. I took over the medical directorship of the facility and took some bigger trauma cases from my senior partner to carry my fair share.

I relocated to my second position in another state and met a second "Piggy," whom I called "Piggy Two," also a general surgeon, who couldn't do enough cases, couldn't get them done fast enough, even transporting the patients to and from the holding room to the operating room, not to help the staff, but to hurry things up so he could get more cases done and go looking for more. He handed out Gideon's Bibles to our doctors' offices.

He finally got kicked out for, among other things, doing a sham operation (appendectomy) when, in fact, he hadn't taken it out. Interestingly, that patient later came back with abdominal pain, and the case was confounded by the fact that the patient's symptoms were typical for appendicitis. He had the nickname analogous to, but not actually, "Speedy Gonzalez." Not so good to be called that when rushing through a thyroidectomy and cutting the recurrent laryngeal nerve causing permanent vocal cord paralysis. (Mutual patient who was sweet enough I don't think she sued.)

Speaking of rushing through a surgery, I heard through the grapevine that Piggy One had a bet that he could do an open gall bladder in fifteen minutes, skin to skin (this was before the laparoscope), but then had to go back in for postoperative bleeding. It reportedly was kept hush-hush. Piggy One was a big player in town and at the hospital, so it probably was never reported.

I approached attorney Johnston about setting up an irrevocable trust for my children to be sure my children would have some money for college and as an integral part of estate planning. It was during this time that things started to quickly unravel with Mindy. The more successful I became from an earnings standpoint, the more brazen she became.

Jerry Jacobs and the Firewood

I remember coming home one night after work, and I saw all this fire-wood stacked up against the retaining wall outside our garage. I learned that it hadn't been delivered and paid for. Rather, Mindy and a guy named Jerry

Jacobs had gone out with our four-year-old son in Jerry's pickup truck to get it. Funny thing, we seldom used the fireplace. Jerry was the aimless, shiftless brother of one of the family practitioners in town who referred to our group. Jerry's profession was potter. Seriously. A potter. Mindy had developed this running craze, and Jerry was sure interested in "running" with her.

"Now this is very interesting," I thought as I reflected upon the pile of firewood. "Since *when* did Mindy ever do a lick of work, much less physical work like hauling and stacking firewood? Only when you're 'in love.'"

This event was my earliest cue to think about filing for divorce. I guess the only satisfaction I got was that Sean had gotten sick and thrown up in Jerry's truck that day.

Little did I know that Mindy, sensing my grumbling about her inactivity and running around with her training partner, had soon sought out an attorney in town to draft what she thought would be an uncontested divorce settlement. I wish I'd had a chance to copy that thing, because it was unbelievably outrageous. It was not a formal filing for divorce but rather a separation agreement or contract. She proposed I lavishly support her until the children were grown, plus give her the lion's share of property and custody of the children. In short, her view was that I flat-out owed her a living. It was so outrageous that I went immediately to Guy Johnston to change course from a trust to a divorce.

Mindy explained to my partner's wife about the amount of time she was being seen openly in public with Jerry. "Well, I figured the more people saw Jerry and me together, the more they'd realize we weren't romantically involved because we weren't trying to hide anything."

Huh? The last straw came when she invited Jerry to spend the night downstairs at our house so they could get up early to go running together. I finally pulled her aside upstairs and said, "Listen, you treacherous, lying, manipulative bitch, I don't care how much you and Jerry are screwing around outside the house. I don't ever want to see him here again."

She hung up a picture of her and Jerry crossing the finish line together after we separated, and I suppose it hung there until she realized that this guy was a deadbeat loser who didn't make any money. Interestingly, Mindy had been married briefly to her high school sweetheart and divorced. Youthful indiscretion, I rationalized. In her deposition, her reason for filing for divorce was that her ex "was a musician who wasn't making any money and I didn't want to be in that position."

Mindy was the consummate opportunist. Since Jerry's brother was a family practitioner in town and a source of referrals, she figured I'd have to tolerate her relationship with him. You'd think that Jerry would have used some discretion under these circumstances, but he was an asshole, and even my attorney Elaine Skyler remarked after taking his deposition "He's got a chip on his shoulder," and "I think we represented his father."

Top Gun

I had acquired my private pilot's license shortly after starting practice, but I guess in part due to stress of the breakdown of the marriage, I suddenly had an anxiety reaction when flying during a routine two-hour cross-country flight in a single engine Piper Warrior. Totally unexpected. Wave after wave of anxiety. Raw, naked anxiety. Nothing I had ever experienced.

I had been flying level at 4,500 feet, on course, with not a thing to do but sit in that cockpit and look out over the landscape on that beautiful, sunny day. I landed in a small airport, walked around the cornfields, and finally flew home, fighting off the relentless waves of anxiety. I remember Mindy's fellow resident having to suddenly leave an airport moveable boarding ramp tunnel from anxiety/claustrophobia. I couldn't believe it then. I do now when patients say they can't lie down in an enclosed MRI. I think 14 percent of patients in one study were shown to be claustrophobic, hence the new open-air MRI design.

More telling of her treachery than the firewood was her sudden willingness to schedule and draw up in great detail, a very neat, concise, and thorough itinerary for me to go flying in California. She did this even after knowing about my recent anxiety reaction and how I did not know if I could even keep control of the plane if it progressed. This itinerary was done in unprecedented meticulous detail by Mindy. I even have it placarded as a memento of the flying itself, including videotapes of the air-combat flights, but also to prove how devious and manipulative Mindy was.

I had never seen her devote so much attention and detail to anything involving me or for any kind of paperwork as this itinerary: not for license application, taxes, checks, bills, loans, exercise-equipment invoices, race-entry forms, children's school enrollment, not for our trip to Alaska just before I started practice. She simply wanted me away so she could have some free time with Jerry.

I was determined to deal with this new onset anxiety attack, and I figured I would have a spot pilot with me for the aerobatics in a super decathlon flying out of John Wayne Airport in California and Top Gun Air Combat USA in Fullerton, California, so I went. I just couldn't believe that she didn't think I knew her motives.

Fortunately, I had a great time in California. It was quite interesting when I was focusing on actually doing aerobatic maneuvers or engaged in mock aerial dogfights in the SF-260s pulling up to six G's, rolls, loops, hi-lo yo-yos, Immelmann's, split S's, inverted spins, and so on, all of my anxiety vanished during that time. When I tried to go back to solo straight and level flight, the anxiety attacks returned.

After our separation, Mindy caught up with another runner from the 10K circuit. He was a meteorologist from the city. Mindy probably thought she could get some TV publicity from the association. Yes, she is that histrionic. I got the impression that her new boyfriend was actually a nice guy. Our next-door neighbor Leonard remarked how her new boyfriend spent time with our son in contrast to Jerry. The relationship with the meteorologist lasted a while, but since weathermen don't make any money either, eventually Mindy moved on. (I had an orthopedic sales rep who changed his last name to get a spot as a meteorologist on a TV station but then quit because he was starving due to the low pay.)

Mindy had essentially abandoned any pretense of ever working as an anesthesiologist, being a mother, or for that matter, being faithful. There were so many men to chase on the 10K circuit. She became obsessed with running and fitness. She entered each and every race. One day, she even entered two races. She just loved getting those trophies she won against those sedentary housewives and showing them off to our son. My partner's wife was also a runner, but she kept it reasonable. She had four kids and had recently given birth. It took her a while, but I remember someone thanking (not just congratulating) her when she finally beat Mindy.

Mindy purchased all kinds of exercise equipment, even though we had a membership to a very nice fitness facility in town you would normally find only in the big city. She stashed a Nordic track, Nordic bicycle, Nordic rowing machine, and mats downstairs in the split-level basement, except there was a problem: the basement leaked and the floor carpet was soaked. Mindy didn't care. After all, she wasn't really going to use the equipment. I continued to come home to a wet basement after work.

This was my first realization that she was hoarder. She also needed to reassure herself that she was a fitness queen, because after all, she had all that exercise equipment in the basement. She had all of Jane Fonda's exercise tapes, magazine subscriptions, and the latest fashion accessories (which had essentially nothing to do with her fitness or actual training, you realize), including the leggings, tights, cute little waistband, gloves, and head band accessories. She even entered a "fitness" contest in the city—part beauty/costume contest, part exercise/dance routine from what I could tell on reviewing the video, which I still have. There were only two other contestants who were probably as insecure, delusional, and self-obsessed as she. Mindy took third. See? Even back then, everyone was getting a participation trophy.

This obsession in some ways reminded me of my father who did no work, never got board certified, never published, and needed some self-reassurance that he was steeped in knowledge, work, and research. He bought every book on every subject there was—chemistry, physics, astronomy, ham radios, art, music with thousands of CDs, and of course all kinds of medical journal and books, which he stamped with his very neat but "oppressive" (my English teacher's description) cursive signature: *Jeffrey M. Sterling, MD*. The house and basement were swamped with books and journals. We could barely walk in the rooms.

He never cracked a single one of those books. They were all thrown in the dumpster with great relish after he died. Reminds me of the HMS *Bounty* mutineers gleefully throwing the breadfruit overboard after Captain Bligh had been set adrift in the launch. I must digress and admit that I have a very strong identification for the ordeal of Fletcher Christian. He was the first officer who mutinied on the British Admiralty ship HMS *Bounty* after leaving Tahiti with breadfruit and bound for the West Indies. After his mutiny, he could never go back to England. He sought refuge for the rest of his short life on an uncharted island called Pitcairn. He had enjoyed an upper middle-class lifestyle in England prior to that fateful voyage, but now he was an outcast. It is theorized he was eventually killed by the Tahitian natives whom he had brought with him to Pitcairn.

It was not a good life. He would hike up to a small cave and spend hours either lamenting, or some theorize, on the lookout for the English navy looking to bring him back to England to hang for mutiny. I could never get back into the mainstream of medicine after my medical-malpractice disaster. I had to visit Pitcairn Island and Easter Island, the latter a microcosm of failed societal planning, misuse of resources, and an example of the ultimate desperation as a result of isolation: the ritual of the Birdman, and, some report, even cannibalism. When I stumbled upon this trip, I booked it on the spot.

I'll be the first to admit I almost engaged in Mindy's aerobics/running level of frivolousness back in medical school with my bodybuilding contests, even to the point that I went on a single four-month cycle of anabolic steroids. However, I could justify my self-indulgent narcissistic ego trip on the grounds that it occurred before I had any responsibilities or kids, and I was focused and generally performing very well in medical school. I was able to immediately extinguish my muscle-head interest after medical school.

The second time I visited Guy Johnston, I announced that the trust was off and that I wanted a divorce. I think I came back a third time to further discuss the divorce, this time I thought to discuss strategy. I assumed he would be handling my divorce. At that third visit, he still withheld the fact that he didn't do divorces.

I remember him saying verbatim, however, with both his hands making a downward motion, palms parallel facing each other: "Now you're going to have to give her some maintenance," meaning I was going to have to pay her alimony (*maintenance*, as it is known in legal jargon). He knew she was a doctor, and yet he made that statement. My understanding from that was I had to pay alimony because she had not worked for two years since we'd left residency training. Much later, I learned that under the subsection of dissolution of marriage in the domestic relations, even temporary alimony was flat-out statutorily prohibited under these unique circumstances. Not much else was covered during that visit, certainly no strategy or my concerns.

Oh yes, one more thing. Johnston for some reason reminded me to be sure that Mindy "gets an attorney who will represent her interests and not his interests." *Now WTF was that supposed to mean?* In closing, he told me to see the movie *War of the Roses*. He and his partner had been divorced too.

Later, on the forth visit, I informed him that Mindy had retained Bernard Mitchell. Johnston seemed quite satisfied with that. Did he know that Mitchell was aggressive enough and, being local, would exploit the commissioner's known stupidity so that the case could be thrown into a long, coordinated, and drawn-out battle for his firm's financial benefit?

Later on, those people whom I talked to, and will mention later, were actually very unhappy with their attorney Mitchell and Judge Lattimer. Were all high-profile divorce cases getting dumped into Judge Lattimer's court? All my cases wound up in his court: office manager's embezzlement, divorce, medical malpractice, and none in the reportedly more competent judge's. I wonder.

And Now Presenting Nathan Salazar

On my fourth visit to Johnston, he informed me that he had filed for the divorce when, in fact, I had not even discussed it much further with him other than to inform that the trust was off and I desperately needed a divorce. I was surprised that he had done this so soon without talking a bit of strategy, which jurisdiction (court) to file the case, or my motives, desires, or intentions. Then he suddenly informed me that he didn't do divorces! This is like me going to doctor whom I believe is a surgeon. He makes the skin incision and then suddenly tells me he isn't a surgeon and that his partner will now perform the operation.

At this point he introduced Nathan Salazar and said, "Nathan does the divorces." And then I saw this slime ball son of a bitch: short, curly black hair and skin graft on his nose.

"Hi," he sheepishly said and announced he would need a $15,000 retainer. Remember: that is in 1991 dollars. My stomach churned. I was stunned. I was being led to the slaughter. These fucking lawyers! Johnston had not only given me dead-wrong advice about maintenance, he had misrepresented the scope of his practice and now was doing the classic bait and switch. This should have been grounds for disciplinary action by the bar for ethics violation.

But since the legal profession does not recognize specialties of law practice, apparently a lawyer can string along a client. I should have immediately walked out of the office that day, and I certainly regret not having done so.

Salazar and I started talking about the divorce. I remember two things we talked about. One was the value of Mindy's upgraded diamond engagement ring. I realized that Mindy was all about appearances, trophies, and displays. She had upgraded the ring five years into our marriage by $9,000 to $12,000. I wanted to recover the cost of the ring out of principle: An upgrade is rejection of the original gift and therefore reflects no sentimental value. It should therefore be treated as mere property. Yes, we were already fighting in the mud for recovery of marital property.

Salazar pooh-poohed my concerns and said he would "deal with that at the end." He never did. He had it appraised, but that amount never entered into the settlement total, nor was it addressed again.

I voiced my second concern with specific instructions/warnings: "Do not underestimate Mindy. She will go to the four corners of the earth to screw me out of every cent she can. I want a full court press." I made it very clear that this was going to be a hotly contested divorce and that I expected a no-holds-barred defense of my interests. Even Salazar admitted this statement in later interrogatories (written acknowledgements under oath).

My concerns and opinion of Mindy, as will be seen later, were well founded. I was not asking Salazar to do anything illegal, fraudulent, dishonest, or in violation of the law. I made it absolutely clear that he was to aggressively protect my interests pursuant to the obligations any attorney has to his client's interests. If Salazar did not feel comfortable with this intensity of legal representation on my behalf, he should have declined the case and referred me to a more appropriate lawyer. In two minutes he understood the dynamics of this case: Two doctors, one who had made every sacrifice in good faith during the marriage and was working and paying for everything including third-party care, while the other was running around, not working, placing the children in third-party care and who clearly had demonstrated seven years of treachery and manipulation.

As will be seen, Salazar disobeyed my explicit instructions at great cost to me financially and emotionally for the remainder of my life.

When I later tried to sue these lawyers, it was implied that essentially, a lawyer merely had to claim he had been acting in his client's best interests if he disobeyed his client's explicit instructions, no matter what the result, even if the attorney had failed to inform his client of other options, or in my case, the range of settlement possibilities. This is tantamount to carte blanche forgiveness of legal malpractice or legal ethics violations. It begs the question, what were my best interests?

Starting Small

When Mindy and I got engaged, the original diamond ring wasn't good enough for her. *Stop!* That should have been a warning to drop her like a hot potato. The problem was, with my upbringing, I really didn't think the ring was a big deal, almost like buying her clothes or some sporting gear, which if she didn't like or didn't fit, could be returned. Five years into our marriage, she wanted another exchange/upgrade on her engagement ring. But wait. There's more. After our divorce, she remarried. Her new husband didn't, wouldn't, or couldn't pony up for yet another upgrade. No problem. Mindy just used the money from the settlement to buy herself another upgrade/addition to her ring that she'd retained from the divorce. I have a copy of her canceled check used to pay for her post-divorce upgrade.

I followed up in Salazar's office before the date of the first court hearing to establish *pendent lite* maintenance (temporary alimony). Both lawyers from the firm were present. Salazar informed Johnston that I had landed in Division II. Johnston immediately groaned. "Oh no! Not him." I sensed a bit of drama in this.

"Why?" I asked. "What's wrong?"

Salazar explained. "It takes this commissioner months to make a decision. I have a client who has been trying to get through his divorce for over two years with this commissioner. He cannot rule. He … can … not … rule."

Salazar, of course, denied making these statement during his deposition when I later tried to sue him, changing it to simply, "Oh, he (the commissioner) rules." A blatant lie under oath. I think these attorneys were putting on a show to mislead me into thinking that I was going to get screwed because of this commissioner and judge, not because of my lawyers. Blaming the commissioner was nothing less than a convenient excuse for their misrepresentation. If my lawyers knew that I would be skinned alive in the local court, they should have filed it in another jurisdiction.

I remember actually seeing that aforementioned client of his in the courtroom on the very left front-row seat during one of our motions and Salazar mentioning that he was still stuck in this commissioner's quagmire. Later, I learned this guy's ex-wife was a nurse at my hospital and was using an attorney from the city to clear things up that her former counsel, Bernard Mitchell, had messed up. Bernard Mitchell, as you recall, was Mindy's attorney. The lawyers kept recycling through this small-town divorce court. It was quite the little club.

A radiologist at the hospital where I practiced had also been represented by Mitchell in his divorce, and he was always pissed. He'd lost custody of the kids he'd claimed, even when his ex-wife's boyfriend had been involved in an incident with a gun, and the kids at one point had had to hide in the closet. He said that his ex's boyfriend had "…almost fucking killed the kids." He also stated that Judge Dwayne Lattimer was as "smart as a VA (Veterans Administration) patient." He made the remark that all the judge and commissioner would do is look at their watches to see how much longer they had to hear the case until lunch recess.

This radiologist was a grump, but for some reason, he had my partner's sympathy: "Bryce, understand that Dr. Minkle has just been through a bad divorce." I never got that kind of sympathy or support, only hearsay criticism via my staff who later told me this partner was upset because I was suing his attorney. "And Sterling, can you believe it? He's suing Johnston."

Johnston, you see, was the relative of the former state senator who later became a court of appeals judge who would later adversely rule in my medical-board suspension appeal, to be discussed later.

In preparation for the temporary support hearing, Salazar merely instructed me to get a list of our household living expenses, including utility bills, credit card, banking statements, and tax returns. That was it.

I spent many hours getting the expense list prepared. Mindy had never done a lick of recordkeeping. She had taken out multiple loans for her education, including the rotary club and several state higher education assistance loans, various banks, and so on. She didn't know how much she owed, to whom, or when she had to pay these. (I had no premarital debts.) Receipts from her shopping were scattered in her apartment, and some had been thrown in the trash when I met her. This pattern of course had not changed during the marriage. I'd kept the financial records as a result.

I went through our checking accounts, IRAs, credit cards, her loans, utility bills, insurance bills, and so on and determined down to the penny our standard of living. It must have been inferred from this degree of completeness that I was a miserly bean counter who spent all day counting my money.

My next appearance was at the courthouse in front of this commissioner for the hearing on temporary alimony (*pendent lite maintenance*) that my attorneys had already said emphatically I had to pay. Mindy and her attorney, Mitchell, were ready. This appearance was a flashback to the movie *The Deer Hunter*, where the first half had been spent in a seemingly disconnected story of working-class life in the steel mills of Pennsylvania (our residencies where we were working together), and then suddenly, the second half abruptly began with these former coworkers semi-submerged in a bamboo cage and being forced to play Russian roulette while their captors, the Viet Cong (the lawyers and commissioner), placed their bets.

This was remarkably similar to what the lawyers were doing to me now, a captive of the legal system. I was financially and emotionally caged as these slime ball lawyers made a fortune off me as they took advantage of this commissioner's incredible stupidity and incompetence. I cannot stress enough how incompetent, naïve, and stupid this commissioner was—and these attorneys knew it. My expenses for the divorce wound up being $93,000 (again, 1991 dollars) and Mindy's $54,000 for this divorce. Then I spent another $18,000 for post-divorce damage control with yet another group of attorneys.

Salazar showed up seemingly hungover, although I could not smell any alcohol. It certainly appeared to me that he had been up half the night, but I can assure you, not preparing for my case. He was very subdued in contrast to the obnoxious, bullying, bloviating Mitchell. Salazar had a small stack of papers that were my work product for the household expenses. The financial records were unusually straightforward for a divorce, because in this case, there were no longer any debts, car payments, or mortgage. There was nothing except just daily living expenses, well summarized and organized, which should have simplified the court's task.

Incredibly, Salazar had generated only one piece of paper in his preparation for this crucial hearing, which would set the tone not only for my divorce, but also for my career and life. No notes. Nothing. He had walked into this hearing cold.

I was still unsure of what was at stake in this hearing, other than establishing marital living expenses so the court could make a determination of how much I would have to pay. My lawyers had already told me that I had to pay everything because Mindy had not worked in two years and we'd had an "agreement" to such. I didn't even understand the meaning of an affidavit, a sworn statement supported by documentation, that she was required to submit to the court if she wanted to make a request (motion) for alimony.

My impression of what I wanted to pay or what Mindy requested did not matter. It was basically that I was going pay Mindy and the children's living expenses during the divorce and was to hand our records over to the court, and if Mindy disputed those amounts, then they would be sorted out. But Mindy had never kept any records in our seven-year marriage or, for that matter, in her life.

Mindy's attorney was a real asshole. He never once mentioned that his client was a board-certified, fully licensed, fellowship-trained (open-heart and obstetrical fellowships) anesthesiologist who had graduated nearly the top of her class (second), was AOA, and already had several publications, which allowed her to be accepted literally on the spot by the residency program director of anesthesiology.

More ironic was that I had applied for, and had been rejected, for her spot in medical school, and that other working single mothers paid taxes, which, in addition to my income earned during our marriage, had paid for or subsidized her medical school education.

Mindy showed up to the hearing dressed quite out of character in her Little Bo-Peep dress, a soft, frilly sundress to make herself look as feminine and helpless as possible to this buffoon commissioner. Mitchell made it clear by inference and omission that Mindy was entitled to support. He started out by pushing our postnuptial verbal agreement that Mindy would stay at home and not work while the kids were young. This, of course, I later learned was absolutely nonbinding in a divorce action, but it stuck. Incredibly, Salazar did not object—egregious legal incompetence. It was not even an agreement. Mindy had basically reneged on her stated intention to work when she got back home after her residency. Salazar had charged me a $15,000 retainer and abandoned me right from the start.

With absolutely no mention of any statute to support his arguments, Mitchell painted me as a controlling, tight-fisted husband who kept our standard of living artificially low, and that therefore, his client was entitled to a level of support higher than ever enjoyed during our marriage as compensation for her implied sacrifice. Mitchell established that his client had not worked in over two years, made only $2,000 the entire year (working one day in the surgical center) and was, therefore, reduced to a full-time housewife who was automatically entitled to support.

Again, no mention of any of my good intentions or sacrifices by my attorney Salazar at this hearing to rebut these outrageous accusations. What did he (the commissioner) think Dr. Mindy did, asked one of my office workers, collect cans? Mitchell tried to portray me as self-centered and extravagant because "I was going to buy myself a plane." Wrong. Actually, Mindy had promised she would buy me an airplane after we'd finished our residencies. Her offer was not to show appreciation for everything I had done for her during our marriage, namely choosing her residency and returning to practice near her hometown, or to make me happy, as flying was something I had always wanted to do, starting from a ground school course I took during high school, but rather to make it appear she intended to work as a physician. She could easily afford a plane, but only if she was working as a physician.

I could have been accepted to my hometown orthopedic program. The chairman's son went to my prep school and knew my references. He told me to wait before accepting the program where Mindy wanted to go. The other reason Mindy didn't want me to go to my hometown for residency was that she was afraid I would want to stay there afterward, and I had an old girlfriend there, whom I now confess I treated very badly, essentially abandoning her as Mindy locked her talons into me. My old flame wanted me to stay in town, not become a doctor, and instead live a simple life and work a regular factory-type job, which I just could not do. She visited me at medical school a few times. She arranged for a small plane ride for my twenty-first birthday, and I still have the picture of us in front of that plane.

Of course, Mindy's argument that she needed a good anesthesia training program was total BS. It didn't matter whether she received good training or not because she never intended to work from the day she'd applied for medical school if she could find a rich sucker husband to support her. She only wanted an MD degree to hang up on her wall to impress people like a trophy and to disguise her real intent as a gold digger. Even if she'd worked, it would have been in academia. She talked tough about how she viewed residents and the academic environment of residency: "I expect everyone to make a contribution, even if it is just tearing tape (to secure the endotracheal tube)." Of course, Mindy would not consider an academic position unless it had residents. She did not want to have to do any work herself. She wanted the residents to do it all. Quite the hypocrite.

Mindy did buy me a plane all right. It was a toy remote-controlled airplane. It was laughable in a cynical way, just like in the movie *Flight of the Phoenix*, starring Jimmy Stewart, when Richard Attenborough broke out in hysterical laughter when the German engineer disclosed that he did not build real airplanes, only toy airplanes. This toy airplane, like our marriage, ominously crashed on its maiden flight as my four-year-old son, Sean, watched and remembers.

In his direct questioning, Mitchell asked Mindy how much she needed to live.

Mindy replied, "I figured I would need, like, a percentage of his income."

"To provide for your reasonable living expenses?" Mitchell asked.

"Yes," Mindy confirmed.

Later on, in another hearing when asked by Mitchell, "And Mindy are you able to live on the amount Bryce has provided?"

Mindy replied, "I don't see how."

Then she was asked why she had spent so much money at the separation, skewing the living expenses. Her answer: "Because Bryce hadn't bought me any Christmas presents." What? We are in the process of bitterly divorcing, and I am supposed to be buying her Christmas presents (exercise equipment)?

She lectured this idiot commissioner from the outset and during her depositions that she expected the court "to respect her right to be a full-time mother and not have to work."

My attorney Salazar objected only to Mindy being allowed to ask for a standard of support *higher* than she had enjoyed during the marriage, and that any motion for alimony, even temporary alimony, by statute had to be accompanied by an affidavit setting forth the basis for her request, meaning Mindy had to establish, with proof or documentation, how much it would cost her to maintain her standard of living.

Salazar then handed the commissioner that single piece of paper he had photocopied. I didn't know at the time what was on it. Later, I learned that it was a copy of the statute that required Mindy to provide an affidavit with evidence to support a claim for temporary support. She couldn't just say, "I need 35 percent of his income." She needed specific proof—bills, checks, statements, and so on, an affidavit.

So, what proof did Mindy offer to this commissioner in response to Salazar's cross-examination on this affidavit issue?

"That's what my friends say they need," she said. "You can check their computer printouts."

Huh? Not only is that pure hearsay, but it was a blatant lie, especially coming from a doctor. How stupid did she think we could be? Mindy never checked anyone's computer printouts. She is a pathological liar and manipulator. Incredibly, Salazar never even asked her to name those friends or produce those printed out amounts to expose Mindy's lying, which might have helped my case.

Then Mindy accused me of having all the records so that she couldn't prepare for her motion for temporary support. She was trying to give the false impression that I was withholding information from her so I could falsify our living expenses. In fact, she exploited my recordkeeping efforts during our marriage to make it appear that I was controlling throughout our marriage. I had kept records simply because she would not. I am quite confident her current husband, a CPA, would attest to this.

When Salazar asked me to recite the financial records I'd prepared, even Mitchell had to acknowledge that I had, in fact, given him copies of the checks, checking account statements, credit card records, utility bills and the numbers in the accounts checked out "right down to the penny, Your Honor." Why would I have not handed them to Mindy? They were accurate and indisputable. There was nothing to hide.

In summary, there was absolutely no dispute over the accuracy of these records. Therefore, the court should have been required to adopt these numbers in its decision on temporary support if indeed by law I had been required to pay support. This commissioner mentioned my exhibit, indicating that my numbers showed an "approximate" living expense number. No! I had calculated all of our previous year expenditures down to the penny. Even Mitchell had agreed, but that did not stop him from asking for a higher amount for Mindy in his exceptions to this commissioner's ruling.

Except there was another problem: By statute, and in fact, printed on that very same piece of paper that Salazar handed this idiot commissioner regarding the need for an affidavit in order for Mindy to request alimony, was the statute stating that maintenance (temporary or permanent alimony) could *only* be awarded to a spouse if he or she was unable to provide for herself, through reasonable employment, or had insufficient property apportioned to him or her to provide for his or her reasonable needs according to the standard established during the marriage. This applied even in a temporary situation before the final divorce decree.

Salazar's whole affidavit argument was mooted. The motion for even temporary alimony should have been *dead on arrival* in view of Mindy's extraordinary and undisputed *immediate* earnings capability as a physician. My attorneys, Salazar and Johnston, had been telling me flat-out wrong on the most basic issue in divorce. They had repeatedly and unequivocally told me I had to pay Mindy temporary alimony. Why?

Alimony is generally divided into two types. One is temporary. It is designed to give a spouse time to train or get educated so she can enter the workforce and no longer be dependent on her ex-husband. The other is permanent, or the "life sentence." This is awarded to a wife who is elderly, disabled, or who has no hope of ever reasonably being able to secure the training or skills to become self-supporting according to the standard enjoyed during the marriage, and often is awarded to the wife after a long-term marriage.

Husbands usually whine and complain about having to pay this, but by statute, this ex is entitled to collect permanent alimony. An uneducated housewife who has been married for forty years and at age sixty faces divorce simply has little hope of ever realistically supporting herself through work. Generally, long-term marriage is considered ten years or more. Mindy and I had been married a little over seven years. Five of those had been spent in residency, during which in each of those years she had actually out earned me. This commissioner's ruling had boiled down to effectively a very short two-year marriage.

In Mindy's case, any award of alimony, even temporary, worked directly against the very rehabilitative principle of temporary alimony and the statute. Mindy was being encouraged to sit idle and let her skills deteriorate so that she became less able to practice.

Salazar told me in his correspondence "not to talk to Mindy during the divorce," and that he had twenty-three years of divorce law experience to back up this recommendation. How then could these lawyers claim such experience and yet be so unaware of the most basic rule in divorce law—that any award of temporary alimony, especially in a case like this, was prohibited? Was it ignorance, or was it intentional to throw this divorce into a long-contested ordeal that would ultimately consume me financially for the benefit of the lawyers? Or had the domestic relations adjudication process drifted so far from the original statutory guidelines over the years that these lawyers no longer were aware of the law? Or was Salazar trying to portray himself as a high-profile, high-society, "proper" lawyer who would not stoop to the indignation of fighting out a divorce in the gutter? If the latter was the case, then he should have practiced in the city, not in a small town.

Finally, yes, the thought that there might have been some sort of arrangement between these attorneys to throw the case did cross my mind. Yes, Salazar's representation was that outrageous. It was impossible to distinguish his representation of me from outright collaboration with the opposing party.

Once Mindy was set up on a generous alimony stream, she had every incentive to delay the divorce as long as possible so that she wouldn't have to return to work. This was economic coercion and is how a divorce becomes more toxic, especially when one party realizes that the other party never entered the marriage in good faith. I would have to keep paying her and these lawyers, especially in the event of an appeal. The property settlement would continue to grow, assuming I continued to work and could still accumulate assets from which I would have to pay her half, thus getting penalized again. On the flip side, if I spent any additional income that otherwise could have been saved, I would be accused of squandering marital assets. Indeed, Mitchell later accused me of doing this.

A divorce between two doctors. Now what kind of dollars do you think the lawyers are thinking? Mitchell had already asked me for $15,000 up front. Yet this case should have been the ultimate quick, textbook slam dunk for a divorce court to adjudicate for the following reasons:

1. Both children, ages four and two, were healthy and had no special needs. The court did not have to be concerned whether under *any* scenario, they would not be provided for. Both parents were doctors, same age, healthy, same income potential well off the charts, and had agreed there were no special needs or issues involving the children's physical or mental health. Either parent alone was capable of supporting the children well above the standard established during the marriage. A

lower standard of living was arguably a healthier lifestyle anyway. The kids would less likely be spoiled.

2. As an anesthesiologist, Mindy did not have to even set up an office or hire staff to return to work. She could return to work *immediately*. She just had to show up at the hospital or surgical center the next day. The equipment was already provided. She already had her license in hand, and malpractice insurance coverage. She had already standing offers for positions at the hospital and at the surgical center. She could literally start up on a 24 hours' notice, which she, in fact, did a few weeks later after being awarded an incredible amount of temporary alimony, and began double dipping as she earned $23,282.00 on the side. It was almost as if she was rubbing it in to prove what a complete fool this commissioner was. If she did not want to affiliate with the current group at either facility (the hospital or the surgical center), she had a wide-open path to start up her own group, with all-out hospital or surgical-center support. The hospital was looking to terminate the current group's contract, which was shortly done, in fact, the minute another group moved into town. My medical school classmate was later hired by the surgical center. Mindy made excuse after excuse. She claimed she couldn't trust the four-man group, especially the leader. Two of the members were very nice. Two were not. The leader, Dr. Alex Abulencia, turned out to indeed be a pathologic liar—just like Mindy. None of these four members of anesthesiology group were board certified. Mindy was far better trained and qualified. Then she claimed that if she worked, she would have to pay taxes on her income. Every doctor, including me, pays taxes. That is a nonsensical argument. But again, this unbelievably incompetent commissioner bought it. Ironically, it was Mindy who thus had identified the issue of taxes in the divorce, at least using them as an excuse to not have to work. It was my attorneys who later failed to address the impact of taxes on the marital estate at trial (settlement). More on this later. The surgical center was less than a mile from our house. One flashing stop light. No weekends or call. Home by 1:00 usually, 3:00 at the latest. The position paid nearly $200,000 a year, which was way above the amount needed for Mindy to maintain

herself according to the standard established during the marriage. Not bad for part-time work. We had stock/part ownership in this entity. Don't you think Mindy would have at least wanted to support it? When it came time to give a promotional presentation at the surgical center, the topic Mindy had originally selected was the female athlete. After all, she was now a big-time runner, collecting trophies in races against other housewives throughout the area and had even won the city marathon. She suddenly refused to follow through with the presentation and arranged a conflict with a visit to her family in New Mexico. The updated schedule of speakers showed her name had been removed. If Mindy wanted to go full time, then the hospital position was open just two miles away, and her income would approach mine.

3. The issue of fault could not lie per the state domestic relations statute, meaning, the fact that Mindy had been unfaithful had no legal bearing on the division of marital property or her fitness as a mother. This part, I understood and accepted. However, the law stated that an equitable division of marital property could be based on the relative contribution(s) by each party toward the accumulation of marital assets. The state was not a community property state in which property acquired during the marriage had to be automatically split fifty-fifty. Overwhelming undisputed evidence existed that would have made it virtually *impossible* for the court to award Mindy greater than a fifty-fifty split of the marital property.

4. I had already in good faith removed the often-contentious issue of temporary custody by allowing Mindy to have temporary custody of our children and to allow her and the children exclusive use of the paid-for marital residence so that the children's lives saw minimal disruption. (In retrospect, this was a mistake, but no advice by Salazar given on this.) Salazar mentioned Mindy's exclusive use of the marital residence in passing and said that I should receive credit for her use of the house. But it was no use. I never did. This commissioner had already decided the minute Mindy walked into that courtroom that I was simply going to pay for everything. Salazar was totally passive during that critical temporary support hearing except for mention of the law requiring

Mindy to produce an affidavit to support her request for maintenance, but which was really a nonissue. He had already agreed that Mindy was entitled to temporary support. "She's certainly entitled to some reasonable support." As my mother remarked when I showed her the videotape of the hearing, "He's just sitting there flipping through the pages." Salazar slipped me two written notes during the hearing. One was "Don't show any emotion. Keep a poker face." The other was written as Mitchell directly questioned Mindy about her need for temporary support. Salazar *quite ironically* wrote, "This is not a good presentation for temporary support."

5. Despite her proclamation and demand to the court that she should not work so that she could focus on being a full-time mother, Mindy already routinely (five to six days a week) relied on *substantial* third-party care for the children—which I paid for. This offered her substantial childcare relief, and should have freed her up to work.

In hindsight, any reasonable attorney should have been on high alert in representing me in this divorce. I was a very high-strung, highly stressed young doctor starting out in practice who was visibly upset at Mindy's incredible treachery and betrayal. I had no family support, and I was viewed as an outsider divorcing a homegrown gal. Furthermore, I would appear very unsympathetic to the court because I was so angry and was making so much money. The fact that this was only a temporary alimony hearing and not the final divorce still did not excuse the total negligence of Salazar in arguing several mitigating issues at this critical time:

- I went to Mindy's residency program instead of the one where the one I had been raised.
- Mindy got excellent training at her residency, whereas mine was substandard. It was placed on probation my final year. I had obviously made a sacrifice to accommodate Mindy and her stated intentions of working.
- I agreed to relocate near her hometown after residency, always under her assurances that she was going to work. If she never had any

intention of working, then I would have been justified in choosing a location other than near her hometown. Once we returned, I agreed to let her renege on her promise to work and instead stay at home as a full-time mother for the next six months even though she had spent many years and gone into debt to fund her training and insisted she needed a good anesthesia program if she was going to work.

- I had been trying to set up an irrevocable trust account for the children with Guy Johnston until it had been derailed. This would have placed assets beyond my reach. How could I be accused of being self-centered, controlling, and greedy if I had been trying to do this?

Mindy finished her residency and fellowships one year ahead of my training. Our last year there, Mindy worked as an attending (a full-fledged doctor), and made a much larger income. That extra income continued paying her premarital nursing and medical school loans on schedule, and the remainder went into her retirement account. With the exception of new cars to replace my badly won out 1966 Impala and her 1970 Nissan hatchback, our standard of living did not change.

Within about two years after finishing my residency and working, I had paid off all of Mindy's remaining premarital debts. In contrast, I did not have any premarital debt. Mindy did not toil and put me through professional school as is often the case for wives who work and sacrifice to put their husbands through professional school. My parents had already paid for my schooling. I graduated with my MD before we got married. Mine could not be described as yet another case of the doctor bemoaning the fact that he had to pay his ex-wife alimony when she had worked to put him through college, grad school, medical school, and so on. No. This was quite the opposite, and this special situation needed to be emphasized by Salazar to this moronic, incompetent commissioner. I just cannot overstate the incompetence and stupidity of this commissioner.

I allowed Mindy exclusive use of the marital residence and temporary custody, which should have gone a long way in mitigating additional conflict. It showed that I had the children's interests in mind. Why would I otherwise let Mindy have the house?

This benevolence is analogous to King's Solomon's ultimate decision to give the baby to the woman who wanted to spare the baby's life whereas the other woman, jealous that it was not her child, agreed with King Solomon's initial threat to simply cut the baby in half. A King Solomon, this commissioner was not. He could not recognize the facts and say, "Wait a minute. This father actually sounds like a pretty good guy. He has done everything for the family and children. Maybe we should cut him some slack and keep him in the children's lives instead of screwing him over."

I kept our living standard low but still upper middle class as I paid off the house, new cars, Mindy's premarital debt, and despite Mitchell's attempts to paint me as a greedy, controlling, penny-pinching tightwad, the fact is there was now a larger property settlement as a result of my saving. The court was essentially punishing me for my thrift by having me pay both ways: a higher property settlement and a higher alimony standard based on a presumed higher standard of living we would have enjoyed had I not been paying off Mindy's debt or saving.

In short, I had put everyone else's interest first. Yet I was painted as the bad guy and punished. The commissioner stated it was "unusual to pay off all the marital debt" as quickly as I had, and used that in part as justification to award Mindy a higher standard of living during the divorce than she had ever enjoyed during the marriage.

There is a fundamental inconsistency. Salazar, on one hand, was willing to educate this fool commissioner about the requirement of the party asking for maintenance to set forth the reason and amounts requested in an affidavit, so why didn't he also argue that any alimony, permanent or temporary, to Mindy, a doctor, was flat out statutorily prohibited? He stated in his exceptions that the commissioner had awarded this level of maintenance in violation of a statute. What about the more relevant statute? That statute was on that same piece of paper he handed this commissioner! This was not obscure law. It was the most basic fundamental statute recognized in divorce law. If it did not apply in this case, it would never apply anywhere and was totally meaningless.

I remember this commissioner trying to figure things out at the hearing. "Let's go around the barn again," he said at one point. That's all he could handle: working in a barn. He obviously had no command of the statutes, no insight into the age-old tricks of spouses trying to increase living expenses before a support hearing to extract a higher level of support, and he let this fat, vociferous, windbag loser of a lawyer, Mitchell, bully him.

In contrast, Salazar just sat there, totally impotent. In hindsight, what a convenient excuse for Salazar's incompetence. Just blame everything on the commissioner. That was part of their defense when I later tried to sue them for legal malpractice. Johnston and Salazar tried to turn it around by saying, "We informed Dr. Sterling the court was going to award Mindy maintenance." No! I was hanging on every word they said. I did not miss that. They said I *had* to pay her maintenance, implying that it was the statutory requirement. They straight-out lied and continue to lie to this day. If this court was going to award her maintenance in violation of the statutes, then the case should have been filed in a different jurisdiction where I would have been treated more fairly according to the statutes. As will be seen, the issue of *pendente lite* maintenance was actually stone simple in my case.

The Commissioner's Recommendations re: *Pendente Lite* Maintenance

I received the letter from Salazar after the hearing and basically said it was good news and bad news. The bad news, as he'd predicted, was I had been assigned total child support. The good news was that it had not been extrapolated higher. The court goes by a table whereby the costs for raising a child (children) are predetermined by guidelines that are periodically revised. The total amount to be assigned is determined by the number of children and the income(s) of the parents as listed on child support tables or guidelines. In certain special circumstances, such as off-the-charts income(s) by either or both parents, children with behavior or health problems, special needs or interests requiring extra expense, the court can exceed, or extrapolate, above the tables and order a higher level of support. There were no special needs identified by either party in our case. Both incomes, assuming Mindy had been working, were off the charts. The commissioner assigned 100 percent of the top amount, $1,500 a month to me (1991 dollars). I also had to pay $4,500 a month temporary alimony. Mindy would pay zero.

But this commissioner wasn't going to let Salazar out-stupid him. In his ruling, the commissioner cited, or rather parroted, the very statutes that expressly prohibited any award of either temporary or permanent alimony to Mindy! He just cited them to make it look like he had looked at them, but he never applied them. It was an example of purely going through the motions of reciting the statutes and then turning right around and ignoring them. "Recite, then screw" will be my eternal refrain. This judicial smoke screen tactic will be revisited later in every legal action. It's done to give you the impression that your case is being addressed according to the statutes. It isn't. Remember: by this time, the house that Mindy and the children were living in and all the contents were paid for. Her car: paid for. Her school loans: paid for. Investments: all paid for. There were no debts. This was in 1991 dollars.

Incredibly, Salazar later wrote in response to my state-bar grievance that he was "well satisfied" with this amount, implying that my dissatisfaction had no basis. He defended his inaction by saying that if I had pressed the statute on Mindy being prohibited from receiving any maintenance, "It would have cast me (Bryce) in such a bad light that it would have poisoned my whole case." Other lawyers I talked to said Salazar's explanation was total nonsense, and if my case could be poisoned on one hand, then why was no effort made to cast me in a favorable light by reciting all the beneficial and accommodative things I had done throughout the marriage? Salazar couldn't. He had walked into this hearing cold. He left me absolutely defenseless and completely vulnerable at this critical hearing which would set the stage for the entire divorce and beyond.

Salazar's only written exceptions to this commissioner's ruling was that Mindy was being awarded an amount higher than had been established during the marriage. "Certainly, as a board-certified and fully licensed anesthesiologist, she is capable of making $200,000 or $300,000, but that is not the question and that is not in issue." It was absolutely unbelievable. That was the single, most fundamental and dispositive issue of the whole divorce.

Had I been sitting on the bench, my admonishments to Mitchell would have been something like

> Counselor Mitchell, how dare you come to my court with a motion on behalf of your client for alimony when she is a board-certified anesthesiologist who does not dispute that she can earn immediately, by her own admission, a standard of living much higher than enjoyed during the marriage without burden or difficulty, and her spouse has already made generous provisions for her and the children's exclusive use of the fully paid-for marital residence, with all other debts paid for, including her premarital professional loans while he had none of his own, has already allowed her to take more than half of the checking account, and then have the temerity to make this request without even an affidavit? Get out of my court. Furthermore, this court recognizes Bryce's over whelming consideration for the children's well- being during this process.

So how did this commissioner come to this maintenance of $4,500? He remarked that Mindy and I had divided our joint checking account before the separation, and she had run through the equivalent of $6,000 per month in a post- separation spending spree lasting not quite two months. Mindy raided the account and withdrew half. Well, actually, she first withdrew another $4,500 off the top because I hadn't bought her any Christmas presents and then split the remainder of the account. Her remaining "half" was still over $18,000.

I had not commandeered all the finances to counter any such move. Our financial arrangement was unchanged right up until this withdrawal. A lot of Mindy's expenses after this bank withdrawal were for one-time purchases like extra clothes and frivolous expensive exercise equipment. It is surprising in hindsight that Mindy did not drain the entire account. This commissioner totally ignored the undisputed day-to-day living expense summaries that I had spent many hours compiling. Instead, he calculated that since $1,500 of

Mindy's burn rate of $6,000 per month over our post-separation period was automatically for child support, then $4,500 was left for alimony.

The court looked only at my income, and everything else went out the window. Mindy's incredible earning capability, all other evidence, and statutes were ignored.

Elaine Skyler, the lawyer I later retained as a second opinion, ultimately would try to justify her representation (but not alerting me to Salazar's gross incompetence) by implying that I was totally unreasonable and unrealistic in wanting to "punish" Mindy. She wrote "but the court, by its actions and inactions, would simply not let you do that." Remember: my state was no fault, so indeed, there was no direct punishment for infidelity. But that was the point. I didn't *care* about her affairs. I was beyond that. I was trying to get out of the marriage as quickly as possible, keep custody of the children and move on, unencumbered by Mindy. No fault divorce in the state was explained and understood by me early on (probably the only thing that was explained), and I accepted it. In theory, if division of marital property is based on relative contributions by both parties, then there is a potential element of punishment there, in that the one who in bad faith makes no contribution to the marriage should not be entitled to greater than a fifty-fifty split. I understand fully that if Mindy had actually been the devoted full-time mother she tried to portray, then the court could have awarded her a fifty-fifty property division, even if she hadn't worked. Without exception, all attorneys I talked to, without even hearing the details of Mindy's "contributions" to the marital property, said that the court would have just split that estate down the middle, probably no matter what. But they could not, with a high degree of probability, have awarded Mindy more than a fifty-fifty split.

In my opinion, there is a blatant type of punishment meted out to husbands if they are good providers. Since I was at the time a successful high earner (near $350,000 including the dividends from our investments), accommodative, and had been looking after everyone else's interests first, I made the rope to hang myself. Because I worked, I was by default a father *in absentia*, Mindy claimed, and, therefore, an unfit father and, therefore, undeserving of custody, which meant that I was to be put out to pasture as a cash cow. During the divorce, Mindy scolded me in her letter trying to claim I had been a peripheral father who had no responsibility for raising the children. "You had no responsibility for the upbringing of the children, especially Sherri. You were not around while we were together. Consequently, they don't miss you now." Her treachery and backstabbing as evidenced by this letter were incredible. Indeed, the court was essentially telling me: Bryce, we don't care about you as a father. All we are interested in is your money and that you pay full child support and alimony. We are so righteous.

On the basis of my personal experience, I simply cannot recommend that men who are good providers and of good character ever, ever, enter a legal contract called *marriage*. Marriage is the *crappiest* of deals, and the risk of divorce is too high. Husbands in dual professional relationships should never start or relocate to a practice of your wife's or fiancée's choosing unless your wife already has a job lined up and is working, especially if she is a doctor and you are relocating to her home. Better yet, delay your marriage until she has actually started working. Even if you think you have a solid prenuptial agreement (which sure puts an end to happy hour), the courts can potentially circumvent it by awarding overly generous child support that allows your ex to live off the children. Child support is treated like a sacred cow and cannot be limited by a prenuptial agreement. The court may also assign lopsided property valuations that clearly favor the wife to circumvent statutes requiring either an equitable or mandatory 50-50 split.

I would even go as far as recommending men first getting a vasectomy and only after the marriage appears stable consider getting a reversal. It is well worth the extra expense, even if it is considered bad faith, because it affords the husband at least some last-minute-think-it-over protection.

The cold reality is, once you are divorced, your children are highly likely to be lost, and you will wind up with at most peripheral involvement in their lives—hardly justification for going through the traditional route of marriage and having kids. No doubt this advice will draw howls of protest and indignation, especially from female readers. But in fact, I later followed my own advice. After the separation, I immediately underwent vasectomy.

Dumb and Dumber: Judge Affirms Commissioner's Findings and Conclusions

Judge Dwayne Lattimer barely read—if he read it at all—his idiot com-missioner's recommendations. He rubber-stamped the report with the classic generic response: "Having reviewed the record, the court finds the commissioner's findings and recommendations are based on applicable statute and established precedent."

So, just what *were* Mindy's "contributions" while we were married? Let's go back to Mindy's first affair with Jerry. It seems that at one point, Mindy and Jerry went to some show several hours away while I was at work. We learned about this from Jerry's deposition. What about the kids? In this case, her mother probably came over. How she condoned this type of behavior by her daughter is beyond me. I guess Mindy really had spun some tales about me, although just looking at the big picture you'd at least think that maybe, just maybe, Mindy was lying. Mindy usually dropped our daughter Sherri off at the health club so "she could see me" (265 days a year per sign-in, 1990–1991 records) while she worked out in the morning, dropped our son Sean off at Montessori school the entire day, and had various other third-party-care situations that afforded her substantial relief from childcare so that she could pursue her interests. I was working and paying for all these. However, if I had custody of the kids and necessarily employed the services of a nanny or helper, I would have been judged an unfit parent who was paying others to care for my kids. I also paid for the housekeeper, who remarked to me that Mindy got dressed up some afternoons as if she was going on a date. (Well, she was.) In her deposition, Mindy's second attorney (Mindy's counter to my second attorney, Elaine Skyler) tried to object to Skyler calling Mindy's trip with Jerry "a date."

"Well what you would call it?" Skyler asked.

"An outing," Mindy's attorney countered.

"You can call it peanut butter and jelly if you want. It was obviously a date. The facts will certainly speak for themselves," said Skyler.

Mindy used her mother in a pinch. Her mother (a bitch most of the time, but nevertheless possessing a work ethic born of harder times back in small-town New Mexico) would drive to our home to help out. She was paid. How else could she afford her new stove, new furnace, the quarter-mile dam they built on the remainder of their property to create an artificial lake so that Mindy's useless, spoiled, brother Brad could enjoy his fishing and bass boat?

Mindy's mother didn't make that much money as director of Head Start in that rural small town. I must remark that Mindy's mother showed far more interest and expended a lot more energy with our kids and the kids at Head Start than Mindy did with Sean and Sherri. A friend confided to me that our daughter had almost drowned at the pool because Mindy couldn't be bothered watching her.

Mindy's brother Brad didn't have any money. He didn't work. He was supposed to be working his father's hobby farm that was drowning under the high-interest-rate debt in the early eighties. The corn was not harvested in a timely fashion. It would fall down and so could not be harvested. The hogs were seldom tended. Mindy's father was a state building inspector and was on the road a lot and couldn't watch the farm. He relied on Brad, except that Brad was useless.

There were a lot of heated arguments between Brad and his father. I remember in the middle of winter, his mother and I were hauling salt licks out on the farm. Brad was nowhere to be found. I have pictures of me working with his father, clearing the farm of trees and unclogging the combine. The first time I met Mindy's father, I had to descend into a hog run-off pit and wade up to my midthighs in pig sewage to rescue a pig that had fallen in. Where the hell was Brad? Both Brad and Mindy had no sense of responsibility or duty.

Mindy's Contributions

Starting at our orthopedic office, one partner's wife helped out as a tem-porary x-ray tech and did yard/garden work. My other partner's wife had no skills, but she too worked on landscaping and did various paperwork tasks in the office and was a regular. What about Mindy? Well, nothing, except she would sneak in the office at night to use the FAX machine to correspond with her track coach or use the phone to make secret phone calls to Jerry. One of these, the records showed, was forty-five minutes.

When asked how she contributed to or enhanced my practice, Mindy first fired back with a predictable excuse. "I tried to bring guests to our house to entertain, but Bryce would say no." (Well, Mindy did bring Jerry over without warning to spend the night.)

She was then asked, "Other than inviting guests to your house, did you help out at the office?" Mindy answered no, but that she did community service at the hospital. When asked to elaborate further, it boiled down to her having performed a single function through the hospital's Women's Medical Auxiliary where she promoted the exclusive sale, via auction, of Jerry's pottery. Jerry was the featured potter and received ninety percent of the proceeds. The remaining ten percent went to charity.

Surgical Center

Mindy withdrew her name to be speaker at the surgical-center sympo-sium on the topic of the woman athlete, but she never failed to attend the center's Christmas parties, even after our separation. The last one she attended with her boyfriend, later husband, Ben Holcomb. Mindy refused to work at the surgical center except for a brief period of time, maybe five occasions, earning $23,282 right after she'd received the award of $4,500 a month alimony, which showed how her inability to work was pure BS. She justified stopping work thereafter because she would have to pay taxes. This moronic commissioner again bought this excuse. I don't see how he could make it in a law practice.

He even fell of his ladder and broke his ankle trying to paint his house. So, he wouldn't have survived as a handy man either.

The surgical center at one point had to coax my mother, almost age seventy, to work there as a temp anesthesiologist. My mother was a workhorse. She had done thousands upon thousands of cases over her career, which was extended because she had started so early, having gone to a Canadian medical school right out of high school, I believe because of WWII need. Her opinion was that the two certified registered nurse anesthetists were so good (and they were), taking care of everything, that there was nothing for her to do.

They told her, "Oh no, Dr. Airene, you don't have to do any of that. We'll take care of everything. You just relax in the lounge, and we'll call you if we need anything." Because my mother didn't pay them, she really had no choice in the matter. She felt totally useless and didn't see how any self-respecting anesthesiologist could work there.

The surgical center had unknowingly hired an anesthesiologist out of Illinois who was discovered to have had some issues on his record. It made the local and state newspapers. He told me he'd been sued/wrongly blamed for a massive deep vein thrombosis (DVT)-related death (blood clot that threw an embolism) that had occurred during a D&C (obstetrical procedure). This may have been yet more egg on the state medical licensure board's face for having given him a license, but I saw nothing wrong with his performance, and from what he told me, I could not see how he could have been blamed, especially to the point his license should have been acted upon. He seemed competent. I had no qualms about working with him. He sent a Christmas card to my mother for helping him out.

Now the Rehab Facility

The rehabilitation hospital was attempting to recruit a pain management specialist around 1991. Mindy had done some pain management training at the end of her residency in addition to her fellowships in open-heart and obstetrical anesthesia. In fact, pain anesthesia may be her specialty at the university where she is a full professor *with tenure*. She refused to apply for this cushy pain management position at the rehab hospital. In fact, she never entered the facility. After all, she was a full-time mother.

When she learned that this candidate was a runner and the recruitment dinner was at a fancy downtown club, Mindy just had to go—with Jerry. Mindy first checked out my schedule and saw that my partner and I had an elective Harrington Rod spinal fusion scheduled for that Friday, which would take several hours, and therefore, we could not make it to the dinner.

Mindy talked my other partner's wife out of going, saying that it was just a boring meeting talking about medical stuff and sales pitches. My other partner, however, did attend and took Mindy. I don't know if he knew about Jerry. Mindy's problem was how to get Jerry through the door without arousing suspicion. They couldn't arrive together. Jerry, a nonmember, arranged to enter with an acquaintance who drove him there, got him through the door as her guest, and then promptly left, leaving him and Mindy to enjoy the festivities together.

My partner had to drive Jerry and Mindy back home thirty-four miles away because Jerry's car had been left back at our town. Jerry and Mindy sat in the back, and my partner noticed that this was more than just Jerry needing a lift. When I confided to him that I was divorcing Mindy, he said, "Yeah, we kind of knew that was coming."

The IRA Shell Game

Mindy and I each had $2,100 in our IRA accounts under MFS money market accounts on deposit with the local bank left over from residency. To make a secret cash withdrawal (for her mother or to help Jerry out or for a trip?), she raided this IRA account. She did not simply write a check for a cash withdrawal from our joint checking account. That would have been too obvious. Instead, she cashed out her IRA account and put the $2,100 cash into her pocket. Then she withdrew $2,100 in cash from our joint checking account and deposited it, in cash, into a third bank to complete her IRA rollover.

There was no need for the rollover in the first place. Mindy made the IRA withdrawal and the rollover in cash. Why? To disguise the transaction. If she had simply withdrawn $2,100 out of the checking account and put it into her pocket, I would have naturally noticed such a large cash withdrawal. Mindy *never* paid for anything in cash, and that was what tipped me off. She always scribbled out checks to pay for everything, once even for an item costing less than a dollar.

In this special situation, though, she obviously could not just write a check to the beneficiary. She needed to set up a confusing trail. She did this via an IRA transfer done with cash, thinking I would forget to ask where was the $2,100 that she had withdrawn from her IRA. Don't laugh, my attorney Skyler could not follow this simple money trail deception. When I saw the $2,100 withdrawal from the checking account, Mindy claimed that it was for the IRA rollover and tried to deny and changed the subject and accused me of being nuts. When I followed up with the third bank they confirmed that she had deposited the IRA rollover in hundred-dollar bills.

It was deception in plain sight. Good thing her husband Ben Holcomb is an accountant. The poor sap. I just can't believe how he has put up with Mindy all this time. This event caused my mother to finally understand the level of Mindy's treachery. When I showed her the receipts of Mindy's IRA transactions, I heard her swear for the first time in my life: "Why, that fucking little bitch!"

My undisputed figures had proved conclusively and indisputably that the amount the commissioner had awarded Mindy and the children, taking into account projected taxes on Mindy's maintenance payments exceeded the amounts required to maintain our documented marital standard of living. This would also pay for the health club and fitness membership fees and health insurance premiums with money left over.

Nevertheless, Mindy came back and requested that I also pay for her and the children's health insurance and their fitness-club membership fees. The commissioner granted her motion. This is the problem when an itemized list of marital expenses is totally ignored and a single amount of maintenance is derived from a single bank withdrawal and a one-time spending spree, in this case $6,000/month over a less than two-month span. These items were never identified from the start and, thus, I wound up paying for them twice.

Next, Mindy unsuccessfully filed a motion to freeze my assets and put me on an allowance with the remainder of the money I earned during the divorce to be placed into an escrow account and divided at the settlement. Mindy came back yet again and requested an advance on the distribution of our rehab center dividends even before any of the valuation of that asset had been performed. Again, the commissioner said, "Okay."

This is why it was imperative for Salazar to have made sure that the statutes were followed and that Mindy return to work immediately upon our separation. The judge, probably hearing the scuttlebutt locally about this divorce, finally got a hold of his idiot commissioner and nixed this, saying, "The court will not piecemeal a case." Salazar stated that he expected Judge Dwayne Lattimer to deny this latest motion of Mindy's. The judge finally overruled and acknowledged, "The standard of living of the petitioner (me) has declined, whereas that of the respondent (Mindy) has not."

This commissioner then suddenly recused himself from the case. Was this because of all the publicity in town that he was hearing, how wildly unfair it was that Mindy was running around literally (10K races) and figuratively (dating the runners), with the kids being placed in a continuous stream of third-party care/activity situations that I paid for while I was having to work? She was driving one hundred miles to a neighboring city to spend the whole day getting a makeover in time for her dates. A total embarrassment for the court? I considered this possibility, because people were asking me in amazement, "Bryce, who in the hell is your lawyer?"

I wrote an *ex parte* (meaning I did not inform Salazar, Mitchell or the Judge Lattimer of this communication) personal letter to this commissioner, demanding to know why he had recused himself. He wrote back to Salazar "because he had some clients who had also used my orthopedic services and might later require my testimony on these patients' behalf, and therefore to avoid any conflict of interest, he would have to recuse himself." In other words, he wrote, Mindy could accuse him of giving me favorable treatment in expectation of

Bryce Sterling

favorable depositions for his clients. This commissioner identified two mutual clients/patients, but they clearly would never need any of my testimony. This was a lame excuse. The commissioner had to have known about these before hearing my case. He must have known that I was pissed at him already. He could hardly now expect me to ever give his clients favorable medical opinions. Why did he decide that he suddenly needed to recuse himself now? I am confident that the word had gotten out that he had really, really screwed up this divorce, that the lawyers and Mindy had made a fool out of him, and now he wanted out.

The first follow-up court date arrived, and predictably, Mindy and her attorney Mitchell had done no work on the divorce as far as discovery (not even identifying financial or custodial experts or scheduling depositions). No rush, of course, since Mindy was receiving all-out support, and she taunted me that she was going to stall and stall. Mitchell asked for, and was granted a continuance by the commissioner over our supposed objections. But Salazar hadn't done much work either. He had contacted two experts to appraise items of the marital estate, namely Mindy's ring and the household contents for which I would be credited for only pennies on the dollar.

I requested Salazar to make a motion to address the unfairness of the current situation and revisit the temporary award ruling that had been allowing Mindy to go shopping for clothes and more exercise equipment, indulge her exercise fanaticism, and chase men on the 10K circuit. Salazar scheduled this and it wound up being totally useless. He arranged it only as a *deposition*, meaning it was not a formal court motion. He did not tell me this, nor did he tell me the court would *never* consider a change in temporary alimony, absent any new major, major developments. Salazar was again misleading me.

Other attorneys, particularly Henry Souvent, whom I later contacted to review my divorce case in preparation for suing my attorneys, were amazed that Salazar had left me having to so pathetically and desperately fend for myself like this through such a "deposition."

I still did not grasp that the current situation was the most egregious violation of divorce statutes by the court (i.e., the most blatant abuse of the court's discretion.) Salazar did not argue on the basis of this statute violation during this deposition. He just sat there and let me flail trying to express my dissatisfaction, to which Mitchell countered simply: "Bryce, all you are doing is rambling. Nothing but rambling. These are just meaningless ramblings."

Of course, Mindy continued to ramble about how she expected the court to respect her right to be a full-time mother and not have to work. Salazar just sat there during this deposition. He did not even try to salvage the extraordinary damage he had allowed the court to inflict upon his client. The problem obviously was that if he now tried to address/correct this glaring issue, he would have exposed his legal malpractice.

The second pretrial court appearance arrived, and again, no work had been done. It wasn't until the third court appearance that Mitchell finally announced that he had identified an expert to appraise the marital property, particularly my orthopedic practice and the rehab center. His expert was Dale Hastings.

Because of my dissatisfaction at what even a third grader could see as totally unfair, and numerous comments about how Mindy was out having a ball while I was having to work, I decided to get a second opinion. Sounds like a reasonable thing to do, right? The joke at my hospital had become: "I don't want to marry a doctor; I just want to divorce a doctor."

I asked our rehab hospital attorney, the very high-priced lawyer, to recommend a fairly aggressive female attorney to look into my divorce. I figured a female attorney would have more insight into Mindy's treachery and manipulation. She gave me Elaine Skyler's name.

I called Skyler and told her over the phone in a nutshell the current status of the divorce, specifically that I was seeking a second opinion and had some grave concerns about whether Salazar was properly representing my interests. I told her Mindy was a doctor, enjoying the use of our fully paid for marital residence, no debts, with 100 percent child support paid by me plus $4,500 a month temporary alimony, and that she had *not* paid a penny for my medical-degree training. It was I who had paid for hers. Her first response over the phone was "Whoa!"

She then said it wasn't proper for her to criticize another attorney's performance, or it wasn't considered good legal etiquette to do so, something like that. Skyler was always about appearances, *never* about substance. Even recently, when I saw her website, her new Suze Orman hairdo just reeked of phoniness. She always worked in the fact that she had adopted two children and therefore, knew all about custody issues. I pity those kids if their plight was so destitute that they had to be rescued through adoption by her.

But her inaction or, arguably, maintenance of the deception of Salazar's incompetence seemed to underscore the fact that a client truly has no recourse against his lawyer, no matter how bad a job he or she is doing. Lawyers protect their own. Here I was, going to her expressly for a second opinion, and she was hiding Salazar's incredible passivity in the handling of my case. In contrast, in medical-malpractice actions, there is no difficulty paying a doctor to testify in a malpractice case against one of his own peers. That is why expert witness doctors who testify against their own in medical-malpractice cases are commonly referred to as whores.

I scheduled a meeting to see Skyler. At that visit, I noticed two immediate things: One, that damn short, curly hair—just like Salazar's. Two, she sure wasted a lot of time asking me ridiculous questions such as if I had a home and, if so, what the address was; if I had a phone and, if so, what the phone number—almost like she was taking a deposition. All the things that I usually did when I filled out an information sheet at the front desk when visiting the doctor or dentist.

I said to myself, "Why is she wasting time taking down this information herself? Let's talk about my case!" Little did I know that this secretarial work was about all she could do.

The bottom line: Skyler did not inform me but, rather, concealed from me Salazar's gross incompetence, negligence, and arguably even maintained a conspiracy in his handling of the divorce at the critical temporary support phase, and then proceeded to bill me double, much of this arguably fraudulently, for hours that she could not possibly have expended as claimed. Thirty thousand dollars was ultimately billed as review of file and preparation for trial.

In many lawsuits, this would merit triple punitive damages. Her act was deliberate, and the conspiracy to maintain Salazar's screwup of the case was maintained right to the end, culminating in a sudden abandonment of me at the trial by suddenly convincing me to settle, with no new information having become available to change the strategy, or necessity, of trying this case for weeks prior. There had been no sit-down review of the status of the divorce or tabulation of the property valuations before trial. I had no idea of where I stood.

After the divorce settlement she would claim that she had informed me that I could pay one-half of what Dale Hasting's had appraised my orthopedic practice and the rehab center. That was materially false because it did not include all the other items of marital property. That was a vague number, not even a dollar amount. It was only meant to scare me, not inform me, into settling.

After informing Salazar that I had retained Skyler, he said that it was important to delegate tasks specifically so that one attorney was not assuming the other had dealt with a certain issue of the case.

In her letter to Salazar, Skyler proudly produced her scorecard she used in her divorce cases. She just thought she was so clever in devising it. Even a third grader made a more informative table. No response from Salazar. I am sure he was thoroughly amused. Skyler was a total lightweight, and this was her ticket stub from the idiot farm.

Goodwill? What Goodwill?

It didn't take long for Skyler to really screw things up. Salazar had retained a local building appraiser to appraise the marital residence, the orthopedic practice, the rehab hospital, and so on. The problem was this appraiser had experience only with property evaluation, not business appraisal, and had no accounting degree. However, he had recently been certified to appraise businesses. Mine, I later learned, was to be his first.

Salazar assured me and Skyler that the local court would attach great weight to his evaluation. Salazar had initially asked me if I knew of anyone who could evaluate the property, and I mentioned this appraiser because my partner knew him and I think was doing business with him (condo construction, which was a break-even project after sale to my partner's banker buddy).

Salazar stated he immediately retained this appraiser because he was so highly respected in town. To this day, I too think he was a very reputable and highly respected building appraiser, and a nice guy, but he was not an accountant.

I heard from Salazar that Mitchell had secretly apologized to him in advance that at trial he was going to have to make him appear unqualified to appraise a business. However, even Mitchell's hired-gun appraiser of my practice and the rehab hospital, Dale Hastings, a CPA, did not dispute my appraiser's work product, except he added an intangible value or goodwill onto my practice. Hastings did no generation of the actual raw numbers or data of the practice or the rehab hospital. He merely scrolled down to the bottom line and accepted my appraiser's numbers.

Did Hastings do any work to derive this goodwill number? Not really. It was basically an add-on appraisal gimmick called *excess capitalization* that automatically presumed a business had intrinsic value above those of its peers if it was more profitable. A simple tacking on a number. The price for this work by Hastings outlined on his two-page letter? Fifteen thousand dollars! This guy had even Skyler beat in the ghost hours billing department.

Hastings was the epitome of the slime ball hired gun, well, maybe with an exception to be mentioned later. In total contrast, my appraiser had produced extensive work product with blue legal-sized folders showing his methodology, raw data, incomes, accounts receivable, profit/loss numbers, pro forma analysis, and other calculations.

What was the effect of Hasting's assignment of goodwill on my orthopedic practice? It more than doubled its value from about $300,000 to $630,000. What a convenient out for a biased court to adjust a property settlement in favor of a scheming underserving female spouse. It could just conjure up goodwill out of thin air to the point that any legitimate evaluation could be rendered insignificant. The fact that it was such an outrageous number should have actually alerted one to the obvious fact this guy was a paid hired gun who should have been dismissed as such. He wouldn't have minded. After all, he had already made his 15,000 dollars. But Skyler was convinced he was the real deal, or, was she using this appraisal as a weapon so she could conveniently threaten me to settle so that she wouldn't have to try the case?

Skyler eventually prevailed upon my appraiser to assign a goodwill number greater than zero on the practice "to withstand potential appellate review," even though Salazar and my appraiser were adamant that my small-town practice had no goodwill. My appraiser was of firm opinion that the practice had no goodwill because our practice was in a small town, and we physicians worked hard. No one outside our town knew about our practice. It was not advertised. We earned at the ninetieth percentile of practices at the time because the area was underserved. We had no competition. We made money because patients agreed to be seen and treated by us. Patients couldn't be treated as cattle. They simply could not be treated as goodwill.

My added argument was that I as a physician made no money unless I personally actually saw and treated patients on a day-to-day basis. I could not have someone else do my work for me in the future. In contrast, in a retail business, for example, the owner may no longer work at the store or business, but instead sit at home and let others do the work from which he collects profits and the business grows.

Our practice had no competition or special name recognition. I was the lowest producer of our group. Anyone of reasonable skill and ability who set up in our town would have done as well. Conversely, had anyone else tried to set up a practice and compete against us, our practice would immediately have been negatively impacted. Finally, per my original contract when I joined the group, in the event of my leaving, no goodwill would be recognized on the sale of my share.

This indeed was how sophomoric Skyler was, in my opinion. Skyler later tried to justify her act on the basis of "withstanding appellate review," but this was pure baloney. Rarely will an appellate court disturb a trial court's adoption of an expert's valuation of marital property because appeals judges simply don't have any expertise in property valuations and they admit it.

Fast forward two years for a moment. After the anesthesia malpractice event, which occurred before the divorce was finalized, my share of the practice would certainly have no goodwill nor would my ability to earn money as an orthopedic surgeon ever realistically exceed others in my specialty. In fact, after the divorce settlement I wound up having to sell my share of the practice for $100,000 less than book. (As sort of negative goodwill for which my attorneys made no provision in the final divorce settlement.) As an insurance policy against this lawsuit, I entered a buyout/indemnification deal with my partners where I would accept a price of $100,000 less than book value if they agreed to indemnify me for two-thirds of any amount in the medical-malpractice suit over $300,000.

For example, if I was hit with a $300,000 judgment, then the first $200,000 was paid by the limits of my insurance, and the additional $100,000 paid solely by me as excess judgment. If the suit went for a million dollars against me, the insurance would pay $200,000, then I would have to pay the next $100,000 and then one-third of the remaining $700,000, or $233,333.00, for a total of $333,000.

Combined with the $100,000 I had already surrendered in the buyout of my share of the practice, a million-dollar verdict/judgment against me would have cost me a total of $433,000. A huge hit, but maybe survivable, I thought. I really had no idea whether the suit would be settled, or, if not, what the jury would award. The plaintiff family was very uneducated, untruthful, and vindictive. They wanted the case to be tried to put me on public display. They were essentially accusing me of murder and the case was sensationalized throughout the media. I figured that with all the state and national publicity, the award would be high.

I did not use a lawyer to draw up this buyout agreement. My partners, still convinced that Johnston was a great attorney, reportedly used him on their side of the deal. As the trial date approached and it was uncertain whether the family would settle, my senior partner became very panicky. He said that I had a duty to try to settle the case. He was now afraid of a catastrophic award if the case went to trial to the point that he would be on the hook for a substantial amount through the practice. Of course, I had heard no complaints from him earlier about the discounted buyout price. Obviously, he now realized that he could be holding the bag for easily over $200,000. So my indemnification buyout agreement wasn't based on any overreaction or unrealistic perception on my part. We were all very anxious at the end and had no idea what would result from this case.

My office manager asked me to write down what I predicted the final amount to me would be. I think I wrote $1 million. She wrote down something more than triple that. My senior partner then reminded me, "Bryce, we didn't have to cut you into the rehab." That was true, but then again, he didn't expend much time or effort acquiring it either. I am sure I paid my share of attorney fees to our attorney who represented us as we collectively wrestled thirty percent of the operation from Dr. Ahmar.

It is important to remember that this malpractice event had occurred *during* the divorce whereas the malpractice settlement was made *after* my divorce. As part of the medical malpractice final settlement, I paid $100,000 excess judgment to the family payable over ten years ($833.33 a month for ten years.) Combined with the $100,000 loss I took on the sale of my practice share, I took a nominal hit of $200,000. The practice (my partners) agreed to pay $50,000 over ten years. So, I really negotiated a fairly reasonable deal in that my partners netted only about $50,000 savings on the purchase of my share, since they had to pay $50,000 on behalf of practice of the $100,000 they saved on buying out my share. My partner's wife certainly had no misgivings about the settlement, saying that it was money well spent (avoiding a trial and possible catastrophic award), but she forgot where that $50,000 came from. I was already paying for it.

Lesson to all doctors: Don't believe for a minute that medical-malpractice lawyers only go after the money in your malpractice-insurance policy. They will go after your personal assets in a heartbeat. This is called an excess judgment, and I was hit with it.

My share of the practice would be reduced to a fraction of Hasting's extrapolated value of over $630,000. I think I actually cleared less than $30,000 net from my practice after expenses and taxes. Again, my attorneys made absolutely no provision for this malpractice case in the divorce settlement or in the arguments/discovery prior to trial or how it would affect my future career and ability to earn. They may claim they had discussed it with the commissioner who would hear our divorce case during pre-trial discussions, but I never heard a word about these discussions or how the malpractice event would impact the value of my practice or future earnings. Skyler and Salazar would conveniently claim they had addressed all these issues using hearsay--that they had discussed them with the commissioner—but no proof. They certainly did not address these issues with me. I am asking these lawyers to this day, if you had discussed them, that means you had identified the issues. If you had identified these issues, then where were the numbers?

Back to the Divorce and Shooting Ourselves in the Feet

Skyler finally prevailed upon my appraiser to assign a goodwill value on the practice. He arbitrarily assigned a value of one percent. This number was based on no generally accepted accounting methodology. Mindy's expert, Dale Hastings, stated in his deposition that he had never heard of this practice of assigning an arbitrary percentage of the book value of a business as goodwill. He argued it had to be derived from a generally accepted accounting methodology. My appraiser had now compromised himself needlessly to criticism of his methodology and, therefore, credibility as an expert.

Skyler repeatedly expressed her "serious reservations about the expert retained by Salazar and his unique methods of valuation." But it was she who had caused him to suddenly become compromised by her insistence that he assign some goodwill on the practice. If my expert had stood by his original opinion, he would have remained a very credible expert, especially in the local court. He could have argued that my practice had no goodwill or, alternatively, that there was a goodwill number, and that number was zero.

Appellate courts do not like to disturb expert opinion valuations that the trial court adopts. They are more inclined to remand or reverse cases only where violations of statutes, procedural rules or courts' abuse of discretion have occurred. Skyler's concerns of the case being able to withstand appellate review were unfounded, confused, and served only to shoot ourselves in the feet.

My impression was that Skyler wanted to make goodwill a factor to make it appear she was a real expert on legal aspects of business appraisal and a sophisticated lawyer. If Skyler had expressed concern about Salazar's handling of the choice of expert for property appraisal, why hadn't she expressed concerns about his glaring legal malpractice in the handling of the temporary support hearing right from the start?

Even more aggravating was the fact that my lawyers failed to apply Hasting's own goodwill tactics against Mindy. Mindy was not practicing, and therefore her extraordinary skills and qualifications, above those of most anesthesiologists, were shielded from any goodwill assessment. If goodwill was to be assessed against me, then goodwill would have to also be assessed against Mindy based on her increased earnings potential which was above usual anesthesiologist range of $200-300,000. To my knowledge, my attorneys were only interested in establishing Mindy's baseline level of income to rebut an award for maintenance, but not a higher level in view of her extraordinary training and qualifications which would have allowed her to earn more than the average anesthesiologist. This would qualify as a sort goodwill which could have been used to offset mine. In other words, because I worked, I was exposed to a goodwill penalty. Because Mindy did not work, she had no similar exposure and was rewarded.

Mindy's Deposition, Friday, February 28, 1991

I never gave my deposition on any motion by Mindy. Why not? Because there wasn't anything that Mindy could use against me. I was clean. I was not running around, drinking, or drugging. I was not diverting marital assets. I was not an unfit father. I was not beating or abusing her, nor was I engaged in any other untoward behavior. Any deposition by me would only recapitulate Mindy's treachery and underscore my overwhelming unilateral generosity and sacrifice.

Mindy had been collecting maintenance for a year by the time her deposition was taken. Skyler showed me her notes and preparation for this deposition.

I later reviewed her file in her office as part of the discovery process during my lawsuit against her. I saw no notes showing a net totaling upon which to base any settlement proposal to Mindy. For example, on the issue of recovery of premarital professional school loans, Skyler was unaware of the issue, never mentioned it once to me, never demonstrated that she had entered it into her calculations, never gave any evidence that she had been aware of the domestic case law that established the precedent for recovery of premarital professional school loans. She had asked Mindy in the deposition whether she had any premarital school debt and, if so, how much, to which Mindy said yes, and to end the subject she acknowledged that it was the amount "whatever Bryce said." (Again, Mindy never kept any records and, therefore, could not dispute the records I had.)

Skyler initially objected to my attempts at discovery in my lawsuit against her because it was her work product. Was it because there simply wasn't any?

Why do lawyers get to review our office medical charts when we doctors are being sued? Aren't these records work-product too?

Skyler did show me her line of questions for Mindy's deposition. In my opinion, Skyler covered enough ground based on the information I supplied her for Mindy's depositions that a court would have looked very negatively toward Mindy's character and contributions which were laughable on one hand but absolutely incredible on the other, coming out of a highly educated, board-certified anesthesiologist's mouth.

What few contributions Mindy had made to the marriage assets were nothing more than confirmation of acts of infidelity. She continued to admonish the court that she had a right to be a full-time mother and not have to work. Of course, I didn't have any right to be a full-time father. Skyler covered Mindy's contributions to the office, the rehab center recruitment dinner, and the surgical center as already mentioned. Mindy made zero contributions to these. I indirectly was making contributions to the children because I was paying for substantial third-party childcare. Mindy certainly was *not* a full-time mother, but Skyler did not specifically confront Mindy with her hypocrisy in her use of extensive third-party care. Skyler did, however, at least submit the health-club nursery sign-in records and other third-party care bills as exhibits.

Skyler also established for the record some of Mindy's impressive credentials as a board-certified anesthesiologist with a double fellowship, and that I had been very (overly) accommodative toward Mindy during the marriage, going to her residency, relocating back to her state, not making her work initially, and so on. Interestingly, Mitchell was not present for Mindy's depositions. Mindy had hired this female attorney it appears solely for these depositions. How the "peanut butter and jelly" flew between Skyler and Mindy's female attorney. Tee-hee. All the ferociousness of a pillow fight between these two lightweights.

After the deposition, the court reporter quietly told me she was absolutely amazed that Mindy was collecting full alimony on top of her use of the marital property and no debt. "Never seen anything like it," she said. She also told me Mindy never paid her court reporter bill.

March 1, 1991—The End

On that day, a twenty-one-year-old man died, my career was ruined, my children lost, and my life forever changed. I had spent the whole day sitting in on Mindy's deposition that had been scheduled on very short notice. I had to postpone my surgery scheduled for 7:30 a.m. until about 4:00 p.m. I had a back surgery and an elbow fracture repair scheduled. I was also on call.

After the deposition, I was called to see this twenty-one-year-old man, Arthur Smith, who had arrived at the emergency room around three o'clock. He had been transported from Mindy's hometown with a table-saw cut to his index finger that involved skin, tendon, and bone. I informed him that it would take several hours before we could get his finger cleaned out and fixed up. He seemed very pleasant and agreeable, and generally, a nice guy. His mother was very concerned as she reportedly made inquiries on the floor about my abilities, to which she claimed that one of the nurses said I was as good as a world-famous hand group whom she apparently knew about. The nurse also blurted out, "And he (Dr. Sterling) is making the megabucks." That phrase seemed to really rankle the mother. She repeated it in her various testimonies.

My partner by now had been called up by the army reserve to Saudi Arabia in preparation for the first Gulf War. Therefore, I was busier than ever trying to cover for him. The last thing I needed was to waste my day in what in retrospect was a needless deposition. If a scheduled deposition was postponed, it was no problem for Mindy. She just canceled the babysitter or her mother. I, in contrast, had to reschedule my office or surgical schedule. Again, this was blatantly unfair to me. I had to drive to the city to take all kinds of psychologic profile testing for child-custody evaluation. I showed up very early, tired, and hungry. I also had to do the same for Mindy's psychology expert, Leroy Rathbone.

Even my nemesis, the state's newspaper, called me at my office asking how my practice was being impacted by the departure of my partner for the Gulf War. Basically, I said I had to get up earlier, work longer hours and take more call. Meanwhile, an anesthesiologist had been called up, so, in the same way as orthopedics, anesthesia was short staffed. Mindy worked for several days but then refused to help out thereafter. After all, she was supposed to be a full-time mother. She was afraid working might jeopardize her full maintenance entitlement status.

This one anesthesiologist from the four-man group had been approached by the armed forces to join the reserves a few months earlier. He even tried to tell other doctors how it was such a good deal. For the extra money, all he had to do was report to duty one weekend a month and two weeks during the year. But it wasn't long before he was called up. I suspect he lost on that deal.

When he returned, the surgical center tried to terminate his contract, and he had to sue to get his job back—more legal expense. The surgical center finally dropped the case because by law he could not be terminated if he had been called up for military service. This anesthesiologist was a good guy. So was one of his partners, who unfortunately suddenly died from an MI. The other two were assholes and liars. One of them died on the table during open heart bypass surgery.

It was around 11:00 p.m., February 28, 1991, by the time I finished the elective back and elbow surgeries. At the end of the elbow surgery with the chief of the four-man group, Dr. Alex Abulencia, who was the head of the anesthesia department and the senior member of the four-man group, begged off this finger case. He said, "You don't need me to do that case, do you?" (I later learned he had to give anesthesia to his partner's wife the following morning.) You have the nurse and the two techs to help you."

I wasn't happy about it because I was tired too, but I reluctantly said okay, since I had plenty of help. Even the patient's mother testified that I looked tired.

The RN (registered nurse), asked me what medication I would need for the Bier block in the presence of Dr. Abulencia as we concluded the elbow case. The RN was fully aware that the medication would be given intravenously and, therefore, rather important, to say the least. A Bier block (the technique first described around 1908 by Dr. Augustus Bier) is a time-honored form of regional anesthesia that numbs the arm without putting the patient to sleep. It has an excellent safety record, as long as the proper anesthetic is injected. An IV is placed in the hand. The entire arm from the fingers to the upper arm is wrapped with an elastic bandage called an Esmarch bandage to squeeze all the blood out of the arm. While the bandage is still on and squeezing the blood out of the arm, a tourniquet placed around the upper part of the arm is inflated, (like an inflatable blood pressure cuff) so that blood cannot reenter the arm. The Esmarch bandage is unwrapped. The arm is now totally pale as there is no longer any blood in it. With the tourniquet still inflated, dilute numbing medicine (0.5 percent xylocaine) is injected through the IV at the hand, and the medicine fills up the veins of the arm where the blood used to be, and the arm becomes numb. The tourniquet remains up until the procedure is completed. At the completion of the surgical procedure, the tourniquet is released briefly and then intermittently reinflated a few times to prevent a sudden bolus of xylocaine from rushing into the central bloodstream.

It was undisputed I'd asked the RN for the correct medication and dose at the end of the elbow case: 40 ccs of 0.5 percent plain xylocaine. It is a very common drug used for numbing skin to sew up cuts or to lance abscesses at bedside, especially in the emergency room or at the doctor's office. It is clearly marked by a blue label. The RN read the order back to me *verbatim* after she had written it down on her scrubs, and even asked me if I wanted it in two thirty cc syringes or a single sixty cc syringe. I returned from the recovery room having talked to the family from the previous case. The tech had set up the tourniquet. I started the IV.

After the tourniquet had been inflated, the RN handed me the syringe. I did not check the medication. I started injecting what I thought was xylocaine. I don't think I checked the tourniquet to see if was tight/inflated. I do remember that there were about a dozen tourniquets used in the operating room at the hospital, which were checked after this mishap, and they all reportedly leaked, which is one reason why only xylocaine can be used for this block. If the tourniquet leaks and xylocaine rushes into the bloodstream, the patient can get a brief seizure but *never* a cardiac arrest.

My senior partner acknowledged he had a patient who'd suffered a seizure from sudden escape of xylocaine into his patient's bloodstream, but with no sequela. All medical literature, especially from a previous five thousand case review study in the *Canadian Journal of Anesthesiology* reported no deaths or significant sequelae as a result of Bier blocks, even when seizures had occurred—as long as xylocaine had been used. If the tourniquet leaked or was released all at once at the end of the procedure, the patient may seize briefly but always came out of it quickly because xylocaine does not impair heart function. In fact, back in 1991, it was commonly used intravenously (slowly) as a drip to treat heart arrhythmias.

I had just finished the injection when the patient suddenly gave out a quick yell and then went into full violent seizure, restrained by the operating room table belts. The RN and the techs freaked.

I said, "Oh shit! The tourniquet's not up." I had relied on the other tech's verbal acknowledgment that she had inflated the tourniquet. I assumed she had checked it out beforehand to be sure it was working. I think she had not switched the valve, and I had not checked the tourniquet to be sure that it was inflated. It is not rocket science to test a tourniquet function. If you inflate it, and the meter registers increased pressure (as occurs when you record someone's blood pressure), and it feels tight, then it has been inflated, or "the tourniquet is up."

Mr. Smith convulsed for a few seconds. I told everyone to stay calm, that the seizure would pass, and he would be all right. I tried to verify his pulse, but there was none. He stopped breathing. I did mouth to mouth. The tech ran back to recall Dr. Abulencia before he left the dressing room. I was alarmed. Why had he stopped breathing and his heart stopped? This wasn't supposed to happen! Within thirty seconds, I asked in panic, "This can't be! What the hell did this guy get?"

Either the tech or the RN pointed to a bottle sitting on the counter in the far corner of the room. It had a green label. Marcaine (also called Sensorcaine or Bupivicaine).

"That's not what I asked for. That's the wrong medicine!" I did not know at that time just how extremely toxic Marcaine was to the heart or how it would cause an irreversible cardiac arrest. I just knew it was *never* indicated for a Bier block. I grew more and more panicky as the seconds ticked by with no signs of life.

Dr. Abulencia could not detect any signs of heart function. The cardiologist was called in. I told him immediately as he entered the room that the patient had inadvertently received intravenous Marcaine instead of xylocaine for a Bier block. He could not resuscitate the patient either. After an hour or so, we accepted the grim reality. Arthur Smith was dead. As the patient's father later said to the press, "It was all so useless." I just couldn't explain it in any more humiliating terms than that. I was embarrassed to be called a doctor. We were indeed a ship of fools.

As I left the room to talk to the family Dr. Abulencia told me, "Bryce, tell the family it was an allergic reaction."

I said, "But, Alex, it wasn't an allergic reaction." I was stunned that he would lie to cover this up. I was even more astounded that he did not apparently realize that a simple toxicology test would confirm the cause of death. There was no way this could have been hidden, yet this pathological liar persisted, as I was to find out a year later, even after I thought my response would have extinguished any thought of pursuing such an outrageous conspiracy.

I was accompanied by the cardiologist and another nurse and patient representative as we headed to the waiting room to talk to the family. I approached both of the parents and asked again to be sure, "Are you Allen and Doreen Smith?"

She quietly said yes. I then said very concisely that her son had died during the procedure due to a medication error. She asked two times, "He'll be all right, won't he?"

I again repeated very deliberately, the third time "No. He died from a fatal reaction from the wrong medication. We'll have to get a toxicology report to confirm."

As I was saying this last sentence, she burst out hysterically, uncontrollable. The nurse offered to give her an intravenous sedative.

She screamed, "And how do I know you won't give me the wrong drug too?"

In contrast, his father sat there, stone silent, fuming, with the look of pure absolute disgust on his face.

I retreated to one of the holding rooms in the hall, exhausted, but I could not sleep. After several hours, I called up my partner and told him what had happened. I asked if he could take my call for the remainder of the weekend.

I called my mother, also an anesthesiologist, that weekend and informed her what had happened. She ominously responded, "Oh, Bryce, that will be the end of you."

There was a continuation of Mindy's deposition the following week. Skyler made no mention of this event or how it would impact the divorce or my practice/career—not during this deposition, not in later discovery, not in the remainder of her preparation for trial, not during settlement negotiations on the day of trial, not ever. Unbelievable.

I think Skyler now realized that this temporary-maintenance situation Mindy enjoyed would now have a not-so-temporary devastating effect on my career, and that this case had really gotten away from her and Salazar. *Here I was, not only having to pay Mindy total all-out support, but I was doing her fucking job too!*

I came to Skyler out of concerns about Salazar totally mishandling this temporary support hearing. She covered up for him. Salazar tried to downplay the whole thing by saying the maintenance was only temporary. The fact was, Mindy could drag out the divorce for years, especially through an appeals process, even if she knew she would ultimately not be successful, merely to keep the temporary-divorce *pendent lite* alimony payments coming in and collect half of any accumulating marital assets through my continued work. This is why the *pendent lite* hearing is so important. It determines the entire course of the divorce and indeed the future of the parties and the children. If the parties are not on a level playing field per the statutes from the outset, the divorce escalates, as one party exploits and prolongs the temporary situation, and the other becomes increasingly bitter.

I still really get pissed thinking about this commissioner said how he claimed to "hate delays" when Mindy's motions for continuance after continuance were granted. Who was he trying to kid? Salazar had warned me it took him forever to make a decision.

So, a man needlessly lost his life, and my career was about to be destroyed. I was paying my wife all-out support in violation of the *most fundamental* statutes as she sat home while I was doing her job in the middle of the Gulf War while my orthopedic partner and an anesthesiologist had been called up. I was having to work harder to cover for my partner. Anesthesia was short staffed and could have used Mindy's services.

My partner's wife by this time was full of scorn for Mindy. She couldn't believe Mindy's reaction to this event. "And Bryce wants me to work? That could have been me."

The next few months leading up to the divorce trial were problematic enough. Now I was having to deal with the imminent lawsuit from this event, the negative publicity, and so on. But the most devastating factor had yet to be realized: The medical board was soon to be calling. I would be caught in a triple pincer of divorce, medical malpractice, and professional licensure-board action, all because I had tried to be so accommodating.

Mitchell would make a comment at the third court hearing in front of the commissioner that Bryce was "just mad at the world." You think?

Back to the divorce

Bryce Sterling

Skyler as far as I can see, even after looking through her work product after the fact, had not made any net total calculations to the define the high and the low range of the marital estate. She never completed her simpleton scorecard, which had the following items, all of which, except my new residence, had been paid for.

- my orthopedic practice
- my extramarital residence
- the marital residence and contents
- Mindy's IRA and Keough
- my IRA and retirement
- rehabilitation center stock
- surgical-center stock
- life insurance policy cash values
- vehicles
- ring

The only values listed on these items were Mindy's and my experts' *pretax* values on some of the items. This scorecard was deficient and simplistic. It was never completed and never reviewed with me prior to trial. Other items, like Mindy's upgrade of her diamond ring, the contents of the house (Steinway Piano, Thomasville Oak furniture in all rooms, her premarital professional loans, the fact that the marital residence was paid for whereas my "more valuable" extramarital residence had a large mortgage outstanding) were not even discussed.

The temporary support I had been paying Mindy was absolutely statutorily prohibited as a most extreme example of abuse of the court's discretion on the issue, and there should have been a provision for this additional $4,500 a month payout (after her paying taxes on this maintenance, Mindy would net at least $3,000 of this $4,500 over fifteen months) or $45,000 net gain in her column, whereas I would have retained maybe 60 percent of this amount had I not been paying her because I would have paid higher taxes on my income tax rate of 40 percent. I would have saved, after taxes $40,500. Therefore, these maintenance payments had already built in a discrepancy of around $85,500 in the settlement column. (She gained $45,000, and I lost $40,500.)

But worst of all, my attorneys failed to make *any* provision for the highly publicized looming medical-malpractice event and the impending medical-licensure-board disciplinary action that would cripple me for the remainder of my career. They totally ignored this and instead focused only on my recent past short-term earnings history to justify this settlement, implying that it was not unconscionable nor unreasonable because it appeared at the time I could afford it.

Bifurcation? What's That?

But wait! This anesthetic death of Arthur Smith occurred *after* **the divorce** had been *bifurcated*, meaning Mindy and I were already officially divorced, but issues of custody and property settlement had yet to be determined. A bifurcation allowed Mindy to date other men/continue her relationship with her boyfriend, Ben Holcomb, or even legally remarry before the divorce was finalized. Mindy could continue to enjoy her alimony payments as a legally divorced woman while I worked.

But most critically, did it allow her to lock in the valuation of the marital estate, including a potential doubling of the value of my practice due to goodwill having been established prior to the malpractice event? As of 1991, few states had addressed this issue. Must a trial court make its equitable distribution award based on the time the divorce is entered, or base its value at the time of the property settlement? Does it base its determination of the valuation of property at the time it had been appraised, or can it base its determination in view of new events which have occurred since the divorce, but before the actual settlement? In view of the new devastating malpractice event, my practice and my earnings capability would clearly have to be reassessed.

Salazar just agreed to bifurcation without consulting me, so I don't know the rationale behind it, but I never heard it mentioned again, especially after the anesthetic death. Had Salazar allowed Mindy to have it both ways—*again*? She would already secure a larger property settlement because a mutually self-imposed lower standard of living had allowed us to save and accumulate property. She had already enjoyed a higher standard of living through *pendente lite* payments to make up for this sacrifice. Now would this huge settlement be preserved by her having closed the deal before the anesthesia event?

My only layperson counterargument would have been that during this time Mindy had been enjoying all-out total support from me and, therefore, continued support and property settlement were dependent on my financial and professional viability. Property settlement should have been based on this new set of circumstances, but the consequences could really only be determined after the malpractice case had been settled and the licensure board action finalized. The amounts at stake were so great that the settlement phase of this bifurcated divorce necessarily should have been delayed. Skyler and Salazar however wanted to ram it through. They had made a complete mess of my divorce and wanted out -before I fully realized how big a mess it really was.

Salazar had communicated to me by letter that Mindy was "making a serious mistake" (by bifurcating the divorce) but don't breathe a word of this to her." Why was she making a mistake, Salazar, and how was it beneficial to me? He never told me the reason. My practice was later about to be rendered worthless, yet at the time of the bifurcation, her expert had appraised it for $630,000. Was Salazar figuring that bifurcation would end Mindy's claim on half of my ongoing earnings during the divorce and any additional buildup of the settlement amount? Without a bifurcation, would Mindy have gotten another sweep of my personal extramarital bank account and taken another half of my savings at the final settlement?

My analysis is that if Salazar had simply made the proper argument that Mindy was ineligible to receive any maintenance right from the start, Mindy would not be playing these games. She, too, would have wanted to proceed with the divorce as quickly as possible to get her hands on her share of marital estate and would have had little incentive to bifurcate the divorce in the first place. She could have lived off this settlement for years without returning to work by her own choice, not at my expense.

As stated earlier, Mindy had even filed a motion to freeze my income and put me on an allowance whereby the remainder of my income would be placed into an escrow account for the pendency of the divorce, to be later divided at the final settlement. However, her monthly maintenance amount and my needing to duplicate the residencies were limiting any buildup of a larger estate through my continued working anyway. I needed to build up savings simply to pay for the impending settlement payout, yet if I tried to save, half of it would be scarfed up by Mindy in an even larger settlement. The more I worked and saved, the more I would be assessed. If Mindy had been working, I would have gotten half of her earnings and offset this cash drain. There was no way I could get a break. The judges and lawyers were too stupid to understand this.

Another Boyfriend, Another Runner, Another Accountant

As would be predicted by Salazar's initial remarks ("this commissioner cannot rule and it takes him months to reach a decision"), the divorce was dragged out as Mindy asked for continuance after continuance until the time came when she needed the cash property settlement. Mindy hadn't known Ben Holcomb, a CPA and a runner, for but a few weeks before she barged into our orthopedic practice accountant's office with him to look over the books. I got a call in the middle of my office from our accountant who informed me this weird guy who was very quiet, and whom he had never heard of, had just showed up at his office with Mindy, and she wanted him to look over the books. He remarked this guy had a flat personality, didn't say a word.

I called Salazar, and he said that yes, legally, Mindy could have him look at the practice's books. This was very unusual, and my partner's wife was *very pissed* that Mindy was inviting a perfect stranger whom she hadn't known but two weeks and who wasn't even an expert named in the divorce to look over the practice's books.

I have already established that Mindy never lifted a finger to do anything about keeping financial records, or any work for that matter, unless there was an ulterior motive. Her lawyer had already retained an expert to appraise my practice for the divorce, and his name was Dale Hastings. Salazar flat-out called Hastings a paid, hired gun. Skyler quite hypocritically accused him of grossly overbilling.

I can confidently say I know Mindy better than anyone, even her current husband of twenty-five years. I know exactly why she brought Holcomb to our accountant's office. It wasn't to double check Hasting's work. She wanted to entice Ben into marrying her by showing off how much money she had coming to her through her divorce settlement. Ben had recently quit his job as CEO of a local fast-food or 7-Eleven–type chain and was unemployed except as a cross-country coach, but was fairly financially conservative and had also paid off his house. He was a runner and just a few weeks earlier had met Mindy on the starting line at the annual mini marathon. "Fast starter Ben Holcomb wins Mini Marathon" read the headlines. He won, because after all, he was in love, at least at the time.

By now, I had recognized the pattern. Mindy and I were dating while I was still in my fourth of year medical school, and she was doing her general surgery internship. She suddenly had an eye out for this short plastic surgeon with a hairy back who was doing a hand fellowship and who came from a wealthy Jewish family. He tried to impress Mindy by running on the YMCA track with his shirt off, revealing his hairy back. Ugh. I later learned she had agreed to secretly pick him up at the airport after he'd returned from a conference. Mindy didn't drive a very nice car and didn't want to be seen driving a clunker, so she visited the Toyota car dealership and requested to test drive a new car for the afternoon under the false pretenses of buying it. The dealer saw right through her scheme and said no. At least Mindy hadn't been trying to test drive this car to learn how to drive a standard shift (and grind through the gears) with her mother as she had done when she was sixteen.

As quickly as the interest between them had started, it ended, and the next morning Mindy was calling for me outside my first-floor med-dent dorm window. Pathetic that she did that. Even more pathetic that I took her back.

Now that I think of it, this older hippie (affectionately using the term) psychiatrist, Fred, and his wife, who lived on the same street as Mindy, had discreetly tried to give me warnings about her.

"I shouldn't be too serious about getting into a relationship with Mindy" had been the sum and substance of his laconic remark.

His wife remarked, "She was already wearing her beanie (the Jewish cap) the next day she met this guy (plastic surgeon)." I had been too stupid to heed or hadn't inquired further. I wonder what profiles Fred could have identified in both me and Mindy, based on his observations.

Custody, Evaluations, and Psychological Profiles

Before our separation, Mindy had asked me if I would agree to fly our minister we'd become friends with during residency to reconcile/mediate. The only reason Mindy did that was because she had fully expected him to take her side. Our minister was a graduate of Princeton Theological Seminary and was the minister of our American Baptist church. He'd baptized me by submersion in front of the congregation. I'd played golf with him; we'd had social outings. We'd visited each other's homes. He was a true gentleman and a Christian. His wife was a very nice person. They'd sponsored through the church a refugee from Africa, whom I think eventually went to medical school. To make a long story short, after our discussions, our minister reluctantly sided with me and thought Mindy's goals ("wanting to find the meaning of life" was her final answer) were very narrow and self-centered. He left somewhat dejected, knowing he had failed. We never saw him or heard from him again.

Then Mindy had wanted me to see a relative of hers in the city who was a marriage counselor or a social worker. I remember at one point during this interview I complained about how this self-described full-time mother never cleaned the house. Mail was all over the place and was even stacked on top of the stove burner. Iced tea had been left in the fridge in an open cup for over a month until she asked, "Do you want some ice tea?" Even when we had hired a housekeeper to clean, the place was always a mess.

This counselor had agreed and said something to the effect, "Mindy, the least Bryce can expect is to come home to a clean house." Basically, this counselor had been at least somewhat supportive of me, whereas I was unable to detect *any* support for Mindy. Mindy did not go back to her either. Mindy not only wanted to wear two hats, but also to switch them whenever it suited her. She never wanted to take care of the household because it was beneath her as a doctor, yet she refused to work as a doctor because she was now a full-time mother.

Finally, Mindy briefly saw a psychologist in the city. I don't know how many times she had seen him, but I suspected this had been part of her pattern to shop for support. Mindy had been even secretly calling my two sister-in laws and mother, trying to recruit them to side with her. Mindy asked if I would mind seeing this psychologist. I said, sure, no problem.

I went and talked with him for maybe an hour, relating what had transpired. After a while, I was no longer interested in pursuing his questions and telling my story. He finally asked me, "Do you think she is having an affair?" I said no. He looked at me, stunned for a few seconds, I think surprised at my flat affect.

Of course I knew she'd been having an affair, you twit. The fact was that I didn't care. I just wanted to get out of the marriage. He perhaps picked up how little emotional attachment I now had for Mindy, or if I had any, it was overshadowed by my florid hatred for her, a hatred born of her treachery and the control she now had over me. I had maybe gotten through to him enough about Mindy's treachery that he realized what a monster Mindy really was. As far as I know, Mindy stopped seeing this psychologist shortly afterward, and I never heard from him again. He was never identified as an expert witness nor deposed during the divorce.

I can't remember in which order the formal custody-evaluation experts were done. I was getting the suspicion that custody had already been prede-termined, or that unless unusual circumstances existed, custody was always given to the mother. When I asked Salazar about getting a house in town, he gave a very vague and evasive response, such as that it would be... okay. I mentioned it because the decision was based almost entirely whether I had any chance of custody. It was another catch-22 dilemma: if I showed no interest in getting my own house, then it would suggest I had no serious interest in gaining custody. On the other hand, the question was whether to stay in town at all if there was no chance of my getting custody, in which case I certainly wouldn't buy a house. Men, this is why you don't get married or start families.

Salazar flat-out evaded this important issue. When the topic of custody evaluation came up, I thought it strange that he really didn't seem to think it was an issue or even a good idea. He never suggested any psychiatric/psycho-logic evaluations, in contrast to Mindy who, was always, always, shopping for support and asked me to present for evaluations by her expert.

Did Salazar mean that it was a waste of time because Mindy would get custody anyway? Did he figure that Skyler would be assigned that task of custody evaluation? He should have come outright and said, "Bryce, you will *never* get custody, whether physical, legal, or joint. It will never happen in this court. You are getting screwed, and the sooner you accept it, the sooner you can get on with your life."

Once I bought my house, it now had to be appraised by both experts as it became part of the marital estate. What made it even more frustrating is that when I finally did buy this similar-sized house (before the big anesthesia event—I would have never purchased it if the anesthesia event had already occurred), Mindy's attorney Mitchell lit into me and accused me of splurging on myself.

To paraphrase Mitchell's rant: "Bryce, how much money do you make?" It was always that question repeatedly at the start of every hearing: "How much money do you make? How much money do you make? What has been your income these past six months? Is it true, Dr. Sterling, that you have just purchased a house, furniture, stereo equipment, and so on, on Barnard Drive?"

"And how much did you spend on that house, the furniture, the stereo equipment, remodeling, and so on? (I had to pay full freight for the replacement furnishing costs for my new residence but was credited only for pennies on the dollar for the same already in Mindy's house, at least according to the appraisers, but that somehow was irrelevant. I ultimately would never receive a penny of credit for any of our marital household property, or even the house.) So you spend all that money and you are complaining about Mindy getting maintenance?" I had been living in a $400/month one-bedroom apartment for a year, but of course, Mitchell never brought that up.

Actually, I had to borrow $40,000 from my parents to help pay for an almost-identically sized and priced ($90,000) house. This "more valuable" house was not paid for, unlike Mindy's (marital residence). All Skyler had done was get an appraisal on the value, but when I sued her, she claimed that as part of my "good settlement," I had "retained the more valuable residence." Skyler never stopped lying or trying to obscure the blatant facts.

Salazar finally stepped in feebly and argued during a pretrial hearing, "Mindy, Mrs. Dr. Mindy, you too could buy that if you worked, couldn't you?

You are using that agreement (the inadmissible postnuptial verbal agreement that Mindy would not work) as an excuse for not working, aren't you?"

Salazar again failed to hammer home that it was absolutely statutorily prohibited for Mindy to collect any maintenance with her extraordinary earnings potential, which she admitted was $200,000–$300,000 and which she could start earning immediately. This postnuptial verbal agreement that she would not work was totally inadmissible and irrelevant in a divorce, but again there was no objection by Salazar.

Again, no change in the commissioner's opinion. Yes, he was that incompetent, naïve, and stupid—or if he realized he had really screwed up, he didn't want to admit it.

My Psychiatric and Psychological Profile Testing

I remember showing up at my expert psychologist's office (for determination of child custody) early one morning after having been up half the night. I began taking a battery of tests. The Beckman Depression inventory, Minnesota Multiple Personality Inventory (MMPI), Rorschach inkblot test, and so on. He had me write a short essay on my child-rearing and marriage philosophy or something like that. He seemed to be a reasonable guy. He was my expert that Skyler had retained.

Mindy, our two children, and I followed up a few weeks later with a series of more in-depth personal-encounter evaluations by his associate, Cassandra Canada, a licensed clinical social worker. She was so full of self-importance, especially for a two-bit social worker—excuse me, LCSW (licensed clinical social worker). She always tried to give the impression that she possessed profound wisdom, expertise, and insight into our situation. Kind of like Skyler. Another lightweight. The Tupperware Party Twins.

Later, an accountant Skyler retained to act as a rebuttal witness to Dale Hastings also proved to be a lightweight. Skyler just never seemed to get it. She couldn't even get decent experts.

I remember two of Canada's remarks that were true. To both of us together she said, "You guys are pissing your money away, because you think you can always get more, and Mindy, I don't think the court is going to let you sit on a medical degree."

In my one-on-one session, I outlined the history of our marriage, reciting how accommodative I had been, Mindy's infidelity, treachery, and so on. She finally interrupted me and said, "Bryce, don't you realize you have been had? Mindy has you hooked." Of course, I realized that. That was why I was so anxious and angry.

She did not discuss any of my latent anger or frustration, my exacerbated tendency to brood, or my relations with the children. I did not really display any anger during this protected evaluation. After all, she was supposed to be my expert. She later evaluated my interaction with the kids, acknowledged in her testimony how freely they would approach both parents, and so on. There were no specific or discernible issues with me being an unfit parent.

But then I read her depositions. She recommended custody to Mindy. She mentioned my tendency to brood, I think, and my low threshold for frustration, possibly some depression. Then the ultimate back stab: She criticized me for being motivated by *quid pro quo*. Any good act or intention was to be disregarded because I expected something in return. Unbelievable.

So, one minute I have been hooked by Mindy and her treachery and manipulation, acknowledged, at least certainly not disputed, by this expert, and then suddenly I am the bad guy because I wanted her to work?

So, what showed up on my MMPI? It was normal. What were the findings on Mindy? Her MMPI was flat, meaning she was trying to fudge the test. Manipulate. Gee, where would that come from? Other psychology tests showed Mindy had traits of being histrionic, narcissistic, and hedonistic. These are traits found in sociopaths. A sociopath is, by broad definition, someone who has no empathy for others or one who is incapable of having any concern for other people's feelings. They use people, manipulating for their own personal gain—people like Suze Orman and her Visa debit card scam she sold people to enable them to build up their credit scores. You don't build up a credit history with a *debit* card. You build it up by borrowing and paying back in a timely fashion through a *credit* card.

Studies suggest that up to twenty-five percent of bankers and CEOs match this sociopathic profile. People forget these people can outwardly appear very pleasant and agreeable in social situations, but when not having to wear the façade in public, they can be downright treacherous. While I was in in my final orthopedic job, one of Mindy's former residents was working as a *locums tenen* anesthesiologist. He seemed to think she was nice. "Oh yeah, little Mindy, I remember her." But go back further in time to when she was in high school or medical school and ask about what they really thought about her, it was a totally different story. I found out too late.

I was even asked during the divorce, "Does your ex-wife really hate you that much?"

I said, "Oh no. You've got it all wrong. Mindy doesn't hate me. She has simply gotten all she can out of me and has no further use for me. She never loved me, and it was no matter for her to put me out to the curb like the weekly trash. You don't hate your trash, do you? Once you have used something and it is no longer of any value, you throw it away. Mindy couldn't care less if I wound up penniless and shirtless out on the street, or if our children never saw me again, not out of hatred or revenge, but simply because she had no further use for me." This is the personality of a true sociopath. Reassuring to know she is a doctor isn't it?

After Canada's findings and recommendation, I guess it really didn't matter what the psychologist or Canada's other testimony was. Surprisingly, Mindy admitted that I was one of the most ethical doctors she had ever known. I can't believe she volunteered that on record. Then this psychologist remarked about how much he liked my essay and had not seen one so moving and insightful or something like that. Then Canada remarked that it was "very unusual for husbands to be as open and forthright about themselves as Bryce." Finally, this psychologist even stated off-the-cuff in his deposition, "I like Bryce."

To this day, I think there are two very important preliminary questions to ask any expert who is expected to testify on your behalf in custody evaluations.

The first is the obvious one involving the usual due diligence: how many of these custody evaluations have you done?

The second is really the one that matters and is subtler: how many times do you recommend custody to the mother—and why? I maintain courts have an inherent bias in awarding custody to the mother. It is assumed that mothers get custody of the children unless proven otherwise. Knowing this, custody experts bias their recommendations toward what they think courts want them to say so that they will be assigned cases by the courts or sought out as paid hired guns by lawyers in custody cases.

Leroy Rathbone, a psychologist, was another of Mitchell's hired guns according to Skyler, who had dealt with him before. She failed to inform me of any of his background prior to my evaluation. She called him Leroy "Rascal." Tee-hee, Skyler, you are so silly, calling him "rascal." Maybe you might want to call him "peanut butter and jelly"? How about Leroy Ratshit?

I have to admit Rathbone had it pegged right when he testified, "Here is a guy who should have behaved as if he were applying for a position of sainthood but who was so angry the people could hear him screaming from downstairs in the other offices and were asking me for a week what was going on in your office that day?" I think he even claimed that I was drooling. The problem was, he only interviewed Mindy and me together (never separately), and Mindy was so brazenly controlling, manipulative, and dishonest that day I could not take it and exploded.

Rathbone laughed, "You really know how to push his buttons, don't you?" Mindy nodded yes, with a smirk. That evaluation was a sham with no acknowledgment of any of my claims or concerns about Mindy. The outcome was no surprise to Skyler. Rathbone characterized me in his deposition as "abusive and scary." The divorce had certainly deteriorated.

I doubt if it is true, but I heard through the rumor mill that shortly after that evaluation, Rathbone stopped doing them. I don't see why. He was almost laughing at me when I saw him down in the cafeteria during a break. He even winked at me. He reminded me of Joe Pesci in *Home Alone*. Could he later have learned about the type of person Mindy really was through the medical community grapevine? Judging from his type of character, I doubt that would have been the reason. I could sense he was the type who would sell his mother for a dollar.

Post-divorce Financial Consultant

Being a doctor makes you a target for all the money experts, particularly financial consultants. I had already had my taste of them in medical school, one being a classmate who was a self-styled financial consultant who must have sucked in about a dozen of my classmates, me included, into his MDIC, or Medical Doctor Investment Club around my fourth year of medical school. I recall giving him about two thousand dollars to invest.

Things did okay for a while, and then during my internship, well, let's say the distance grew, from both him and my money. I asked for redemption, and all of a sudden, I received a lot less than I had invested, and in fact, I first learned what the parentheses meant around a number on a financial statement. It meant a loss. I don't know what he had been doing with his money, but apparently my classmate had bailed and left his fund manager to run the show.

As the old saying goes, he got the money, and I got the experience. I shortly figured out he was a pathologic bullshitter. He always said he worked out so he could keep his bench press up to three hundred pounds, even though the few times I saw him at the university gym he never tried to show off his advertised prowess. I mean, come on. Guys always want to show off their bench press in the gym.

He also claimed the surgeon he worked with as a senior in medical school let him do all the cases and that he would let him ask for the instruments as he needed them and so on. Pure BS! Then in residency, I heard that he had to do an extra year. Was he spending all his time dabbling in real estate, or was he a slow learner? He at least was able to show me his real estate card stating such. (But never any three-hundred-pound bench press.)

A financial consultant approached me shortly after my divorce had been finalized. She said she specialized in divorce financial planning. I thought this was either a unique angle or just a gimmick, but I agreed to see her in my office. Just what I needed, I thought sarcastically, another financial planner. I had lost money on investment with my former medical classmate and then again during my internship when a financial planner-medical student advised me strongly to invest in MFS's ninety-ten fund, which had a 7 percent front load and ultimately lost a lot of money. Shows you how naïve I was about financial matters.

I came prepared with the settlement, financial records, and appraisals. After giving this consultant the rundown on some of the numbers on the practice, the rehab unit, the price paid on the marital residence, and the divorce settlement, she started asking me some questions about premarital school loans, the cars, retirement accounts, what Mindy did, how much child support and alimony I was paying, and so on. She then asked me for a few numbers on how much we invested in the rehab ($60,000) the surgical center ($23,000), and the brain-injury unit ($7,000), and looked at the appraisals on these and other items of marital property, both the high and low ends.

After about an hour, she asked (paraphrasing our conversation), "Dr. Sterling, did you agree to this settlement or was this a court decision?"

I said that I'd agreed to it. The case had been settled.

"No, what I mean is did you agree to give her this, or did you contest it?"

I said, "No, this case was bitterly contested on all fronts at the cost of over $90,000 in lawyer and expert fees (that's in 1991 dollars) over fifteen months."

"But did your lawyers advise you to settle at this amount?"

Yeah, I said. They said I had to settle because my exposure was so high, and Salazar told me during the settlement negotiations in front of my parents that I could pay over a million dollars if the case went to trial. Skyler later had a number written in her correspondence to me in which she informed me, "We always told you the court could have awarded Mindy up to one-half of what her expert Dale Hastings appraised your practice and the rehab center."

The problem was an itemized summary of all other the individual marital-property items had never been totaled to give me an idea of the cumulative total.

"And what about all the items of marital property? Those were part of the divorce too."

"Those were appraised but not individually negotiated," I said. "It was a 'package deal.'"

Then the adviser asked me if I had gotten a tax consultant for the divorce, and I said, "Yeah, Skyler got this guy from a hotshot financial firm with a sickening gold-embossed letterhead to look over the numbers as a rebuttal witness on the issue of goodwill on the practice."

Then came the bomb. "Dr. Sterling, do you realize that Mindy ran off with the entire marital estate?"

"What? Wait a minute," I said.

She came right back and asserted, "Your lawyers didn't tell you that she gets her settlement free and clear of any taxes while you get stuck paying the taxes on both yours and her shares? You're going to have to liquidate some of these properties to pay her settlement, aren't you? You'll get a tax bill."

She showed me that even using Mindy's expert's high-end, inflated property evaluations numbers, with a rough estimation of capital gains taxes of 30–40 percent factored in, I still would have clearly paid less than the amount my lawyers had urged to me to settle. The lawyers clearly had not factored in the taxes.

When a more probable midway evaluation of the assets was taken into account, plus the tax basis, the difference was even more glaring. In hindsight, I wonder if this financial adviser had already looking for this critical error right from the start. I can't remember if she said that this has happened before, but I suspect she used this insight to get her foot in the door when approaching a new client who was in the process of getting or had recently been divorced.

She spelled out the impact using the rehab valuation as an example. If the marital parties have taxable property that is appraised at $600,000 of which only $60,000 is principal and the rest is capital gains, then my ex-wife gets $300,000 of that tax-free. (I later verified with our orthopedic accountant with a formal, printed analysis that there was a total of 33 percent tax on all gains on all of the marital property if liquidated at that time.) In her example, my half of the rehab hospital was derived from a simple series of calculations. I would have to pay $600,000-$60,000 = $540,000 x 33 percent or $180,000 in taxes on the capital gains appreciation. So, assuming I have given her $300,000 which she gets tax-free, I have to pay $180,000 in taxes for both. This leaves me with $120,000 to her $300,000. And taxes consequences didn't matter? (As my attorneys still defiantly maintain to this day.)

And this lightweight accountant whom Skyler had retained as a rebuttal witness (but only to dispute the issue of goodwill) hadn't looked at any of that. What in the hell did I pay him $3,000 for? He was as bad as the lawyers, and I still see that phony gold-embossed letterhead of his company.

Again, Skyler never stipulated at the settlement hearing, nor would stipulate after, *any* value specifically, either the high end or the low end, of anything individually or collectively in a cumulative total except for the Mindy's expert's high-end appraisal pre-tax numbers of the rehab unit and my practice at $600,000 and $630,000 respectively. Her and Salazar's strong recommendations could not be distinguished from just a wild guess on the settlement payout number. As stated earlier, taxes sure seemed to apply as an excuse when Mindy was trying to get the idiot commissioner to forgive her earning $23,282.00 as an anesthesiologist right after she had been awarded her maintenance based on her zero-earnings capability.

Interestingly, on my trip to Africa a few years later, there was a domestic relations lawyer who *immediately* declared, "Yes, absolutely. That (omitting tax basis in recommending property settlement to a client) is legal malpractice." I later saw an article on this subject in a legal newsletter, so it was hardly an obscure issue. It was argued that in property settlement, assets, and *debts* are to be taken into account, and *taxes* are the quintessential inescapable *debt* to the government.

This financial adviser then clued me in on Mindy's medical school and nursing professional school debt for which I should have received credit, but nowhere in my attorneys' work product/records, depositions or Skyler's half-filled scorecard had this amount been taken into account. Skyler later stated erroneously that premarital debts are not credited to the other party in divorce. Yes, they are if they are professional school debts.

And of course, this financial planner was astonished that I had been paying Mindy $4,500 in support payments plus 100 percent of the child support while giving her exclusive use of the paid-for marital residence with all debts, even the car payments and her premarital medical school loans already paid off.

"She's a doctor. She isn't entitled to any support. Not even temporary support. How did she get that? Didn't you get a second opinion?" I told her Skyler was the second opinion. I explained that during the divorce, after seeing my ex-wife running around, not working, having everything provided for her while she sat on her medical degree, the word got around and back to me, no less than from my children's pediatrician: "Who in the hell is your lawyer, Bryce? Why isn't your ex having to work while you get stuck having to work and pay her alimony?" This had prompted me to get a second opinion from Elaine Skyler.

Sensing now that this case had been a disaster, she asked me if any provision had been made for this medical-malpractice case, and I said no. She then said, "Oh, Dr. Sterling, I wish I had been able to talk to you before you settled. Your ex-wife has wiped you out. Here she is talking about goodwill on your practice and this medical-malpractice suit is going to cost you more than your policy limits of just $200,000. Your practice may end up not being worth anything, and your lawyers made no allowance for this in the settlement? Didn't they even ask what were your medical malpractice insurance liability limits?"

"Nope." I fumed. I later realized that the lawyers hadn't even made any provision for the impact the future medical-board suspension would have on my career and future earnings potential. The trial should have been delayed until the magnitude of these losses had been realized, despite my being under economic coercion with these apparently non-recoverable temporary support payments.

Indeed, this planner's predictions were spot on. After paying for hastily negotiated indemnification insurance in case of a catastrophic award in the malpractice suit after the divorce had been finalized, my practice was for all practical purposes, worthless. I received $150,000 (no goodwill), and from this I had to pay $100,000 over ten years for the excess judgment exceeding my malpractice-insurance limits. I am now already down to $50,000.

Then, of course, there was the absolute three months' downtime imposed by the medical board when they suspended my license, and the lingering effects of career underemployment and unemployment. That would cost me *millions!* And don't forget that to pay Mindy the $365,000 tax-free cash settlement, I had to borrow and pay interest.

She also got the paid-for house, all the paid-for household contents, car, her much larger retirement IRA, paid-off premarital medical-school debt—$54,000, $9,000 diamond-ring upgrade. Not bad for effectively a little more than two years work. In other words, right off the bat, Mindy collected $365,000 cash tax-free, and I had to cough up $365,000 plus interest to pay her. That built an immediate $730,000 discrepancy. From there, we add to her total all the tangible property and her paid-off premarital debts.

By this time, I knew this adviser wasn't BSing me for business. She was absolutely stunned at what these lawyers had done. In fact, she didn't even bother to follow up or give me her card. I never heard from her again. She knew I was toast and realized that she had just wasted several hours of her time. It was like my later experiences with medical recruiters whose recruitment efforts stopped dead in their tracks once they realized I had a malpractice history and medical-board suspension and that I was uninsurable and could not be credentialed.

I was so furious and so agitated I almost drove over to Salazar's office to beat the crap out of him and Johnston. My hatred no doubt has become pathological because, even to this day, I would still first torture and then kill the whole lot of them, if I could get away with it. As my pilot friend said: "Sterling might as well have not even had a lawyer."

The problem is, this kind of problem doesn't go away. It stays with you; it nags you for the rest of your working career, which is extended much longer out of necessity because of income lost over my working career. I now can't afford to retire. In fact, the reality is that by the time I factored in all the wasted legal expenses, the costs of the malpractice lawsuit, and the future medical-board suspension, the settlement and property payout to Mindy, and so on, I would have been far better off emotionally, financially, and professionally having just literally handed everything—children, house, practice, all marital assets and walking away, except that Mindy would have hounded me for child support.

I don't know how I managed to keep my cool. But one thing I realized: I had to go back and see what these goddamned lawyers had done to me. After all, there is never just one cockroach in a room. And there again, I am prone to sulk and stew on things when I should just put them behind me. Easy for others to say, which pisses me off even more. We, the public, are supposed to quietly submit to this outrageous incompetence and double-standard abuse by lawyers? I don't know how I managed to keep practicing: the kids gone, dealing with the divorce settlement aftermath, the medical-malpractice case, and the impending medical-licensure-board action, all descending on me at once.

I started heading off to the university law library and, with Black's legal dictionary in hand, started reading the state domestic relations statutes and annotated case law, and even looking up appellate cases. I was on notice. My lawyers had screwed up. I was now about to find out how badly they'd screwed up and how they were lying to cover it up. Even worse, this was only the beginning. More lawyers were to come, like fucking rats streaming out of the sewer lines.

Back to Skyler's Office

I approached Skyler at her office about the settlement and asked her point blank whether she had taken taxes into account in the settlement. "Yes, we took those into account," she said, flat-out lying to me straight faced, eyeball to eyeball, as she read back my question verbatim as if to reinforce her answer. If she had come so prepared for the trial, why could she not simply sit down for twenty minutes and show me how she had prepared for the trial and arrived at the settlement number by pulling up any pretrial calculations and summaries for which I had been billed for dozens of hours as preparation for trial and review of file?

That clever little scorecard she had showed Salazar at the beginning of the divorce. Where was it? The fact is, she had come to trial without even that pathetic little piece of toilet paper. There was simply no way a client could have possibly made any informed decision to settle at any amount that day.

All they talked about was a single number, a grand total amount that I might have had to pay if I didn't settle. No specific item or it's appraisal value entered the negotiations.

Skyler showed no work product to me in her office that day for the probable reason that she simply had none. In contrast, had there been a dispute over the bill, she could have produced complete records and amounts paid down to the penny. She did get her secretary to get me one of her fancy accordion-file folders to put all my papers in, though. Then to defuse the tension, she asked if I wanted to take a tour of her office. She introduced me to her husband, a much older guy (or maybe he was her partner?) and her secretary. I asked myself WTF was this office tour for? I mean, why the hell do I want to see her new office? To be sure that she really runs a law office? I left the office and decided to get another lawyer to look things over.

I called an old codger lawyer who knew my distant relative, whose last name was also Sterling, who had been a judge in my town for years and who had been plagued with health problems. Judge Sterling was an alcoholic, diabetic, and had some legal problems (DUI) as well. There was always something in the town paper about him. I met him once at a family reunion. I remember reading in his obituary how one of the lawyers complimented him on how well he understood the law, and would even take a lawyer aside after a trial and inform him how he had screwed up his client's case.

This codger lawyer was "proud to know me as a Sterling," and told me to go see this lawyer in the city

"The Laws Suck."

This referred lawyer said he would review my case, but instead of the usual free consultation, I would have to pay him seventy-five dollars. He came into the office and said he was stoked because he had just won his case. He listened to my story from what at this time was still not fully developed as far as my understanding. In about fifteen minutes, he said I was blowing a lot of hot air, and there wouldn't be anything I could do about it. I remember him saying emphatically why: "Because the laws suck." I really sensed I was getting a snow job and was about to leave the office when he reminded me to pay him his seventy-five dollars.

I later learned the divorce laws in my state, in fact, did not suck but were some of the most progressive in the nation and, if applied to my divorce, would have accomplished their stated objective per the statutes, of mitigating the consequences of divorce. In other words, these statutes, if followed, would have protected me from the oncoming ravages of divorce better than any other state. I think the only deficiency in the statutes was that my state was a no-fault state. Mindy knew a no-fault state allowed her to run around with other men with no consequences in a divorce.

This lawyer was a real sewer rat. He just wanted a quick seventy-five dollars. He didn't care about me. He didn't care if he gave me correct information. Even when I ask people on the street for directions, I usually get more honesty and good faith effort than I did from this slime ball, a real asshole whom you could smell in ten seconds. The legal profession is just full of slime balls and liars, and there isn't anything you can do about it.

Dr. Ahmar's *Ad Hoc* Credential-Review-Meeting Testimony

Dr. Ahz Ahmar's lawyer had been in contact with me to testify before an *ad hoc* hospital committee. Ahz was an orthopedic surgeon who had a checkered past, reportedly with some medical malpractice. As stated earlier, he had initiated the rehab project that was wrested from him by me, my partners, and Piggy. The hospital had been trying to get rid of Ahz for a long time.

I was called in to testify on a case involving a femur fracture he had rodded during which the patient died, possibly from a heart attack precipitated by blood loss. I had met Ahz briefly over lunch to discuss this case just one time in which he asked if I would mind appearing before the panel to give my opinions on the case. I don't recall even looking at the record or x-rays. I walked into the case cold. Strange that he would have asked me to do that, but maybe he knew I was pissed off at the hospital and would help him out. I had never been involved in a formal legal case review as an expert until this one. Based on all the anecdotal reports, mostly on his back surgeries, I figured they would have tried to introduce these, but my testimony was only about this one particular case.

I remember the case because it was unusual. When I looked at the x-rays for the first time in the hearing, I saw that there was also a nondisplaced hairline femoral neck fracture that had been missed, and only the midshaft fracture had been treated with a rod. (Possibly the femoral neck fracture could have become manifest after the main shaft fracture had been fixed, or maybe had been missed from the start as they sometimes are, or maybe the patient had died before that fracture could have been treated.) Either way, I was not questioned on that and I made no comment.

The panel asked me whether the case should have been done in retrospect because the patient apparently had lost a lot of blood and reportedly had died as a result of a cardiac arrest. The inference was that Dr. Ahmar was not competent to perform an intramedullary rodding of this fracture and that the patient had lost an unusual amount of blood as a result.

I pointed out that, in fact, Dr. Ahmar had ordered a type and cross for four units of blood preoperatively and that, therefore, blood loss was anticipated and replacement transfusion available and that a significant amount of blood loss is not uncommon for these fractures. It was clearly the anesthesia's fault for not keeping up with the blood replacement that had caused this patient's demise. My deliberate, spontaneous, and concise opinion stunned the panel who thought they had a solid case. It only underscored the incompetence and inadequacy of the anesthesiology department, as had occurred in my case earlier when Dr. Abulencia had abandoned his post. His partner had also refused to do one of my cases. I should have reported him. (This was the partner who later died on the table during open-heart surgery.)

One panel member then tried to do damage control and asked if I had been paid by Dr. Ahmar. "Yes," I said. "Lunch." Then one panel member (these are lawyers) asked me about my anesthetic-related death, apparently now trying to discredit me. I responded in a bring-it-on manner that demonstrated I was eager to drag the issue out into the open to show how the hospital, through its agents—the nurse, tech, and anesthesiologist, Dr. Alex Abulencia—was the reason for my patient's death and it was more of the same as with Dr. Ahmar's case.

The panel quickly realized that they had stepped into a hornet's nest and that digging up my incident only served to bolster my testimony and Dr. Ahmar's case. It was the anesthesia department that had screwed up again this time, not Dr. Ahmar. They stopped and conferred off the record and then stated that my incident would not be discussed.

The Divorce Trial

I insisted my parents come to the trial to witness Mindy's treachery. My mother loved me as a son, probably disliked me as a person, and initially had actually sided with Mindy until she saw her IRA shell game. I wanted to be sure she fully understood Mindy's treachery. She had assumed I was a bear to live with because of my childhood temper.

Mindy had been contacting my brothers' wives and had them all convinced that I was at fault. This was Mindy's standard MO of witness shopping as she did with our minister, her family social worker, and even her own aforementioned psychologist. My father was more intent on playing with his computer in the courtroom. My mother told him to put it down and listen. My father snapped back, "I'm not going to be unproductive for a minute!"

That was one of the biggest bullshit statements I'd ever heard from my father. He had nothing to do all day. He had done nothing his entire life. He had my mother supporting him both in the household and financially. It was my mother who paid for the house we grew up in. It was my mother's parents who provided the down payment. My mother paid the mortgage, utilities, insurance, laundry bills, groceries, and so on. My father wandered around the house at all hours of the night because he couldn't sleep. Of course he couldn't. He never worked. And my father had tenure, which meant the state university school of medicine could never get rid of him. He was on the dole until nearly age sixty-seven. Mindy constantly criticized my father. But guess what? Mindy wound up in the same cushy academia job with full tenure too. This means they can't get rid of her either. Mindy published some papers early on her career that allowed her to move up in the department. However, now that she has achieved the rank of full professor with tenure, I'll bet she hasn't done a damn thing since, just milk the system for all it is worth. Confront her with this and she will smirk.

I didn't ask my parents to travel over six hundred miles just to see me settle the case. I came to the courthouse that bright sunshiny day fully expecting to try the case, which I was informed by Skyler would last two days. As mentioned numerous times before, we had not gone through any specifics in the case from financial to custody since the original depositions, although at that time I realized that custody was a lost cause, especially since my own expert LCSW had recommended custody go to Mindy.

By this time, Mindy had been given so many breaks by the court I knew that the system was stacked against me. I was a male orthopedic surgeon who was apparently making plenty of money, and the court had been presented with a glorious opportunity to prove how concerned they were for the children in divorce.

Children and mothers often, if not usually, get the raw end of the deal in a divorce. Many times, the husband is not good provider, has been running around, is an alcoholic or drug addict, mentally or physically abusive, or is just irresponsible. In those cases, the ex-wife and children can't get blood from a stone.

In contrast, I was a good provider, responsible, faithful, sacrificing, accommodative in many ways, and most importantly confirmed by my child-custody expert a loving father who was devoted to his children and was in turn loved by his children, especially my son. Mindy's expert had not done any such evaluation of my interaction with the children. His sole purpose was to discredit me as an individual, not as a father. I had not had as much time and contact with my daughter. She had been born while I had been starting up my practice, and I had been busy. But remember: it was Mindy who'd wanted me to join this practice—where she knew I could make a lot of money, be close to her home town, and where she could spring her trap. She would never work again as long as I was her mule.

This divorce nevertheless was a perfect opportunity for the court to show how generous and concerned it is with the children—by raking me over the coals. It seemed to me a makeup call, a practice that would be revisited again by the medical licensure board. In pretrial hearings, the new commissioner, Selig, made it clear he was only interested in hearing what the children's needs were.

It was a beautiful sunny day. My parents had shown up. No new information or summary of the estate numbers had been provided by my lawyers in weeks. Specifically, I had not seen any new additions to the long-forgotten scorecard that Skyler had provided Salazar months earlier. I knew the individual pretax appraisal numbers of my orthopedic office, the rehab, the surgical center, the homes, and so on, but again all of these were pretax, and these valuations had not even been totaled in scorecard format to give me an idea of the cumulative size of marital estate upon which any determination of an equitable division could be made, and certainly not on short notice.

Certain items such as Mindy's premarital medical school loans and her ring upgrade had not even been addressed. I assumed that my attorneys had all this information prepared and we were going to trial and would itemize these one by one at trial. Certainly, if settlement had been contemplated, an itemized total should have been made available to me well ahead of time for review.

From what I can now gather, my lawyers were simply going to wing it at trial that morning if they could not convince me, or more accurately, scare or threaten me, into settling.

Newly appointed Commissioner Lorne Selig made the usual introductory disingenuous remarks that he would be happy to hear this case, but threatened me that this case could go on to the court of appeals (where I would be mired for years with endless temporary support payments). These statutorily prohibited temporary orders gave Mindy tremendous bargaining power and were nothing less than outright coercion.

Selig tried to give the impression that he was going to be fair. He specifically mentioned, *twice* that he did not think Mindy's listing of an electric fence for the dog was a justifiable child support expense. This was the only specific item he mentioned. This was, in my opinion, a pathetic smoke screen to give me the impression that I was going to get a fair shake. Selig had already made up his mind. I was going to pay for everything, *except for that fucking electric dog fence!* Mindy would get custody, and I would have to pay extra in marital-property settlement to be sure that the children were provided for. After all, he surely didn't expect Mindy to have to provide for anything. "But we won't make you pay for everything Dr. Sterling. Look, you aren't going to have to pay for the electric dog fence."

A little background about Commissioner Lorne Selig, who is now deceased. Sometime earlier, he had been riding a tractor with his young son, pulling a bush hog. His son fell off the tractor and was pulled under, chopped to pieces and pronounced DOA at the emergency room. So, in my opinion, Selig had a guilt trip that he took out on fathers by ordering generous child support. He was divorced himself, but I guess he could never figure out that it was in the children's best interests if you don't piss off the father so much that he throws his hands up and walks away. I could tell he already assumed I was at fault. In contrast, women going through divorce always seem to be able to justify their bad behavior because they are victims and have to resort to lying, manipulation, or infidelity as coping mechanisms for survival.

Selig didn't have much sympathy or insight over my medical-malpractice case. He later opined that my leaving my orthopedic practice was "patently voluntary but latently due to the publicity." How could he be so sure I did not have to leave the practice? Or could it have been because my partner was *not* leaving even though had signed a contract to work at the military base or that my license was *not* going to be suspended and probated? Or that despite all the publicity, my practice and my career were *not* going to be impacted? Or that the practice would not have to close? Or was it simply that because my ex-wife was now leaving this town to which she had lured me, it simply no longer made sense for me to stay? He just had it all figured out. He was going to punish me to the bitter end. Fuck you in your grave Selig! His comment in this context made it very clear that he had been out to screw me from the start.

It was interesting that Mindy's female attorney was not present the day of the trial. Remember, Mitchell had *not* been present at Mindy's depositions. Did Mindy not want Mitchell to hear the type of person she really was? On the flip side, had Mindy terminated her female attorney because, after having attended Mindy's deposition and hearing about her "contributions" and treachery during the marriage had voiced her opinions which Mindy didn't want to hear? Or, that Mindy might not do as well at trial as she thought as a result? Remember, Mindy had me see two of her counselors whom she then quickly rejected, and she had rejected our mutual friend, our minister. Therefore, I was not surprised that her female attorney did not show up for trial. I think deep-down, Mindy's attorney was not sympathetic to her at all. Mindy sensed this and terminated her.

So rather than start the trial, Mindy and Mitchell suddenly went back to a separate room. Skyler left me and began negotiating a settlement with Mindy and Mitchell, which was strange because I thought we were there to try the case. I was not even present during these closet negotiations.

Skyler then came back and suddenly started telling me that Mitchell and Mindy were asking for a huge sum of money and that I had better settle the case rather than try it. No scorecards or summaries were presented. No range in settlement amounts had been discussed. Incredibly, Skyler will still claim to this day that she told me the full range my exposure based on her preparation. She is a fucking liar. She and Salazar knew they had screwed up the case from the start, knew that they weren't ready, and now desperately wanted to get it settled so that I could not sue them for legal malpractice. Once the case was settled, it would be buried forever and they would get off scot-free after having ripped me off for tens of thousands of dollars.

Skyler shuttled back and forth just like a used car salesman with his manager to give the impression that she was negotiating a lower settlement.

"Mindy has agreed to a lower amount, but Mitchell is telling her to go higher," she huckstered. "Settle now at this amount and you will be getting a good deal" was her sales pitch as she and Salazar desperately tried to squirm out of this case.

Incredibly, Skyler then approached my parents in the courtroom and inquired if they would be willing to cosign the settlement payment to Mindy! *Unbelievable!* Skyler would stop at nothing so that she could get out from under the case. My parents naturally said "no." So why did Mindy need to get this guarantee of payment from my parents? Was it because she knew that maybe my practice and indeed my entire career were in jeopardy because of this anesthetic death case? If so, neither Mindy, nor my attorneys would ever acknowledge that, even in my lawsuit against them alleging legal malpractice. They would only focus on my past income, which within two years would suddenly drop off the cliff to zero. True, at the time, it had been approaching $350,000 with all the dividends from the investments, but Mindy's nearly equal earning potential was totally ignored.

So what kind of provisions should have been made? Well, let's look to Mindy's tactics. Earlier, she had tried to freeze my income and put me on allowance with the reminder of my earnings to be placed in an escrow account during the divorce. How about Skyler and Salazar merely insisting that any settlement payment be put into escrow until *after* this medical-malpractice action was finalized and the status of my license determined? In fact, I now wonder if it was I who should have insisted on a provision for permanent support! That would have been the ultimate comeuppance for Mindy: having to pay me maintenance for her treachery. Again, Skyler and Salazar didn't want to throw any roadblocks to getting this case settled, so they never mentioned this subject. I was sold out. Premeditated, egregious legal malpractice by any standard or definition.

So, clearly, I was blindsided by my attorneys. What was the basis for this settlement recommendation? I had seen no totals of the estate. Then Salazar joined in saying, "I strongly urge you to settle this case. Your exposure is too high. You could pay a million dollars if Selig rules against you." In his answer to my interrogatories when I later sued Salazar he affirmed in his answers that "I got a good settlement."

"Absolutely, based on what you had to lose, you got a good settlement." The reality: Salazar didn't really know how much I could lose because he and Skyler had never crunched all the numbers. Salazar did not mention this million-dollar number in his answer to this interrogatory. Any specific numbers seemed to disappear into the mist after the settlement. Finally, my parents, convinced by my lawyers' theater, joined in and urged me to settle.

In his explanation to my grievance to the state bar concerning his incompetence, lying, and abandonment of his client, Salazar wrote, "Bryce was a very high-strung individual … and we had to get his case settled quickly." Why did you have to get my case settled quickly, Salazar? Because I was high strung and agitated, or because you and Skyler had really screwed up my case? Here I am getting screwed by this divorce court, by my treacherous ex-wife, facing a ruinous medical-malpractice suit and likely medical-board action, and it is unrealistic for me to be high strung?

It was very simple in hindsight: My attorneys had, at the minimum, botched the case. They were not ready for trial. They had already financially made a killing off me, so they abandoned me at trial and got me to settle, knowing that once the case was settled they were off the hook. I could never sue them for legal malpractice. Once you settle a case, that's it. You can't address your attorneys' errors. You can't go back to court. And believe me: this incompetent Judge Dwayne Lattimer, who had failed to keep an eye on his idiot commissioner, also wanted it buried forever. It was a how-everything -can-go wrong in a divorce case if you wind up in a court room of liars, thieves, and fools.

Salazar never got involved in my case again after that. I tried to go back and get the settlement overturned on the basis that Mindy was rejecting the terms, I think again wanting me to pay additional dividends from the rehab hospital and maintain the children as beneficiaries on my life insurance policy. If I am providing life insurance, then Mindy didn't have to purchase it. This would be yet another form of additional indirect benefit to her. Her demands further delayed the settlement. Lorne Selig mercilessly ruled that I had to pay additional interest penalty on the settlement because of this delay. Judge Lattimer finally recognized the need for damage control and said no. Mindy should not benefit from the delay she has caused.

Skyler initially, and against my instructions, tried to argue that the settlement be set aside on the basis of Mindy having rejected certain terms and thereby would nullify the settlement in its entirety. Even I knew this was a bullshit argument, but Skyler insisted. Shortly thereafter, Judge Lattimer cited a case law precedent that established that a settlement dictated into the record on audio tape is binding, just as a written signed contract. (I had already researched this case law as well as economic coercion.)

Skyler finally had to resort to my original argument that I had been economically coerced by the court through threats of long appeals while I was having to pay what was clearly statutorily prohibited alimony. Judge Lattimer's opinion was that the "property had been equally divided and that since I could afford to pay without difficulty or burden, the settlement was not one-sided."

Huh? He didn't even know what the property division was. Therefore, how could he possibly have determined that the property had been equally divided? He had dodged the whole point. The property theoretically could not have been equally divided if one party was being coerced. And what about Mindy? She, too, could have paid without difficulty or burden. Yet again, her earnings capability was never recognized. This was the classic case of two equal parties, same age, same income if working full time as required by the statutes, with no special needs for the kids, which would not have permitted the court to deviate from the statutes. But here we had a situation where one party was paying for everything and the other for absolutely nothing. This was the purest example of a manifestly and patently unfair settlement that should have been set aside as *unconscionable!*

In that hearing, I read a prepared statement in front of Lattimer in a very belligerent tone to the extent that a deputy sheriff was now present. I was so spot on that the judge could not respond. No one in that court said a word, not a word. Stone silence. Only as we departed the courtroom, the sheriff quietly said to me, "I'm sorry, Doc, but it won't do any good."

The hidden argument, or the elephant in the room, was the fact that I had been represented at trial by counsel, so theoretically, I could not have been coerced into a bad settlement. My attorneys should have prevented this from occurring. They were looking after their own interests and sold me out. Skyler, I'm sure, was acutely aware that my argument on the basis of coercion would implicate her own failure in adequately representing me. Later she wrote that she'd known that I would ultimately turn against her.

The day of the settlement, Skyler tried to blow the most pathetic smoke screen to justify this sudden settlement as we exited the courtroom: she blamed it on Commissioner Selig. "It was a beautiful day, and he just didn't want to hear the case." Then she tried to reassure me that she and her partner (her errand boy) were seriously prepared for a two-day trial. She took me to her car and popped open the trunk to show me that she and partner had packed clothes for an overnight stay in town, just as she would later give me the tour of her office.

I saw Mindy at the courthouse payphone grinning ear to ear as she undoubtedly was calling Ben to inform him of the jackpot divorce settlement she had just negotiated. She and Ben, a CPA, knew that the settlement was a tax-free bonanza and she had nearly doubled the child support to a high enough amount to allow her to spend a considerable amount on herself. Indeed, they already knew what I should have known. I was still dazed, wondering what I had agreed to and what was going to happen to my career.

Skyler kicked into gear again. She would show up at the subsequent hearings, finalizing the divorce with volumes and volumes of paper she had printed out. At one point when Mindy was still disputing the terms of the divorce, Skyler made reference to how much work she had been doing on the settlement, implying that Mitchell had done nothing but obstruct and ask for more benefits for Mindy.

Mitchell snapped back, "Elaine Skyler, you don't know how much work I have been doing on this!" Quite ironically, Skyler had not been doing much herself. She was now trying to make it appear she had been doing a lot of work by the sheer volume of computer-generated paper she was spewing out, and by the amount she was billing, but there had never been anything behind it from the start—an empty suit, an empty briefcase, an empty file, an empty practice, just as she had started out the case in her office: taking down my address, phone number, and all the other nonproductive, useless, busywork. She was ending the case in the same way.

Again, if it was such a good settlement, why couldn't my attorneys have simply sat down and show me how they arrived at their recommendation after the fact and why it was a good settlement? Sort of like how a customer who disputes a bill? Surely, they must have had some sort of tabulation of the marital property, both contested and uncontested, before they recommended a settlement? Obviously, they didn't. For someone who preached against trial as a last resort to resolve a dispute, they did nothing to prevent me from filing a lawsuit against them. Their "evidence" was based *solely* on their *verbal reassurances* that I had achieved a good settlement and that they had been prepared for trial. They asked the court to literally take them on their word that they had been prepared for my divorce trial and that "the facts were most certainly not in dispute." What were the facts, Skyler and Salazar?

In a letter responding to my initial concerns that the settlement reached was woefully unfair, Skyler wrote, "We always informed you that you could pay up to one-half of Mindy's expert Dale Hasting's appraisal of the rehab hospital and your practice." That was it. That was as close to any "number" that Skyler admitted to—no other specifics, no other issues of marital property, property, taxes, premarital medical school loans, only language saying that it would have been ill advised for me not to have accepted the settlement dictated into the record that day because of a trial's "potentially catastrophic result" for me.

Skyler even tried to redirect blame away from her incompetence back to me, implying that I was being unreasonable because I wanted to punish Mindy, which the court by its actions and inactions just wouldn't let me do. No, Skyler, the court would have been obligated to search out a more equitable settlement if you had been ready for trial and made the proper arguments. You were deliberately confusing the issues of my motivation to "punish Mindy" with my extreme dissatisfaction for not getting even remotely adequate representation. You blamed the Court. You blamed me.

I went to Henry Souvent in the city upon recommendation by the nurse who had been dealing with Judge Lattimer and Mitchell, and whose ex-husband had been a client of Salazar's (mentioned earlier). Henry looked things over and after about an hour was able to confirm that, yes, based on my information, court documents and the settlement agreement, Skyler and Salazar had been negligent. It started out with a bang. When Mindy gets over $350,000 cash in property settlement, I lose $350,000 and that builds an immediate $700,000 discrepancy. Then the taxes take over from there. Then I have to pay interest on top of the money I have to borrow to give to her.

Henry mentioned that the postnuptial agreement Mindy had relied upon for temporary support was pure nonsense, nonbinding, and inadmissible in divorce. Finally, if Mindy was refusing to work and contribute her share of child support, then the court would have to consider giving me custody. He wrote a brief letter outlining these issues, although he was very reserved. He certainly wanted to string me along in hindsight, but did not want take the lead in suing my attorneys.

Suing My Attorneys

I hadn't yet found an attorney willing to sue my divorce attorneys, but now that I had a formal written expert opinion that my four attorneys were negligent, I filed four individual complaints on my own, without attorney representation (*pro se*, or on my own accord, to get the ball rolling). Yeah, yeah, I know the old saying: A client who represents himself has a fool for an attorney. I was hoping that if I made a slip on one I could still preserve my actions on the others. But it underscores my opinion. It is very difficult to get an attorney to sue another for legal malpractice! They protect one another. The court immediately consolidated all four actions for judicial economy.

I hired court reporters and took Skyler's and her partner's and Salazar's depositions and wrote interrogatories (written questions to which they were legally required to provide written responses, under oath). Skyler so blatantly lied in her deposition that I gave up. I finally wound up asking her if she was aware that doctors made more money than, for instance, grocery store clerks, and she answered that she didn't know.

Of course, she lied about having taken taxes into account, and insisted that she had come fully prepared for trial. She didn't even know the case law that allowed a marital party to recover premarital professional school loans. This issue had never been mentioned in the pretrial discovery process, nor had ever been listed on her pathetic little scorecard.

But really, this case was so straightforward as far as the facts speaking for themselves that I really didn't need to depose them. They were going to lie under oath anyway, and the real numbers already existed. They just had not been stipulated. But, again, these depositions weren't necessary because Salazar gave me the item that I wanted when he admitted on his interrogatories that "I got a good settlement" and, having to be consistent, therefore also admitted that he and Skyler had "strongly recommended me to settle the case as was dictated into the record that day." He also admitted that I had warned him about Mindy's treachery before the case was filed and "not to underestimate her."

During his deposition, however, he avoided confirming his repeated statement that the commissioner could not rule. He replied evasively, "Oh, he rules."

I should have fired back, "You didn't answer my question. Under oath, did you ever make a specific statement about this commissioner that 'he could not rule?'" That would have been important because it would have been tantamount to Salazar knowing in advance that the commissioner was incompetent, and therefore, it was necessary to rebut *any* award of temporary support to Mindy by *spelling it out,* citing the statutes like he did for the issue of need for an affidavit.

To deflect my accusations, Salazar stated that he had a client who was having to pay alimony to a lawyer. This lawyer was probably fresh out of law school. It is well known that lawyers, except maybe a very, very select few out of prestigious law schools, make practically nothing for years while they set up their own practice or work for a firm. Many have to close shop because they can't make it as attorneys.

Mindy's situation was the polar opposite. She commanded an initial salary of $200,000–$300,000 right off the bat. Had Mindy's and my roles been reversed so that I was a stay-at-home dad sitting on my medical degree, the court would have told me to get off my ass and go to work- immediately, and I would not have seen a dime of temporary support.

Of course, Johnston's response to the complaint was pure BS: the usual answer that I "failed to state a claim upon which relief can be based" (they always say that), that my action was limited by "estoppel, waivers, laches, satisfaction and accord, statute of limitations" and so on. When the supposedly reputable lawyers get pressed, they too, will lie. They will all lie. Johnston is a liar. Salazar is a liar. Skyler is a liar, and they all continue to lie to cover up. Why? Because they can.

In response to my grievance to my lawsuit, Salazar again denied making a statement that he had advised me "I had to pay Mindy maintenance." He and Johnston instead changed their story to they had told me "the court was going to award Mindy maintenance." Salazar's excuse to the bar on the issue of maintenance then changed yet again: If I had contested the payment of maintenance to Mindy, it would have poisoned my whole case.

Judge Hubbell

Judge Hubbell at the trial court level dismissed my complaint against my divorce lawyers via summary judgment. He relied on an old case cited by these defendant attorneys' counsel, but not before he had written in his opinion that "having reviewed the record, the depositions, and having made all reasonable inferences, this court concludes that attorney Salazar was negligent in his preparation for the *pendent lite* hearing, and that Salazar and Skyler were negligent in their failure to take into account the tax basis of the marital property."

However, based on old precedent case law, the court dismissed my complaint by relying on the opinion that, even though my former attorneys were clearly negligent, I could not prevail at trial because my losses were speculative in that there was no single issue of material fact upon which relief could be claimed.

These lawyers scurried like the rats with a motion for clarification of the court's opinion. They wanted the phrase "assumes for the purposes of discussion" inserted in place of the word *concludes*. I objected. Judge Hubbell had not assumed anything. He, like every other attorney I had review the case, immediately recognized and were able to conclude that these lawyers had been negligent. Judge Hubbell also granted their motion that the case be sealed.

The Precedent Summary Judgment Case Law, or the Lawyers-Get-Out-of-Jail-Free Case

In this single precedent (domestic) case upon which Judge Hubbell re-lied, a plaintiff had been injured at work, and his lawyer missed the statute of limitations for filing the lawsuit. But this plaintiff was still able to file in a neighboring state where the company was also in business and the statute of limitations had not yet expired. The case went to trial in that neighboring state and was settled before the verdict was reached. The plaintiff, therefore, received compensation for *material economic* losses such as time lost from work and hospital bills and also *intangible* losses, such as pain and suffering.

Not satisfied, the plaintiff then sued his lawyer saying that he could have gotten a better settlement had the case been tried in the home state. The plaintiff actually won his case against his attorney in the home state, but the verdict was overturned on appeal. The appeals court ruled that any economic losses and intangibles of pain and suffering above and beyond what he re-covered in the neighboring state were speculative and, therefore, not material and, therefore, could not be recovered in the home state, and therefore, the case was thrown out.

In my case, both sets of experts had appraised the marital property only in pretax dollars. Mindy's expert, Dale Hastings, obviously had never mentioned tax liabilities, which would have decreased Mindy's settlement amount. His omission of tax basis should have been grounds to disqualify him as an expert, especially since he was a CPA, but Skyler was too unsophisticated to argue that point. Of course, she could always claim that she would have been ready to argue that point at trial, but the problem was that she had never demonstrated *once* during trial preparation, discovery, depositions, or pretrial conferences that she understood or had incorporated taxes into her calculations, so she was obviously unprepared to argue for tax-basis impact on valuation of marital property in the event of a trial.

The high and the low end of the range of the cumulative marital-property assets were, therefore, established and quantifiable. The court could not have assigned a value higher than that of the experts. The tax basis on the property at liquidation value (like selling of stock) was also quantifiable by standard IRS methodology down to the penny. Judge Hubbell, in a ridiculous argument, argued that taxes were abstract and could not be determined as it would depend upon when the asset was sold.

But that is also like saying that value of the asset itself could *never* be determined because its value could increase or decrease when a party decided to sell in the future. Such an argument would render the whole process of property valuation or expert appraisal meaningless. A court could simply say that an asset could be worth any amount in the future when it is sold. In reality, an appraiser places a current day valuation on a property based on its current and future prospects or both, including profits, losses, assets, pro forma analysis, and liabilities.

But wait! Hubbell's argument on the timing of the sale might have actually helped me by nullifying the higher valuation of my practice and earnings capability in existence before the bifurcation, and provided for a "recalculation" to lower valuations as a result of the malpractice event. This aspect of the law is still unclear.

I argued in my *pro se* belated appeal to the state supreme court that the applicable taxes on the estate would be applicable at the time of the property division, as oftentimes one party has to liquidate or sell property to raise cash to pay his spouse a cash settlement. In my case, I might also have had to liquidate these assets to pay for excess judgment in my malpractice suit and, therefore, would have to pay capital long-term, short-term tax gains and income taxes on distributions at that time.

Thus, there was a threshold amount, or the maximum amount, I could have paid in a worst-case scenario had the court gone with all of Mindy's experts' high-end valuations, including intangibles of good will on the practice, and so on.

I was prepared to demonstrate with a much more elaborate scorecard the settlement recommended by my lawyers exceeded even this high-end threshold, especially with the looming medical-malpractice claim and the medical-board action for which no provision for future income losses had been made. In short, mine was actually a textbook example of quantifiable material loses.

If the valuations had been properly done, the most I could have paid was X amount, but I wound up paying X + Y on my attorneys' undisputed it's-a-good-settlement recommendation. Because I think I could have made a good case in front of a jury that my lawyers had intentionally sold out their client at trial, misled me into thinking that I had to pay my ex-wife alimony, and that Skyler had fraudulently billed me for hours she never performed as demonstrated by lack of any justifiable work product other than what has been identified above, I would have been entitled to recover triple *punitive* damages. This case was not about honest mistakes or oversights by my former attorneys. They knew they were not ready for my divorce trial and that they had compromised my case. They deliberately misled me into settling the divorce in order to get themselves off the hook. Hubbell identified these attorneys' motivation to seek a safe harbor via a settlement in the final sentence of his opinion: "The dispositive feature is that the plaintiff settled his case."

Informed Consent

One of the main arguments my attorneys constantly used in their de-fense was that Mindy's experts had valued two items: (1) my orthopedic practice at $630,000 ($330,000 of which was goodwill) and (2) the rehab hospital at $600,000, which meant I could have had to pay up to one-half of this combined amount.

Really? How likely was the court to take the absolute top of both Mindy's experts numbers in her favor? Every expert I talked to indicated that the court would have most likely split the difference between her expert and mine, especially when one looked at Mindy's contributions, which in my state could be considered in the division of marital property. It was not an automatic fifty-fifty split. My attorneys used this potential catastrophic result as a scare tactic to get me to settle, not because it was in my best interests, but because they needed to bail on this case. Any reasonable person would at least like to have known this middle number before making a decision. Skyler claimed she informed me of all possible outcomes. This was blatantly false. Not only did she not verbally inform me, there were no records to indicate that she had done any tabulation of the individual marital item amounts, with or without taxes factored in.

In a medical analogy, suppose I tell a patient that he has a cancer but that if he undergoes an operation, he could die and, therefore, should not get the operation. *But* suppose I fail to tell him the operation usually has a fairly predictable good outcome, although not guaranteed, and that the risks of dying from surgery are actually very low. I convince the patient not to get the operation and he dies three months later, I can now cast the blame on the patient because he made the decision *not* to undergo the surgery?

In my case Skyler ultimately defended her act by stating in her letter, "You made the decision to settle." This is what informed consent is about in medicine and should be the same in law. I had been informed at the very last minute before trial *only* of the potential catastrophic, but relatively unlikely, result in very vague terms. No middle-of-the-road or best-case scenario or number had ever been discussed. I had been pressed into a sudden last-minute decision to settle when instead I had arrived that morning fully expecting the case to go to trial and that my attorneys had prepared to do so. Any such preparation should have been reviewed and explained to me not only well before trial, but especially if settlement was being contemplated or was a possibility.

At this time, seeing that I had taken upon myself to file complaints, depose the attorneys and file interrogatories, I think Henry Souvent may have realized I needed to get an attorney and that I was serious and willing to spend money on attorney fees, but he was clearly not going to personally sue these attorneys, even though he unequivocally admitted they had committed malpractice. I also think the court's recognition of legal malpractice in its initial opinion, unlike the other attorney's earlier opinion stating I was just blowing a lot of hot air, may have added some legitimacy to my concerns.

None of these later attorneys, in my opinion, ever intended to follow through to the end, however. They led me on, but when it came to crunch time, they would walk away with their money and leave me stranded.

Henry Souvent walked over to another attorney whose opinion he respected. This new attorney asked $3,000 to review the record, including my depositions of Salazar and Skyler and her partner, and wrote a two-page opinion.

Basically, at his office I remember him saying to Souvent, "The case should have been tried, Henry."

"Yeah, Sterling did chase Skyler on the issue, Henry."

"She wasn't ready, Henry."

"If you get Skyler and (Mindy's female attorney) on a case, you'll never go to trial."

But that was about all he ever did. He admitted he stopped reading my summary because the print was too small. So he basically ripped me off for well over $2,000.

In his written letter, this attorney stated that Salazar had negligently prepared for the hearing on temporary support "indeed if he prepared for it at all." (Well actually Salazar did. He had photocopied one page containing the statutes that he used to argue that Mindy needed an affidavit for alimony.)

Also, he concurred that taxes had not been taken into account.

Skyler argued that Mindy certainly would not have accepted less in settlement. This was pure hearsay, totally irrelevant, and inadmissible as a defense, and I had simply argued Mindy did not have to accept less because she and Mitchell knew that Skyler and Salazar were not prepared for trial.

This attorney also wrote, "Nobody wants to call a lawyer a liar, but when I see literally dozens of hours billed (by Skyler) as 'review of file' and 'preparation for trial,' I grow suspicious."

He opined I had grounds to report these attorneys to the bar and dispute the fees. He concluded by walking me back down the street to another attorney, T. J. Holt, and explained the case. All these attorneys agreed that a provision for the impact on my medical-practice valuation, medical license, and future medical career earnings as a result of this medical-malpractice case should have been made at settlement. I don't think there is a single attorney who would argue against this point. Not a single word of this enormous liability had ever been mentioned by Skyler or Salazar at settlement negotiation.

T. J. put some effort into salvaging the case on appeal of the summary judgment dismissal. He had to research and rebut ten foreign (out-of-state) case laws that Skyler and Salazar's lawyers had blindly shot-gunned in defense of their clients. These foreign cases were totally and ridiculously unrelated to my case. The appeals court did not rely on any of these ten foreign cases either. I suspect it did not even look at them. It decided first that it was going to let these lawyers off and then rely on this single domestic case cited by trial court Judge Hubbell to reaffirm the summary-judgment dismissal. It was a classic Alice in Wonderland court of the absurd.

"Stuff and nonsense," said Alice, "Whoever heard of sentencing first and verdict afterward?"

Instead of "off with her head," in the Queen of Heart's court, it was the reverse: "Dismiss the case first." My impression is that a large number of cases are adjudicated by a judge for politically correct reasons or expediency, and from there he works backward and cites a number of non-applicable cases to give the appearance for justification of his ruling. Of course, when these cases are carefully reviewed, one sees that, in fact, they were just shot gunned in and totally irrelevant.

I predict this summary-judgment precedent case, now decades old, will forever remain a permanent backstop for lawyers facing legal malpractice. The inherent ambiguity in this case (in legal jargon called *less restrictive*) allows application to a wide spectrum of cases. Any future legal malpractice complaint can now be compared to this case and, therefore, dismissed automatically as speculative in a clear-cut abuse of summary judgment. In contrast, in medical-malpractice cases, noneconomic damages, which by definition are speculative in nature, are recognized as recoverable by the plaintiff, and a jury gets to decide. Quite the double standard.

Standard of Proof

As stated earlier, in criminal cases, a defendant is convicted only if the jury finds him guilty beyond any reasonable doubt. Better to let a hundred guilty men go free than erroneously convict one innocent man, the saying goes.

In contrast, in civil (noncriminal) law cases like medical malpractice or personal injury, the standard of proof is merely that an act or consequence is more likely to have occurred than not, and damages can even be awarded for intangibles such as pain and suffering, emotional distress and loss of consortium, which are based on subjectivity and speculation.

In legal malpractice, however, it would appear that the standard of proof sets the bar higher than even criminal law because of abuse and exploitation of summary judgment. The court throws the case out before any evidence can be presented or weighed by a jury. All material evidence which might otherwise have led to a favorable verdict for a plaintiff is dismissed as speculation. It is an unapproachable standard of proof.

Summary Judgment

In summary judgment dismissing a plaintiff's suit, the case is thrown out by the court without the plaintiff ever being allowed to present his evidence at trial. It is a presumption that there is no evidence. This summary judgment process, as one might expect, is abused/exploited, and the state supreme court, the highest court in the state, had recently addressed this abuse in a landmark ruling just prior to my case.

Which law firm had been involved in this supreme court landmark ruling? The very one that was representing Skyler and Salazar. This state supreme court case, which should have been controlling, or the ultimate authority in the matter of abuse of summary judgment, was not even cited by these defendant attorneys' counsel or discussed by the trial or appeals courts in dismissing my lawsuit. Why not? It was definitely not an oversight. Because it squarely addressed the issue of abuse of summary judgment in a manner favorable to my case!

This recent state supreme court of appeals ruling placed the burden of proving nonexistence of material fact squarely on the defendant party (my former lawyers) who were relying on summary judgment to get the case thrown out, not on the plaintiff (me) who was trying to recover damages. Even if the court did not think I would win my case, it could not, by this ruling, deny me my chance to produce my evidence, as long as there was at least one single issue of material fact that I could present at trial, even if the remainder of my evidence might be considered speculative. A tax bill from the IRS is not speculation.

The appeals court had jumped the gun. I would have to be unable to present a single issue of material fact at actual *trial*, not during arguments for *summary judgment!* This was a classic catch-22. I could not bring evidence to the summary judgment because summary judgment does not let you elaborate any evidence. When it is abused, it relies on a presumptive judgment.

For these lawyers to have mounted a successful defense through summary judgment, it is they, not I, who would have had to *demonstrate*, not just *claim*, that I could not have presented a single issue of material fact at trial. Therefore, it is Skyler and Salazar, not I, who would have had to go back and identify the high-low valuations on the individual items of marital property, total up the property settlement after taxes and demonstrate conclusively that through their recommended settlement, I had paid Mindy an amount that was still less than the highest amount I could have paid even had the court taken all the property valuations in her favor.

Clearly, had this calculation been performed prior to the settlement with the expertise of an accountant to include tax basis and proper summation of all the marital property, it should have been no burden for them whatsoever. The work should have already been done.

The court also ruled that the impending medical-malpractice suit and the impact of the medical-board action against my license could not qualify as material fact at this summary-judgment appeals stage because they constituted new charges which could not be brought up on appeal during the summary-judgment appeals process—even though the case had not even gone to formal trial and discovery was still in its infancy. If summary judgment had been decided in my favor, I could have simply amended the complaint to add those additional issues of malpractice. Amended complaints are commonplace in law. The deadline for submission of evidence and additional charges was still wide open. I really needed a good attorney to navigate this situation, but that's the problem, the public has no recourse. Attorneys won't sue other attorneys, the Bar tribunal won't sanction attorneys for intentional legal malpractice, and even writing a book about it to inform the public is problematic.

In glaring contrast to legal malpractice, intangibles of pain and suffering are routinely recognized by juries and awarded in personal injury cases that make it to trial, even though the true extent of pain and suffering is purely subjective and, therefore, inherently speculative. Both the trial court and the appeals court dismissed my case on summary judgment in favor of Salazar and Skyler, who carried no burden at all as was required by this highest state supreme court directive. Again, both courts relied solely on a more dated (1977) and less restrictive lower-court domestic case precedent.

Child support was a distinctly separate issue that could not be comingled with property settlement. By this strongly recommended settlement, my 100 percent child support payments, which had been $1,500 a month, had now increased to $2,800 a month in 1992 dollars. I was paying for all of it and more, even that electric dog fence. Maintenance could not be possibly awarded to this doctor and comingled with property settlement either. With child support and maintenance clearly off the table, the issue of property settlement stood starkly alone. I presented the above arguments on my appeal to the state supreme court. What happened?

T. J. Holt Quits

It wasn't long before T. J. Holt informed me that he was no longer willing to work on the case. He cited the fact that the arguments and preparation for the appeal of the summary judgment had taken him more time than he expected. He was also going through a divorce and had four kids (convenient excuse?), so he was going to get clobbered. But the legal malpractice didn't stop there. In his letter informing me of the termination of his services, he wrote that I had thirty days to appeal to the state supreme court. Wrong. It was twenty days.

As I handed the appeal to the state supreme court (written *pro se* and which now included the above arguments) in person to the clerk at the court house, the clerk sat there for a minute, counted the days, and then informed me I had missed the deadline. "What do you mean? My attorney said right here in his letter I had thirty days."

"Well, your attorney told you wrong," she said. I filed a motion for enlargement of time, but of course, the court quickly answered, "The appellant's belated motion for enlargement of time is denied." But my lawyers still weren't done screwing me over yet. Not by a long shot.

A Previous Ophthalmologist Client of Skyler's

I called a prominent ophthalmologist whom Skyler had represented and mentioned in a deposition. I asked him if she had taken into account the tax liabilities of his property in his divorce. He said he didn't know but that he had been put through the wringer. It seems that Skyler had negotiated an all-nighter marathon settlement (again, no trial) with his ex-wife. The problem is, as soon as the settlement was signed, his ex-wife ran off with her lawyer, got married, and per the settlement, he still had to pay alimony. Skyler had made no provision for this to end upon her remarriage. (An OR nurse in my hospital also said her lawyer failed to get her co-signature nullified on the mortgage on the house that her ex now enjoyed after the divorce, so I am sure legal malpractice is absolutely rampant.)

This ophthalmologist said that the next morning Skyler's errand-boy partner came knocking and said, "We can still fix this." But they couldn't. I suspect a double screw up by Skyler: no provision for his ex-wife's termination of alimony upon remarriage (just as no provision for my medical career for the malpractice event) and probably no tax-basis consideration of his marital-property settlement.

Finally, a hand surgeon from a very prestigious group, whom I met socially, also expressed his displeasure over Skyler's billing. I assume that she was also billing him exorbitant fees for work that she may not have done or had served no purpose.

I am perplexed how Skyler can be landing these doctors as clients and be so incompetent. These were not little issues she had messed up on. But the public has no way of knowing through a database or publicly available forum that exists for lawyers as it does for doctors. A lawyer database probably would be of little use anyway because so few lawyers ever get sued or have their licenses acted upon by their bar associations for legal malpractice in the first place. It is simply never allowed to be exposed. Witness the difficulty I had in even getting a lawyer to agree to sue my divorce attorneys. Even worse, these defendant attorneys turn this situation around to their advantage when they say: See? This doctor obviously has no case against his divorce attorneys. He can't even find a lawyer who will represent him.

Judges Eberhart and Hubbell

My girlfriend, Tessie, worked in a bar/restaurant in the city that lawyers and professionals frequented during lunchtime. There was a judge, Eberhart, who liked Tessie. Eventually, we three had dinner together. I told him of my travails and how I was suing my divorce attorneys whom he knew. He said none of them were worth a damn. But he said I needed to get a lawyer. Ugh. Funny how a few months later after Judge Hubbell had thrown out my case on summary judgment, I actually was introduced to him at a semi pro baseball game by Judge Eberhart. Judge Hubbell sat behind us. There was no further conversation during the game. Hubbell looked like an alcoholic and did not seem to recognize my name from his docket.

Downhill All the Way

It didn't take long for Mindy to remarry after the divorce. She moved to a suburb on the other side of the city. I was reduced to the "treat dad" or "vacation dad," meaning that I got to see them every other weekend, if I was willing to drive both ways, and work my hours around Mindy's busy running schedule. It was so "generous" of me to have agreed to move back to her home state after residency. Now she was going to pay me back by moving away almost one and a half hours away.

By the first snowfall, Sherri was featured in the front page of the state newspaper captioned, "Downhill all the way," as her arms were spread out in a crucifix as she was skiing. The picture identified her as Sherri Holcomb, even though her name was Sherri Sterling. Mindy already wanted to give the impression of one big, happy family.

By this time, I knew the kids were gone, and I proceeded to give them up for adoption through Henry Souvent. I was finished career-wise anyway and would have to relocate, assuming I could get a job. Henry Souvent drew up the agreement after an aborted attempt to get child support shared. Mindy was still not working. I guess one could argue that I gave up the kids so that I wouldn't have to pay child support. I was paying all of it while Mindy continued her policy of the devoted full-time mother who didn't have to work and wasn't required to pay any child support.

Of course, in order to get the divorce settlement pushed through since Skyler was terrified of going to trial and would therefore sell her client out in heartbeat she wrote language into the agreement that I would be entitled to "significant input" into the rearing of the children. There were no specifics to this "significant input." It was BS and yet another sell-out of my interests. If you don't have at least joint legal or physical custody, you have nothing except long drives every other weekend and two weeks during the kids' summer vacations. Kids don't like joint custody except in very unusual situations where the parents are already cooperating and living in proximity, which almost renders the point moot. Kids don't like to be torn from their friends, carted back and forth between households and having their activities disrupted.

Then Skyler wrote language into the settlement that after two years, child support levels could be renegotiated. That too was BS. Once established, it is very difficult to get child support levels changed. Skyler had lied to me again with these provisions to quickly dispose of the case.

To rub salt in my wound, shortly after my divorce, Judge Dwayne Lattimer came out with a first-of-its-kind ruling allowing a joint-custody arrangement. It went all the way to the state supreme court and was upheld. On the front page of the state newspaper was a picture of the judge who'd voted yes, and beside it was a picture of Judge Leafgreen, who'd written an impassioned argument against it, properly calling it "a pernicious problem causer."

Interestingly, I had treated Leafgreen's mother for osteomyelitis of her thumb, requiring partial amputation of the tip at my hospital. He hadn't mentioned his name or profession when visiting his mother. He just quietly handed me his card and said to call him if I ever needed any help. I still have his card. In retrospect, I sure needed his help. It is amazing how blinded one can become in extremely stressful situations.

The Waiting Game

From April 1991 until about October 1993, I continued practice, although was hit by the second suit involving the death of a thirty-seven-year-old man who'd initially presented with what was later confirmed as advanced multiple myeloma. It made the local papers. The headlines read: "Doctor responsible for second death." It was written by this same little twerp reporter who had been reporting about the anesthetic death. In yet another coincidence, I met this guy later at Tessie's brother's apartment. Talk about a jackal who slowly walks away with his tail between his legs when he saw me. This reporter was reportedly let go. He reportedly had been previously terminated at another position for falsifying stories.

Then one day my partner called and said he was resigning from the practice. I was hurting the practice. He had already signed a contract with a nearby military base. I told him he didn't need to resign. I would resign instead. I knew the practice had collapsed and I would have to leave anyway.

He tried to get out of his contract with the military but could not. My senior partner was pissed. He clearly preferred my leaving instead, but he was still upset that our partner had suddenly left him. I'm sure my partner received full buyout of his share unlike me. I remember him nevertheless complaining about having to pay full freight to buy back into the practice when he later returned. Well? What did you expect?

I knew my partner had a number of claims, and maybe some malpractice, because I had seen some of his patients and he'd told me about them. One was a female who had a laminectomy redo and he'd accidentally cut her nerve root. "I am ruined for life," she repeated in the waiting room.

Then there was a patient whom he had done a laminectomy back surgery for misdiagnosed hip-joint arthritis. Don't know if that resulted in a lawsuit. He also had a wrong site surgery on an elbow or carpal tunnel (as did my partner in my final practice recently when all of these preventative measures were in place) and had gotten in trouble with state quality assurance because he had put a prosthesis back in an infected hip, which I had previously removed for him because of infection. He got out of that one. I think his first total hip had dislocated, and he had been sued for that. He was a good steady surgeon, however, and I thought he was very competent and still fashioned some of my surgical technique from him. (I certainly didn't get much from my residency.)

He later quit operative orthopedics. I wonder if it had to do with the number of claims he may have had, judging from my own personal experience with a total of fourteen claims in my career. He may have been distracted by all his extracurricular activities: a partner in a roof-truss company, which he ultimately sold after his manager was caught embezzling the business, running a marathon, building condos, and adding on a big addition to his house.

The medical-licensure-board-action storm clouds were gathering. Pernell Drayton, the family's attorney for this anesthesia-related death medical-malpractice suit also filed at his clients' behest a formal grievance to the medical board. He supported the grievance with testimony from one of his paid anesthesiology experts in the civil malpractice case. Immediately, the board's first entry was that this expert "specialized in anesthesiology" whereas I "specialized in the orthopedic surgery." In essence, the board had immediately and properly recognized the different specialties and ordered that the case be sent to an orthopedic panel expert for review.

I was being charged by the medical board with malpractice, just as I was in the companion civil medical-malpractice suit. Malpractice is said to have occurred when a physician fails to follow the same standard of care as a like physician in the same specialty under similar circumstances. In other words, what would a physician in the same specialty have done under the same circumstances?

Thus, the board's charge was very simple. Pursuant to the state's medical-practice act requiring impartiality and holding a physician to the standards within his same specialty, it had to obtain an opinion from one of its preapproved panel orthopedic surgery members. If that expert said I had fallen beneath the orthopedic standard of care, the board would have grounds to discipline me. If this expert exonerated me, then the board would be unable to meet its requirement to provide substantial evidence that I had committed a violation of the medical-practice act. This impartiality was underscored by the medical examiner who testified during the hearing that he explained to the family that it was not the board's position to take sides in a dispute. Its mission was to simply to determine whether a violation of the medical-practice act had occurred.

I was served with a complaint (lawsuit) by the medical board. Some old righteous psychiatrist on the board made the motion to initiate the lawsuit. A fucking psychiatrist! He probably had not been in an operating room, or even a hospital, in decades. His motion was unanimously passed by all the members of the board, just like a herd of lemmings.

I later learned that the statutes required that the board first had to do a thorough review/discovery of the case before a lawsuit could be filed. My attorney, William Goerbing, failed to object to the premature filing of this lawsuit. I had not even given a response to the initial inquiry. The board was under the impression that I had knowingly and deliberately injected the lethal medication. The medical board's own attorney also failed to inform the board that filing a lawsuit was premature. The board's attorney is not supposed to act as an advocate for either the public or the physician. His role as the board's attorney is that of a minister of justice. My case was a classic example of a rush to judgment.

I was only insured for $200,000 by my medical-malpractice carrier on initial advice of my partners. I don't know if they thought that the hospital would be liable for any deficiency or if they simply thought that, back in 1987, awards never exceeded that amount in a small town. Dumb on my part. As an employee, I did as I was told, although I now remember my attorney who reviewed my contract informing me that "$200,000 coverage was way too low, and the big figure settlements from the city simply had not arrived in my small town yet." I think my partner may have already bumped his coverage to $1 million by the time my event occurred as his lawsuits started trickling in, but I was unaware. Today, a hospital will not let you have privileges without at least a million dollars coverage per event.

In yet another incidence of paying twice in property settlement like I had been for alimony, because I had been paying for only minimal malpractice insurance, the savings in insurance premiums were added directly to the practice's bottom line resulting in a higher valuation of the practice and property settlement. Since my attorneys had not made a provision for this lawsuit in the settlement, I would pay a second time with extramarital funds through an excess judgment payment after the divorce.

Doctors be aware. There are two reasons to have good coverage:

1. The obvious one: If you get successfully sued for a large amount, your insurance is more likely to cover before you start having to liquidate your own personal assets.
2. When your insurance company has a lot of its own money on the line, it is more likely to vigorously defend your case and with a more competent lawyer. In other words, you are paying for good legal counsel, not just for the coverage itself.

My insurer appointed William Goerbing as my lawyer in the medical-malpractice case. He was a partner at a prestigious office downtown. His office was in the top corner office, meaning he was one of the top dogs, it would seem. I later heard from the attorney who later tried my case involving the man with the broken finger (that was dismissed after failing to state his claim due to lack of expert testimony) that Goerbing had been assigned because my insurance carrier was intending to settle, not try, this anesthesia-related wrongful-death case. So maybe Goerbing was not the lawyer he was cranked up to be, and had been assigned to my case because he was only protecting $200,000 of the insurance company's money.

Goerbing was single, never had any biologic kids of his own. He had been married once and divorced. He was more interested initially in dating my office manager than discussing my case. She said, "Nope. He doesn't float my boat."

My insurance company then offered to pay for the legal services of Goerbing in my board action as a "courtesy" since he was already representing me in the medical malpractice case and the board action would be a "mirror image" of the medical-malpractice case. Strange. This would counter the argument I made previously. Why would the insurance company expend a single cent on my behalf if it didn't have to?

Goerbing then made the most devastating legal strategic decision impacting my life and career. In response to the medical board's lawsuit and the inquiry into my involvement in the case, Goerbing delayed the answers and requested that my answers be given in the form of my yet-to-be-taken deposition in the companion medical-malpractice case, which might be months later. Thus, this case was allowed to fester and the medical board continued to operate under the assumption that I had knowingly and deliberately injected the wrong drug.

Attention, doctors: When the medical board comes calling, drop whatever you are doing *immediately* and make an all-out response/defense of your license. Cancel your college reunion. Fly home on the first available plane from your dream vacation. Clear all other appointments. The deck has already been stacked against you! Medical boards have an inherent bias in disciplining doctors.

Many members of the board are not in the medical field, and if they are, they are often in nonclinical roles. Both panels of my medical board were headed by the chairmen of the medical schools—academicians who were not in active practice. There was a member from the Department of Public Health, one from a peripheral medical specialty like psychiatry, and in my case one in family practice in a small rural town.

These board member physicians often have very little experience of what goes on in a hospital or an operating room. Our orthopedic group actually rented satellite office space from one board member (panel A) family practitioner whom my senior partner informed me had once referred him a patient with a broken ankle. My partner informed him, "Dr. G, I wish you would have referred me this patient earlier instead of treating him yourself, because he should have had surgery for this, and now it is too late," to which this board member doctor replied, "Dr. Z, I tried to get her to drink her milk, but she just wouldn't do it."

Some board members may want to be on the board for the prestige and public spotlight, others to build their resumes or egos, or simply out of curiosity what doctors are really like and how they screw up behind the scenes. Some quite frankly, need the income. But either way, it is not always about whether there is an issue of medical ethics, competence, or "any act meant to deceive, defraud or harm the public or any member thereof," according to the medical-practice-act directives. It is about board members feeling righteous and important, especially when they are in the public spotlight. They could care less what you as a targeted physician may have to endure because of their sometimes whimsical, uninformed, or righteous decisions.

My medical school classmate, "Mr. Benchpress," said he went into orthopedics in addition to his investment hobby so that he would have a skill that "they could not take away from me." That is dead wrong. A licensure board can take your license in an instant, and then you are no more than a bum on the street. Unemployable. Without a license, you are dead in the water and all your years training are useless. In fact, you are probably even worse off because you have devoted all your time to medicine and have not learned how to fix your car, grow your food, do electrical wiring, or to diversify into an alternative side career. You figured that you would make enough income that you could pay someone to do this for you.

You can wind up like me, literally spending five afternoons a week just riding your bike to the town square and sitting on the public bench for hours, wondering what happened to your life and career.

Furthermore, if the board does take action against your license, it is reported on the NPDB where it is accessed by all hospitals, medical boards, malpractice-insurance carriers, health-care-insurance companies, and managed care organizations (MCO). It goes viral. It is the equivalent of the layman's social security number or driver's license. You absolutely cannot go anywhere without it being checked. When I did a self-query of the data bank,

I saw hundreds of hospitals, recruiters, and health insurers—Blue Cross, Cigna, Aetna, Anthem, Humana, United, and so on—had queried it.

The board later discovered, as reflected in its minutes, that indeed I had ordered the *correct* drug, but I had been given the wrong drug by the nurse, and they now wanted me to appear at a meeting to clarify this. This board appearance conflicted with my recently-booked and paid-for trip to Australia, New Zealand, and Fiji. God knows I needed a vacation desperately after all I had been through. I postponed the board meeting until after my return. Big mistake. The board never followed up and now the public relations pot was coming to a boil. I had missed my only chance.

In the aftermath of the Board action and my divorce settlement, I filed grievances against Goerbing, McCliven (new medical board attorney), and my divorce attorneys for misconduct and incompetence. The reviewer agreed that if I had shown up at that Board meeting in 1992 before the public relations winds had changed, I probably would have been excused by the board.

He encouraged me to send as much information as possible concerning my grievances, and that "he liked to gather as much information as possible before submitting it to the bar tribunal." The bar wants to make you think they are going to thoroughly investigate and act upon your grievance. That is pure baloney. The bar will seldom sanction a lawyer for incompetence or legal malpractice. Send all the information you want, but it will be for naught.

In the end, the bar tribunal's reply was simply that "the tribunal found no need to take any action against any of these attorneys." I did not even learn who the three members on this panel were. Similarly, when I wrote a grievance to the Judicial Retirement and Removal Committee concerning the absolute incompetence of the commissioner and judge in my divorce, the committee simply replied, "The Committee finds Judge Lattimer guilty of no misconduct." But my grievance had not been for reasons of misconduct—it had been about flat-out incompetence.

I had no support from the local doctors at my hospital, not even from my own partners. A neighboring OB-GYN said he knew someone on the board and that he would speak to him about the case. I never received any feedback from him. The reasons I suppose could range from indifference, to not wanting to be bothered, or an assumption that the board would never punish me for something that was so blatantly the nurse's fault. I think this latter may be part of the answer, as even my malpractice-insurance carrier had offered me the courtesy services of Goerbing. They wouldn't have offered this unless they thought it was going to be quickly resolved.

I was anticipating the approach of my trial in front of the administrative law judge before the medical board when suddenly Dr. Abulencia stuck again. He claimed he'd had a stroke and couldn't appear for trial. I protested this delay and asked my attorney, Goerbing, to make a motion to sever the case. (Asking the board to try me first in a separate action and then try Abulencia at a later date.) Goerbing told me directly to my face he couldn't do that. My understanding from his response was that legally or procedurally the case couldn't be severed.

I then wrote an *ex parte* communication to the board and requested that I be allowed to sever my case from Dr. Abulencia so that I could get on with my career, or what was left of it. I had already resigned the practice and had no chance of getting a job while this was hanging over my head. I never heard from the board until after Dr. Abulencia had recovered to the point that he could appear and the hearing proceed.

Goerbing also liked my girlfriend, Tessie, and invited us for an overnight stay at his apartment in the city. In retrospect, this was very strange. I don't know how we got on the subject that night, but he repeated his concern that he wished I hadn't gone on the Australia trip, implying that the board would have let me off, but now it was too late. The groundswell of public opinion had been growing against doctors, and now the board had a public relations problem. At that moment in his apartment, I realized a very simple fact. If that meeting with the board to clarify my role in the drug mix-up was important enough for me to have canceled my three-week trip to Australia, then it was important enough that Goerbing should have responded to the board immediately: That it was unaware of the most salient feature of the case as far as my role in the patient's death: I had *unintentionally* and *unknowingly* injected the wrong drug after having verbally ordered the *correct* one. Goerbing suddenly changed the subject and said it was the nurse who was responsible.

The original board attorney who filed the complaint suddenly resigned. Déjà vu with the divorce commissioner. I don't know the reason. It seemed a little strange that both the board attorney and the medical investigator quit right about the time my case came up and after the lawsuit had already been filed.

The Little Shit Replacement

Sal McCliven was a smug recent graduate out of the state university law school. He had been in some kind of law practice for a few years before accepting the board position. Another aimless lawyer? In my opinion, he had grandiose aspirations of a lucrative law practice concentrating in medical malpractice where the verdicts sometimes can be astronomical. What better place to learn the ropes than as the attorney for the medical board?

The board minutes clearly show that initially the board had recognized me as a doctor who specialized in orthopedics and, therefore, should be held to the orthopedic standard. The medical practice act specifically stated that the grounds for licensure board action required the physician be held to the same standards as someone in his own specialty. If the administration of the Bier block was part of the recognized global orthopedic procedure performed routinely without the requirement of an anesthesiologist, then there should have been no legal grounds to go outside the orthopedic specialty. The board obtained an opinion from their own pre-approved board-consultant orthopedist. As the board's own medical investigator outlined in his testimony at the hearing, "it was not the board's position to take sides in a complaint, but only to determine if a violation of the medical-practice act had occurred." He stated emphatically that "experts testifying in the case for or against the physician could neither be friends of, nor competitors to that physician."

Furthermore, the medical-practice act stated that the board's attorney was not to act as an advocate for the aggrieved party, but rather as an impartial minister of justice.

Sal McCliven nevertheless went on an all-out attack mode, acting as if he were acting as the plaintiff's trial attorney in the medical-malpractice case. It was like Martin Montgomery who saw fit to pack a shotgun and chase speeders instead of performing his assigned job as an unarmed security guard. McCliven withheld the board's predesignated orthopedic surgeon opinion, which exonerated me completely, until very late in the case. Even then, my own attorney, Goerbing, in yet another incredible delay, withheld it from the board until the very last minute to spring a sort of "gotcha" defense. He was quite frankly more concerned about Perry Mason theatrics than protecting his client.

Goerbing did put his foot down and objected when McCliven wanted to submit, as evidence, testimony from the plaintiff's paid experts in the companion medical-malpractice case. This was a flagrant violation of his requirement of impartiality as the board's counsel.

"I do not agree, nor will I ever agree, to the admission of depositions by experts in the medical-malpractice action for the simple reason that these experts have been paid, and paid well, by the plaintiff's counsel to testify against Dr. Sterling. It is just inconceivable that the board would try to do this."

McCliven tried to explain that it was for "completeness." If McCliven was so intent on completeness, why did he not go back and re-depose the RN and the techs as to the specifics of Dr. Abulencia's attempt to solicit a conspiracy? Why did he let Dr. Abulencia ramble through his testimony uninterrupted? I reviewed the tape several times. Only one or two questions were initially asked by McCliven, and then once Abulencia started talking, he was allowed to give his entire rehearsed version of events from start to finish. Specifically, there was no challenge to, or clarification of, Dr. Abulencia's false claim that I had volunteered to do the case so that "he could take off and get a good night's rest." No challenge of his obvious attempt to deceive the public with a conspiracy to call the death a severe allergic reaction. And of course, as long as his lies were unchallenged by McCliven, Dr. Abulencia's monologue testimony was allowed to continue uninterrupted by his attorney, Darrell Forrester, a regular on the doctor medical-board defense circuit. Even the state newspaper wrote an article about the deception and how it was Dr. Abulencia who, by all other testimony, had clearly asked me to do the case.

McCliven resorted to other sleazy-lawyer tactics. All medical expert testimony stated that once the wrong drug had entered Arthur Smith's circulation, his death was certain. There was no medication or procedure that could have saved him. But McCliven wrote hysterical arguments suggesting otherwise, stating "that instead of trying to find a drug to reverse the medication's effects, Dr. Sterling tried to deceive the cardiologist who had been called in to try to resuscitate the patient into thinking the patient had received xylocaine." Then in the matter of trying to tar me with attempts to deceive the family by calling their son's death a severe allergic reaction, McCliven cited a whole page of the RN's deposition from the companion medical-malpractice case where she had suddenly and unexpectedly volunteered testimony that "Dr. Abulencia had pulled her, the two techs and one other person aside, *I know it wasn't Dr. Sterling*, and said that we all had to stick together and call this an allergic reaction, a severe allergic reaction." McCliven lifted the one key sentence "I know it wasn't Dr. Sterling" from her testimony.

I could not have been there at the conspiracy because I had left the operating room to go talk to the family with the cardiologist and the hospital representative. He needed to falsify the facts on record in argument to make his case. Why had he not completed the investigation by deposing the witnesses to this conspiracy?

And why did the hearing officer in his written findings and conclusions just let the whole conspiracy charge drop, stating only that "this had not been clearly proven"? Even more incredible was his justification: "A conspiracy, even if did exist, could not have been maintained forever." But the medical-practice act clearly stated "any act meant to harm, deceive or defraud the public or member thereof … and that actual harm need not have occurred … are grounds for disciplinary action against a physician."

Obviously, Dr. Abulencia solicited a conspiracy, and obviously his intent was to maintain it forever, so the hearing officer clearly erred in his opinion. But let's face it: this was not an inadvertent error—this was intentional. The board clearly deviated from its avowed position of impartiality and was acting as an all-out advocate for the family for public relations objectives. The board had been negligent in disciplining doctors. It had egg all over its face and now needed to serve up a scapegoat to appease the public.

The Other Side of the Conspiracy, or Why the Deceased's Family Was Lying

A full investigation was performed following the death of Arthur Smith. The state coroner's report, complete with a toxicology result, was released, confirming cardiac arrest due to Marcaine toxicity. The family contacted lawyers, and a full investigation was performed by their experts and the board's examiner. Certainly, the questioning of the family would have proceeded along the lines of asking, "What did Dr. Sterling say before the operation and what did he say when he informed you that your son had died?"

No significance was ever attached to anything I had said to the family for a year. No mention or charge of using the word *allergic*, conspiracy, cover-up, and so on, not by any attorney, the board, the press, the hospital, other medical experts, or the family. It was only a year later when the RN, out of the blue, volunteered the existence of this conspiracy. Pernell Drayton, the family's attorney, had asked an open-ended question at the end of her deposition: "Is there anything else you would like to say?"

Only then did this RN suddenly exposed Dr. Abulencia's attempt to solicit a conspiracy to cover up the cause of death as a severe allergic reaction. She testified she responded in disbelief, because she knew this was a patent lie. Arthur Smith had received the wrong drug. I had clearly and loudly announced this error to the entire operating room the minute I realized that the patient could not be resuscitated.

About ten days later, the family's attorney, Pernell Drayton, filed an amended complaint, charging Dr. Abulencia, but not me (yet), with conspiracy. A few days later, a sleazy reporter from an old national TV tabloid and his camera crew piled out of their van parked in the medical office next door. I gave a very brief statement that the court records spelled it all out, and I, therefore, had nothing to say.

Several days later, patients in the rehab hospital suddenly informed me that I was on national television. The TV tabloid had also made sure to inform the viewers that this was not my first mistake and that I had operated on the wrong knee in an earlier case (the surgical-center arthroscopy case). A few weeks later, Dr. Abulencia was named as a conspirator in the medical-malpractice suit as Drayton tried to rebut the hospital's claim of right of sovereign immunity that precluded them from being sued. Then the charge suddenly appeared on the medical board's amended complaint, charging both Abulencia and me with conspiracy. McCliven was certainly an eager beaver.

Finally, the Smith family's depositions were taken in the medical-malpractice case—long after the conspiracy had been exposed. It was interesting that Mr. Smith, Arthur's father, had been stone silent during the entire ordeal from the time I'd broken the news of his son's death until his deposition answering the questions with the flattest of flat affect, simply saying yes or no.

But when asked about whether I had ever said the word *allergic*, he suddenly responded quite out of character. "Yes, he said 'allergic.' He said that." Still later, at the medical-board hearing, Mrs. Smith testified that I had used the word *allergic* when I'd informed her of son's death at the hospital. When asked how could she be so sure I had said that word *allergic*, she said, "Because it was a once-in-a-lifetime event that I couldn't possibly forget."

It begged the cross-examination question that was never asked: "Mrs. Smith, you have testified essentially that you were looking for any way to destroy Dr. Sterling, obviously out of revenge for the death of your son and probably resentment of his status as a doctor and could not possibly have forgotten what was said that fateful night. Yet it appears you indeed have forgotten the critical word *allergic* for an entire year, and now suddenly seem to have 're-membered' it only *after* the RN just recently volunteered the word *allergic* as it pertained to Dr. Abulencia. Why is that?" The board's medical investigator also testified that during his visit to the Smith's home and questioning, the Smiths had never mentioned the word *allergic*.

Obviously, the family was lying to discredit me. Furthermore, Mrs. Smith made no secret of her hatred of me. She admitted during the medical-board hearing that "anything that could be done (against Dr. Sterling), we wanted it done." She wanted criminal charges filed but testified that her attorney, Pernell Drayton, had said he couldn't do that, so she had to accept a civil action.

At some point McCliven figured out how blatantly the family was lying. He suddenly dropped the charge on my appeal, nor did he appeal the hearing officer's incredible exoneration of Dr. Abulencia. Why? After all, McCliven was clearly out to take down as many doctors as he could in his role as counsel for the medical board to build up his reputation as a medical-malpractice-plaintiff lawyer, just like some young DAs press for guilty verdicts in criminal law, even if they know the defendant is innocent.

Had McCliven pressed the conspiracy charge against Dr. Abulencia, his attorney, Darrell Forrester, would have dragged the family into the conspiracy and easily demonstrated that the family was lying. The board was sympathetic to the family and did not want to expose them as liars. Again, this was in violation of the board's stated purpose of impartiality.

Note: Had this been a criminal act, the board could not have gone back and retried Dr. Ascuncion after acquittal. That would be double jeopardy, and such action is protected by the Fifth Amendment. This, however, was a *civil action*, which was not immune to being remanded (sent back) for retrial.

Saved by the Conspiracy

Ironically, the very act of Dr. Abulencia soliciting the conspiracy and the family's taking the bait with their false accusation against me saved Dr. Abulencia.

If the family had not lied in their false accusation against me, and Abulencia had not solicited a conspiracy, the board certainly would have had wide-open grounds to discipline Abulencia on the basis of patient abandonment, even had I agreed to do the anesthesia. Abulencia was automatically required to have done the case once the patient arrived in the operating room per American Society of Anesthesiologists (his professional peer group) and the hospital rules and regulations. He did not "just turn the case over to Dr. Sterling," as the hearing officer opined.

Dr. Abulencia was *not* board certified and therefore, arguably would not be bound by the American Board of Anesthesia Standards, only his professional society, the American Society of Anesthesiologists (ASA). Dr. Abulencia should clearly have been disciplined because he had abandoned his post. He had abandoned his patient. He knew it, which is why he felt the need to solicit the conspiracy.

If the family had *not* lied about the word *allergic* in their new accusation against me, then the board certainly could have also disciplined Dr. Abulencia for attempting to deceive members of the public with his conspiracy. The state medical-practice act clearly identified any act intending to deceive the public as grounds for discipline. The testimony of the nurse was overwhelming and would have been easily verified by deposing the others present. In order to spare the family from being exposed to their perjury, the Board backed off the conspiracy issue altogether, thereby saving Dr. Abulencia.

If I was getting suspended, fined, probated, and ordered to write a letter of apology, then why was nothing, absolutely nothing, done to the nurse, tech, or Dr. Abulencia? It had to have been the most twisted verdict in the history of any state medical board, and I would defy anyone to find such a double standard of punishment.

Incidentally, I was never asked by the board or the Smiths' attorney whether Dr. Abulencia had asked me to participate in the conspiracy. But Dr. Abulencia had indeed asked me, just as I was leaving the operating room, to go break the news to the family that night. Because my deposition was early, the existence of Dr. Abulencia's conspiracy still had not been exposed, and therefore, the question could not have been asked. I figured that surely Dr. Abulencia would have abandoned his efforts to get the nurse and the techs to participate in such a preposterous conspiracy after I had rejected it so quickly as I was leaving the operating room that night.

"Bryce, tell the family it was an allergic reaction."

"But, Alex, it wasn't an allergic reaction."

Thus, I was stunned when the RN suddenly volunteered it a year later in her deposition. I just didn't realize how compulsive and pathological a liar Dr. Abulencia was.

After the RN had volunteered the existence of the conspiracy, I confided to my attorney, Goerbing, that Dr. Abulencia had indeed tried to solicit the conspiracy as I was leaving the operating room. Goerbing told me not to mention it, because then I could be charged with being a party to the conspiracy, even though my sworn testimony would have been that I had rejected it on the spot and certainly did not follow through with it when I talked to the Bond family.

Again, I was never asked about it during my deposition for the simple reason that the plaintiff was totally unaware of its existence. The big question was, did I have a duty to report it from the outset? I guess it was now a moot point because the board never punished Dr. Abulencia for his conspiracy. I could not have been punished for not disclosing something that ultimately was not material to the case.

Then there was a delay in the proceedings as the Smith family, through their attorney, Pernell Drayton, had filed a Freedom of Information Act–type lawsuit demanding that the board's proceedings be open to the public. No. no. no. Just because the public can't get access to legal bar tribunal actions against lawyers doesn't mean it can't get access to the medical-board proceedings against doctors. The statutes in the state's medical-practice act *clearly* stated that the public had access to these proceedings. This was a complete waste of time and a useless lawsuit that caused additional delays for me. Again, the statutes were ignored, whether for divorce or medical-board hearings. They are meaningless.

The Medical Board Hearing

After several months of a second delay due to Abulencia's stroke, the medical-board trial in front of hearing officer commenced. He recited the medical-practice act and the charges against me including "any act that could be deemed malpractice or incompetence … or any act meant to deceive, defraud or harm the public or any member thereof, and that actual harm need not have occurred."

So, the issue was medical malpractice, or at least that was the foundation of the charge against me. The standard of proof should have been along the general guidelines of standard of care: What would a like professional in the same specialty under similar circumstances have done?

Panel A in its minutes initially recognized the grievance was based on an anesthesiologist's opinion, but that I was an orthopedic surgeon. The board stated in its minutes that, therefore, it would get its own orthopedic expert opinion. Thus, they had initially recognized the standard of care of a like specialty: orthopedics. Their orthopedic expert completely exonerated me.

> I have reviewed the case and do not see how Dr. Sterling could be found at fault in this at all. I have no concerns whatsoever that Dr. Sterling's act would require any action by the board and therefore I am canceling my deposition.

This exoneration by the orthopedic standard inferred, argued for, or acknowledged the following issues which were covered in the hearing:

1. It was known that orthopedic surgeons were doing Bier blocks throughout hospitals in the state as an incidental procedure for the definitive treatment of an orthopedic condition, and that a Bier block was appropriate in this case. This expert specifically mentioned he had done his own Bier blocks.
2. I had asked for the correct drug and dose to be handed to me in the operating room. This order was given to an authorized RN.
3. Surgeons routinely gave verbal orders to RNs, and they were expected to carry them out through time-honored standards of care and delegation of duties by the physician to the nurse.
4. Techs were prohibited from selecting or drawing up medications. This act of the tech being allowed or directed to get the medication violated the sacred trust between the doctor and the RN, hospital rules, nursing

rules, and standards of care. Only nurses can select and draw up medications—to prevent the very disaster that occurred.

5. The permits to do the surgery also included permission to perform anesthesia "as the anesthesiologist may deem necessary." If the anesthesiologist deemed his services were not necessary, then that automatically surrendered the entire case to the orthopedic surgeon, and anesthesia was to be performed as an incidental part of the global orthopedic procedure. In a similar situation, in the emergency room, the ER physician does not get an anesthesiologist to inject a wound before he cleans it out and stitches it. The ER physician does that himself as part of the combined procedure. (Goerbing had not made this argument, but I did on *pro se* appeal.)

6. The hospital, as well as those throughout the state in 1991, had no rules or regulations that prohibited orthopedists from doing Bier blocks.

7. Special credentialing of an orthopedic surgeon to do Bier blocks was not recognized or nor required at this hospital or others in the state. (I am not sure if a Bier block was even listed on the procedures for credentialing of an orthopedic surgeon. It was assumed that if an orthopedist was setting a wrist fracture, he was doing so with a block that he performed as part of the procedure, not a separate procedure.) Note: this has changed since this event. Bier blocks are now recognized as separate procedures, across two different specialties, with specific standards of care for each. Indeed, separate permits for anesthesia and surgical procedures were drawn up by my hospital *after* this event, but this was not the standard back in 1991. This is how standards of care evolve. The medical board, in a manner *ex post facto*, was trying to hold me to future standards. (I added this issue of *ex post facto* creation of separate permits on appeal. Goerbing had failed to identify this argument.)

I produced a highly regarded expert orthopedic surgeon who testified that I had not fallen below the orthopedic standard of care. The board did not produce an orthopedic surgery expert to testify on the standard of care or dispute my expert at the hearing because the board's own orthopedic expert had already exonerated me during the discovery phase.

That should have been it, right? The board had no expert, therefore no evidence, and therefore the case should have been dismissed. You can't prevail if you have no evidence. Right?

Malpractice, I learned, is based on the standard of care, except when it isn't, especially when you are in front of a medical board. To advance the board's case, McCliven, the medical-board panel A, or both, switched the standard of care and suddenly held me to anesthesia standards. I don't know if this was done with the approval of panel A, who had previously recognized my specialty, or whether this little shit lawyer had taken it upon himself to commandeer the whole case.

McCliven had initially and formally charged me with specific counts. At the hearing, he tried to introduce a new charge—that I was not credentialed to do Bier blocks—by arguing he could now plead his case generally, which would allow him to add new charges and introduce new evidence. Goerbing objected that McCliven had charged me specifically and now wanted to introduce new charges after the deadline. This revisited itself later during the hearing when Goerbing reminded the hearing officer, "Now you see why I objected to McCliven pleading specifically and then changing to pleading generally and now is objecting to me to introducing the hospital CEO's deposition to rebut this new charge that Sterling had not been credentialed to do Bier blocks?" (The CEO admitted that orthopedic surgeons were doing these blocks at the hospital.) The hearing officer sustained our objection on this minor issue, but otherwise, the hearing was a kangaroo court. The verdict had already been decided in the court of public relations.

Speaking of kangaroos and Australia, one of my favorite films, *Breaker Morant* is based on a true story about a sham trial in Transvaal, South Africa, in 1901 during the Boer War. The Australian Bushveld Carbineers were the only effective fighting force against the guerilla tactics used by the Dutch Boer farmers against the English. The English had been committing brutal war crimes against Boer women and children, even starving them to death in prison camps. To make peace with Germany, who protested the way the English were dealing with the Boers under orders from Lord Kitchener himself, England had to make scapegoats of three Australian carbineers who were charged with these war crimes. The trial was a farce. Two were executed by firing squad, and one sentenced to years of hard labor. Later released, he wrote a book entitled *Scapegoats of the Empire*.

Equally a sham was the trial of Captain McVay of the USS *Indianapolis*. After delivering the atomic bomb to Tinian Island, the Indianapolis was torpedoed by a Japanese sub on the return trip. The navy failed to initiate a search for the overdue vessel for three days. The men floundered in the open seas while they were savaged by tiger sharks and thirst. The navy court-martialed McVay for not zigzagging to evade Japanese subs. Incredibly, the Japanese sub commander testified at the court martial that zigzagging would have made no difference. The Indianapolis was a goner no matter what. The sub commander did not even have to use his Kaitens (human suicide torpedoes). Nevertheless, Captain McVay was convicted. Years later, he committed suicide.

This medical-board hearing officer had a record of *never* having disagreed with the board according to Darrell Forrester's written pleadings. Forrester even formally submitted a motion to have this hearing officer recused from this case. Forrester stated that in all his years dealing with the board, this was the first time he had ever asked for recusal of a hearing officer.

The board's case, therefore, was now redirected to holding me to anesthesia standards of care and producing an anesthesia expert to testify that I had fallen below the anesthesia standard. The hearing officer summarized in his findings of fact and conclusions of law simply: "Sterling was required to follow anesthesia standards of care but failed to do so." Why was I required? This simple question was never answered. So instead of addressing through legal doctrine or precedent why the anesthesia standard of care was now controlling, he legislated from the bench. He decided what was to be standard of care. But why was I required to be held to anesthesia standards when the statutes specified a physician accused of malpractice be held to the standards within his own specialty? My specialty had undisputed internal standards of care involving treatment of finger table saw injuries which involved among other things, the administration of Bier blocks by the orthopedist for anesthesia. If the orthopedic standards were ineffective or fraught with complications, they would have simply ceased to exist as part of the orthopedic treatment and standard of care.

The anesthesiology specialty was also motivated by a turf war. To preserve more business for anesthesiologists, they would be inherently biased in their opinions against orthopedists doing Bier blocks. They were competitors. So much for the Board's stated objectives of impartiality requiring the board's expert be neither a competitor nor a friend of the doctor. Once I was held to anesthesia standards of care outside my specialty, my defense collapsed.

Enter Enrique Stockli, MD, Anesthesiologist and Chairman of the Department of Anesthesiology

Dr. Stockli expressed his condolences to the Smith family for the "trans-gressions of our colleagues" in his written opinion to the board. He opined that Dr. Abulencia was required to have performed the anesthesia per hospital rules and American Society of Anesthesia Guidelines and, therefore was in violation of his professional duties. Thus, it could be inferred that he had abandoned the patient. My mother, a board-certified anesthesiologist, also concurred. "He abandoned his post." Dr. Stockli also opined that I was not formally creden-tialed by the hospital to perform Bier blocks even though I had done them in residency and in the emergency room.

Dr. Stockli stated that, per anesthesiology standards, I was required to check the medication that was handed to me, and to see the actual bottle from which the drug in the syringe was drawn. When asked why this anesthe-sia standard, he replied because there are "so many drugs an anesthesiologist uses, that they have to label them (in this context, I think he meant to identify them) to avoid mix-ups." I argued that there were no other drugs in this case. The only other drug, an antibiotic called Ancef, had been given in the emer-gency room hours prior. There was only one drug in this case, and it was one of the most common and well known and easily identified by its familiar blue label.: xylocaine.

Then Dr. Stockli claimed that the patient wasn't monitored with blood pressure, EKG, and pulse oximeter. Wrong. The patient was monitored with all of these, but still did not alert us to the impending disaster.

Dr. Stockli Cross-Examination

I argued on the basis of a hypothetical case. After a surgical hip proce-dure, an elderly patient has returned to the recovery room where the anesthesiologist is still responsible for following her postoperatively. She suddenly develops a heart arrhythmia, which in 1991 would have been treated with the same drug I ordered: intravenous xylocaine.

I asked whether Dr. Stockli drew up that drug or the nurse? He said the nurse. And who injected that drug in the recovery room? Again, the nurse, he answered. He admitted he might not even be there. But it was okay for him to order the drug to be selected, drawn up, and injected by the RN. He could rely on her *totally* to carry out his verbal order, but it was *not* okay for me to rely on the nurse to carry out my verbal order and hand me the medication in the operating room? Why is it okay for him delegate total responsibility to the nurse? Because he is an anesthesiologist, and his situation is different than a surgeon's in that he may be doing another case when the previous patient developed that arrhythmia in the recovery room. The doctor's specialty, and the nature of the specialty and special situations it places him in, determine the different standards of care between the specialties.

A surgeon is scrubbed and sterile and so has to rely on being handed things he orders verbally without selecting or drawing them up himself. Air traffic control (ATC) requires pilots verbally read back and acknowledge ATC orders to avoid midair collisions. People's lives depend on it. The nurse verbally read back my order *verbatim* as she wrote it on her scrubs. She even went so far as to ask whether I wanted it in two 30 cc syringes or a single 60 cc syringe. That I would not receive what I had asked for, given such a simple order under the circumstances, was inconceivable.

At this point, the hearing officer interrupted to give his confirmatory input supporting Dr. Stockli's testimony, "because in Abulencia's hypothetical case in the recovery room, it was the nurse who injected the medication." The hearing officer had just introduced his own layman standard of care: Whoever actually injects the medication is responsible for knowing what's in the syringe, and that therefore, the anesthesia standard is controlling. This reasoning may sound plausible to the lay person, but this was not the rules of procedure or standard of care for an orthopedist in the operating room.

This is similar to the act of legislating from the bench. The judge cannot determine what the laws or standards of care should be. He can only opine if they have or have not been followed, based on expert testimony. So, his layman interpretation allowed the board to abandon the controlling legal standard of care by a like individual/specialty. Couldn't the board have simply produced an expert orthopedist to say that he would have checked the medication before injecting? Sure, if it had continued shopping for enough witnesses.

If the board's orthopedic expert had stated that he did *not* do Bier blocks for his orthopedic cases, but instead relied on anesthesia to do them, then the board would have had grounds to go outside the orthopedic specialty to identify that supplemental standard. But this was not the situation in my case. This orthopedic expert did his own Bier blocks and therefore the board did not have to abandon the orthopedic standard of care.

By common legal doctrine, a court cannot rely on a more general standard when a more specific and exclusive one (the orthopedic standard incorporated the administration of anesthesia in its standard of care as part of the procedure) had already been recognized and was available. Goerbing failed to argue this critical argument at the hearing or in his pleadings.

In short, the whole issue of rule of law, rules of evidence, and standards of care were thrown out the window. The case was reduced to a lay person's belief that a doctor should know the medication he is injecting into a patient. Indeed, this sounds very plausible and intuitive to the lay person, but it was not based on the formal legal definition of standard of care. Why have a hearing/trial at all? Why even have the statutes? The medical practice act should be rewritten simply: "The medical board can do whatever it wants."

Dr. Stockli quickly tried to distinguish my situation from the hypothetical case of the nurse selecting and injecting a medication in the recovery room on an anesthesiologist's order.

"It's apples and oranges, Your Honor."

Why?

"Because those infinitesimal doses given in the recovery room cannot harm the patient."

Huh?

"If the nurse selects the wrong drug, or directs the tech to get the drug and the tech draws up the wrong drug, and the nurse doesn't check, she can kill the patient."

Dr. Stockli responded, "The medicine goes directly to the patient in the recovery room. It doesn't loiter." Wait. Stop!

So, if I had given the injection immediately, it would have somehow changed miraculously in the syringe?

Dr. Stockli admitted that I had ordered the correct drug and dose, and that whether the tourniquet may have leaked or may not been inflated in the first place was not the issue. Once the arm had been injected with the wrong drug, death was imminent, regardless when the tourniquet deflated.

"If you ask me, it was the wrong choice of the drug. Once the drug gets into the bloodstream, these patients are unresuscitatable."

William Goerbing's Perry Mason Moment for Equal Treatment

In his preliminary remarks, Dr. Stockli had mentioned a patient who had been given an epidural block for child birth by an anesthesiologist in his department with the same drug. She received only a small dose of this drug (0.5 percent marcaine) over the spinal cord. The remainder had inadvertently been injected into the circulation. She had been "damaged" as a result of the prolonged seizures. Goerbing knew about this case. He asked Dr. Stockli "who that doctor was in your department at the university who gave an epidural to a lawyer's wife for her delivery, but who did not monitor the patient or perform a test block before the epidural injection was given to detect if the drug had inadvertently entered the bloodstream?

"Dr. Stacks."

"He just rammed it all in," said Goerbing.

"That's why he was fired," Dr. Stockli immediately countered.

This anesthesiologist knowingly injected the medication (which he drew up himself, I assume, as anesthesiologists do) without doing a test dose or monitoring the patient. Uncontested, undisputed, intentional medical malpractice. That patient went into immediate seizures and had a miraculous but very difficult resuscitation, probably because only a fraction of the medication actually entered her bloodstream, unlike my patient, where all of it did.

It has been reported in the rare instances when patients have been resuscitated from these inadvertent intravascular epidurals, they have reported still having numbness to the lower body, indicating that a substantial amount of the medication must *not* have entered the bloodstream and fortunately instead spread over the nerves to cause the intended anesthesia.

It was at this time—three, two, one—right on cue, that the hearing officer interrupted. "Excuse me. Are we trying that case?"

Goerbing replied, "No, but as Perry Mason says, if you'll give me two minutes Your Honor, I'll make my point."

Goerbing asked Dr. Stockli point blank: "Now was there any disciplinary action taken by the board against Dr. Stacks?" Dr. Stockli hesitated, unsure, or not wanting to answer.

Then came the punch line by Goerbing: "Well, I happened to defend Dr. Stacks, and I can tell you there was no licensure-board action taken." (Dr. Stacks' case was quietly settled without the devastating publicity I had on national TV or the state newspapers, and before public sentiment against the board and doctors had built up.)

The hearing officer asked why it mattered what happened in Dr. Stacks' case.

"We deserve equal treatment," Goerbing replied.

At this point, Darrell Forrester, Dr. Abulencia's attorney, entered the argument.

"Let me step in here for a minute. I think Mr. Goerbing's point is very well taken. How is it that Drs. Abulencia and Sterling are here and Dr. Stacks is not? On what basis does the medical board determine whether a medical malpractice case is addressed by the board in a lawsuit or not? I have been asking the board for years to clarify this standard and have been unable to get an answer. It is well known that the board routinely picks cases on public relations grounds or—"

The hearing officer snapped back "You don't know what the grounds are! You are just making those statements."

"Well, at least Dr. Stacks' patient is still alive," replied Dr. Stockli.

"Well, the mother is paralyzed from the chest down ("damaged," as per Dr. Stockli's earlier description) and the baby was born with severe cerebral palsy—if you call that being alive," Goerbing reminded him.

"Dr. Stockli, if the nurse makes a *mistake*, should you be before the licensure board for that?" (Obviously referring to my situation but with objections being fired off by the board's attorney, McCliven)

"I don't think so," Dr. Stockli had to admit.

The Games Hospitals Play

Dr. Abulencia, the hospital, the nurse, and the techs were all insured by one insurer, State Medical Mutual. I was insured by a different one in the civil medical-malpractice case. This civil case had been settled a few months before my medical-board hearing. Before the settlement, and I don't know where I heard it, it was being suggested that the plaintiff's attorney, Pernell Drayton, was crazy to be focusing all his attention on me. I was going through a divorce and would be sliced in half. I had resigned my practice. I had only $200,000 malpractice coverage, hardly the deep pockets lawyers search out in malpractice actions. Go after the hospital and the nurses and anesthesiologists, not Dr. Sterling. I suspect Drayton was just going along with the family's demand to put me through hell to publicly crucify me out of blind revenge.

The family wanted all the attention in the end to be focused on me. My impression was that the Smith family was so vengeful, so vitriolic, that they couldn't stand the thought of me getting off so easily. Quite interestingly, they never spoke out against the RN, techs, or Dr. Abulencia. I guess they didn't perceive them to be "making the megabucks."

I heard from Goerbing that Drayton had quietly admitted his clients were extremely difficult to deal with. I'll come out and say what I think: I think that the Smiths could not stand the thought of me being successful and "making the megabucks" while their five sons may not have amounted to as much.

I'll be more blunt: It was class envy. Understandable grief for the loss of their youngest son notwithstanding, the Smiths would not hear of any other explanation except that I was *entirely* to blame for what they could only perceive as callous, premeditated murder. There was just no way they would ever have accepted my apology. There was no way I could ever explain to them, no way that they could ever understand, that it had been a terrible accident. I didn't mean to do it. It was not callous indifference. I had been focusing on how I was going to treat his mangled finger, not second guessing whether the RN would hand me the wrong medication. Why would I want to kill their son?

It is not inconceivable that Drayton, therefore, could have made a settlement deal with the hospital, Abulencia, the RN and techs *first* just to leave me as the sole defendant standing, allowing him to focus squarely on me as the reason the Smith's son died. This would have satisfied the Smith's desire to put me in the hot seat, standing at trial alone when everyone else had settled. However, I think that he probably talked them into settling in the end by saying that he could arrange so that I would have to pay out of my personal funds for ten years. That would have given them some satisfaction.

He also no doubt said that if the case went to trial, the jury could find that it was all the nurse's and tech's fault and I would get acquitted, and the Smiths would be denied their vengeance. Of course, Drayton didn't want to go to trial. The big money had already settled. He just wanted his cut from my share of the settlement and then go straight to the bank.

At the medical-board hearing, as stated earlier, Dr. Abulencia was allowed to roll. No questions or challenges to his story, no cross-examination as he rambled. He mentioned that it was quite the double standard that the hospital had suspended a hospital worker for ten days without pay for stubbing a patient's toe while pushing him on the stretcher in the hallway, yet here the RN and tech, in a premeditated fashion, committed an act that cost a patient his life, and no punishment. They were never fired, put on leave, or suspended.

Why not? Because such disciplinary action would have been tantamount to the hospital admitting liability for its agents in the medical-malpractice suit. The hospital obviously wanted to shift all the blame to me. These are the legal games that are played. Same with the board. Any disciplinary action against Dr. Abulencia, the nurse, or the tech would have been tantamount to inconsistency. If the board disciplined the nurse, tech, and Dr. Abulencia, then such disciplinary action would have implied it was at least partly their fault and would have been a reason to give me a less harsh punishment. This would have been perceived as watered-down justice.

Why then, did I get all the blame for this? Remember: the public was pissed off at the board for not being vigilant enough against doctors. The board (and doctors) had a public relations problem. The fact that I was also on national TV featured in a story designed to inflame the public in order to sell their brand of junk journalism made it more urgent that I be found entirely to blame. In fact, I am quite confident many readers will use this event to confirm their opinion that doctors need to be disciplined even *more* harshly. I have anonymously tested the waters through various forums. When I explained the event, and my unsuccessful attempts to get a position at the VA or the Indian Health Services (IHS), a not atypical comment from a reader from Zero Hedge was "so you're going to fuck up those people too?"

In the licensure-board case, I was punished for the result, not the act. If I had injected an innocuous drug through the nurse's error and the patient had suffered no ill effects, I would have never been brought up before the board for the same act—failure to check a medication. If I had checked the medication, determined that it was the wrong one, and reported the nurse and the tech to the hospital, the nurse and the tech would have probably been disciplined for breaching rules of conduct- because the patient would have lived.

But in this situation, it was the result (death) that turned discipline and rule of law on its head. The nurse and tech were not disciplined because it would have been tantamount to admission of hospital liability in a high-profile, costly lawsuit. Had I injected xylocaine into Arthur Smith instead of lethal Marcaine, he would have had a brief seizure, fully recovered, and it would merely be reported as a hospital incident where it remained internally, and would have never reached the board.

Well, actually, the Smith family would have probably reported it to the board and tried to sue me, or encourage their son to sue me since he was twenty-one, out of obvious hatred of doctors, especially if he had bitten his tongue or dislocated his shoulder from the seizure, but even those events are exceedingly rare. I have not seen a case report or heard of a single anecdotal account of such sequelae. In fact, I think anecdotally these patients have been reported to wake up wondering what happened, almost as if having come out of a regular general anesthesia.

The hospital administrator at the second hospital where I later worked said in no uncertain terms that "at this hospital, if the nurse and tech had done that, they would have been fired." They always say that trying to be so righteous, except if that event actually had happened at their hospital, the tech and RN would have been protected also. The hospital will sell the physician out in heart-beat.

In my memorandum on my medical-board appeal, I argued that the board's verdict/order was excessive and duplicitous because I was clearly being punished for the result, not the act, and that the result had already been addressed through settlement payout to the family in the companion medical-malpractice civil suit. The settlement amounts were sealed, which is surprising because the family had already publicly dumped on me as much as possible. My practice and career had been ruined by all the negative publicity and I would have to leave, so sealing the settlement terms certainly didn't help me. I was merely required to "sign the papers." Why then, was the case sealed?

Answer: to protect the hospital, the anesthesiologist, the nurse, and the techs who worked there.

The Settlement Agreement Reached by All Parties in 1994: $1,250,000

Amount paid by the hospital, techs, the nurse, Dr. Abulencia through a common medical mutual malpractice company: $900,000

Amount paid by my insurance company: $200,000

Amount paid by me in excess judgment from personal funds: $100,000 payable over ten years or $10,000/year.

Amount paid by my orthopedic practice over ten years $50,000, or $5,000 year. This amount was deducted from my buyout of my share of practice as part of the indemnification insurance agreement outlined previously. My partners did not pay this $50,000; I paid for it. In fact, even after this $50,000 payout, my partners were still $50,000 ahead because this was part of the indemnification arrangement that did not have to be activated, as the case was settled for below the stipulated threshold amount. An even more disgusting way of looking at it is that since I effectively paid $150,000 out of my own personal funds, at a minimum, I forked over at least one-third of this personal amount or $50,000 (based on contingency ratio) to this attorney.

Now comes the uncomfortable part in which I disclose, without comment, as it invariably makes me appear even more callous. People probably want to know how this amount was arrived, and why it appeared so low. As the public may be aware, awards in personal lawsuits are based on *economic losses* such as lost wages, hospital bills, and cost of future medical care and *intangibles* such as pain and suffering. A third category, *punitive damages,* can be awarded in cases of extreme carelessness, indifference, or premediated awareness or intentional misconduct where it is known an act will result in harm. In Arthur Smith's case, his projected economic losses were derived from lost *future* wages, termed *power to labor and earn money*. These were calculated by a forensic economist based on several factors including previous work history/experience, skills, physical and mental capabilities, education level, and so on.

There were no specified punitive damages, although Darrell Forrester had argued that his client was entitled to these by some argument that I don't remember, but it went something like "because I had subjective awareness that what I was doing was putting the patient's life in danger." Attorneys love to advance punitive damages because, at least at that time, there were no monetary award limits, and it gave a jury an opportunity to be extremely generous and offset any limitations of an award based only on economic losses or pain and suffering. As for the doctor, one of the first things your medical-malpractice insurer will inform you is that your policy does not cover punitive damages.

In Arthur Smith's case, his pain and suffering were unknowable. I recall reading a communication by Pernell Drayton that it was worth at least $100,000. I obviously cannot know if indeed Arthur Smith was terrified out of his wits and suffered the ultimate distress of one who senses in a split second he is about to die, and I would certainly be the first to admit that pain and suffering could not be dismissed. Had the case gone to trial, the jury would have assigned a percentage of blame to each of the defendants. It seems to me that if the RN had followed orders and yet for some inexplicable reason had selected and drawn up wrong the medication herself, and not the tech, and she had failed to double-check it before she handed it to me *and* I had also failed to check it, then a stronger layman's argument could have been made that I should have checked it.

However, this was not the nurse's innocent human mistake of forgetfulness. It was a premeditated act insofar as she knew she was not supposed to be allowing a tech to select and draw up medications. From a probability standpoint, it could be argued that if the RN had done her job, it would have been probably less than one chance in a million that Arthur would have received the wrong drug. Therefore, William Goerbing mischaracterized Frazier's act as a "mistake" on his cross-examination of the board's anesthesiology expert, Dr. Stockli, and pleadings. It was not a mistake. It was a premeditated act of misconduct and should have afforded me another level of defense.

Invariably, the more I try to defend myself and the more distilled my arguments become, the more I am accused of being indifferent to the patient's demise, or showing no remorse (indeed, traits of a sociopath), and the more the arguments against me resort to generalities such as "you should have checked the drug," "you simply blame the nurse," or "Dr. Sterling, don't you have any remorse for this man's death?"

Arthur's father was intent on disparaging *only me* in the media after the board's sentencing—not the nurse, not the tech, not the fact that Dr. Abulencia got off. Only that I had gotten practically no punishment at all. As reported in a state newspaper:

"My son is dead, and he gets three months. The next time it happens, I suppose he'll get six months."

"It was all so useless. My son was in A-1 physical shape."

His mother criticized the board for requiring me "to write a letter of apology, *admitting responsibility.*"

"If he's forced to write it, it doesn't mean anything."

Back in 1994, lawyers would *never* tell their client to express any regret or apology, no matter how heartfelt, for the simple reason that it would be tantamount to admission of guilt. This situation was potentially problematic in my situation in the event that if the medical-board action had preceded the companion medical-malpractice civil suit, an apology could have been used as evidence confirming my responsibility had the civil suit gone to trial. This situation has changed in the last ten years or so as statutes reportedly no longer allow an apology by the physician for an unfortunate event to be used as evidence against him. However, recent studies show that these apologies have not reduced the incidence of malpractice claims. It's still about the money.

Neither Dr. Abulencia, the RN, or the tech ever apologized to me for destroying my career or for the permanent disruption to my family and my life as a result, nor to my knowledge, did they ever apologize to the Smith family. Nurses will take time, though, no matter how busy they claim to be, to write up an incident report on a doctor. They are always lurking in the medical system as potential assassins. (That was the description an ER doctor at my last practice used to describe the nurses who were just waiting to find something for which they could report him.) Nurses are increasingly challenging and confronting doctors, always looking to appear more knowledgeable. Of course, when something does happen, how they quickly scatter and say, "Don't look at me. He's the doctor." Welcome to the modern world of medicine.

We did not get a forensic economic expert in the civil malpractice case as that would certainly been an insensitive judgment on the value of his life. We left the evaluation to be performed by the Smiths' own expert. My defense counsel, Goerbing, did depose the parents. From these sources, the following facts were made evident:

Arthur Smith had a severe learning disability and did not finish high school. IQ in the dull range. Had initiated an application to work at the new factory, but did not follow through because he could not take the written test. Had been arrested once for fighting. Had drifted from job to job. Could not continue with a manual labor job because he couldn't lift the "hod" because it hurt his shoulders. His power to labor and earn money was based on working until he was fifty-five.

His father claims that it was his son's intention to get a driver's license and a car, but there was no evidence that he had even attempted the written test. His parents had been in the process of signing him up for Medicaid until they realized he was still covered under the family insurance policy. His father worked at a large plant until he retired at age fifty-five, right around the time of this accident, and may have also had some kind of learning disability. His mother earned money as a babysitter but was not regularly employed. Lifetime earnings based on the power to labor and earn money was around $500,000, according to their expert. I guess part of this was based on earnings history of similar people who, as laborers, are physically unable to continue after age fifty-five.

I Fired Goerbing

By this time, I absolutely knew that this medical-board hearing was a sham, license suspension was imminent, and Goerbing had missed the opportunity over two years ago to inform the board that my act was purely unintentional. The board probably would have been more lenient earlier before the negative publicity had built up.

I told him in the office he was fired and why. He then had the gall to remind me that I owed him some money, about $10,000, since my insurance company had recently reneged on their offer to provide me with a courtesy defense through Goerbing. They suddenly admitted that the medical-board case was much more involved than they had anticipated. Did this mean that even this insurance company didn't think I would be getting screwed as badly by the board as I was about to be?

Why should I pay Goerbing to undo something he allowed to happen? In fact, why didn't I sue him? His fumbling of my case was comparable to a delay in diagnosis of cancer in a patient to the point that it had now spread beyond treatable margins. Oh wait, my losses would have been speculative.

When I reported Goerbing to the state bar, even the bar investigator who knew Goerbing later admitted per our phone conversation that had I acted in a timely fashion, my license probably would not have been suspended, but now the medical/legal winds had changed.

Another attorney, whom I hired to appeal the medical-board case agreed that I shouldn't pay Goerbing. Goerbing turned all the files over to me. Nothing new, except a letter from the board's attorney Sal McCliven, informing Goerbing months earlier that I had written him an *ex parte* communication requesting my case to be severed from Abulencia's and that I should cease and desist, and that he had no problem with severing my and Abulencia's cases. Also in the files was Forrester's motion to recuse the hearing officer and a bunch of background documents on the Board's lack of consistency.

That son of a bitch Goerbing had been lying to me, saying he couldn't sever my case. And here I had been waiting for months for Dr. Abulencia to recover from his stroke. I could have already proceeded with my hearing and started serving my suspension.

Goerbing simply didn't give a shit. He only said to me that he couldn't do that. He never gave me any reason. Only later did I think about the possibility of the strategy backfiring if I had proceeded with the medical-board action first. The board's guilty verdict would then be used as more evidence against me in the pending civil medical-malpractice case. Talk about getting caught in a double pincer. I might have wound up paying an even higher settlement.

But by his absence of any discussion of this issue of severance of Abulencia's and my cases, I realized that Goerbing didn't care about what happened to me. If he had to be bothered with sending a letter off to McCliven, well, that would be an inconvenience to him at the moment, especially if he was preoccupied with my office manager. Goerbing never asked me to pay this $10,000. He knew he had been derelict in protecting his client and his dereliction of duty would cost me a hundred times that amount over the course of my career, what was left of it. It made Skyler's and Salazar's negligence almost trivial in the grand scheme of things, but in my mind, Salazar's incompetence had set the first domino in motion. I was doomed the moment I first walked into his office.

Judgment Day—Board Sentencing

To get an idea of how screwed up this state's medical-practice act was (and is), you have to understand that there were two panels, A and B comprising the medical board. Each panel had about nine members, including the dean of one of the state's two medical schools, one or two doctors in active practice, a layperson, a person in a medical-related field such as Department of Public Health, an attorney, and so on. In my case, panel A made the rush to judgment and initiated the lawsuit. They had heard only some of the evidence as reflected briefly in the minutes. It was only the hearing officer who actually heard all the evidence, particularly the testimony of the experts.

Once this hearing officer had written his findings of fact and conclusions of law, the case was turned over to the other panel B, who had never heard a bit of testimony or evidence about the case. It was panel B who would listen to hearing officer's verdict and determine my sentence. Correspondence from Darrell Forrester to Goerbing indicated that yet another one of the medical examiners, who was resigning, was dismayed how the panels based their decisions almost entirely on a hearing officer's opinions and recommendations.

Again, I resorted to a last-ditch attempt to save my career by sending again a binder with supporting documents to all members of panel B in advance of the sentencing informing them of the facts so that they would not walk into the sentencing phase uninformed. It was to no avail. At least this time I was not formally criticized by the little shit for another *ex parte* communication, because by this time, I was acting *pro se*. It no longer mattered.

This sentencing phase is like seating a jury in court to hear a case, telling them the circumstances of the case but then suddenly escorting them out before they hear a single bit of sworn testimony. Only the judge hears the evidence. When the judge has heard all the evidence, a new jury is seated and for the first time, hears about the case through the judge's verdict and decides the sentence based only on the judge's findings and recommendations. It is an off-the-wall process. Why have panel A or B? Why have a jury? It is essential a truncated bench trial. The medical profession has surrendered everything to the legal system.

I showed up to the sentencing and was greeted by the new medical investigator. He asked, "Are you Dr. Sterling?"

I replied, "Yes."

"Hi, I am Miguel Arronzo, the new medical-board Investigator." He handed me his card, which I still have. "I heard about this case. Let me tell you: this is *total bullshit* what they are doing to you. I was a medical investigator in (another state), and back there, we would've *never* done this to a doctor for something like this. You know, shit happens. But hang in there, and you get through it."

I heard Doreen Smith laughing and talking about her other son in Oklahoma in the foyer before we entered the conference room. One of the Smiths had attended every deposition and hearing in both the medical-malpractice civil case and the licensure-board case, and she had an agreement with Pernell Drayton that a member of his firm would be present at each medical-board hearing. The press was also in attendance.

Doreen Smith was given a chance to speak at the sentencing. She remarked how everyone had treated Arthur Smith's death "like he was nothing." Of course, some degree of emotional lability would be understandable for a while as she mourned the loss of her son. But now three years later, her display was pure theater as she saw the panel just sitting quietly, unmoved, as she spoke for a minute and then on schedule, broke out in an overacted sobbing fit. Pure drama. The tears were no longer about the loss of her son. They were part of an act to sway panel B to deliver as harsh a sentence as possible. I am sorry, but that is how I saw it.

I made some feeble attempt and asked the panel if they had received or read my communications explaining the case. None of them even answered. They just sat there, unresponsive, and dumb as rocks, so I made no further comment. I knew it was pointless. This case had long ago been decided. Then the panel B chairman, a vascular surgeon, who appeared to me to be a cold and emotionally aloof asshole, read the already-prepared sentence:

1. $5,000 fine to cover costs
2. Three-month suspension
3. One-year probation
4. A written letter of apology to the Bond family, "expressing regret of the circumstances and admitting responsibility"

The latter, when threated with loss of license if not complied with, was nothing less than a coerced confession.

Legal experts dismiss my claim of coercion because I had been found guilty by the board.

The board threw as many different types of punishment me as they could, clearly trying to give the public the impression that they had thrown the book at me. It was really all for show or, as in the military, "fire for effect." Even a suspension for just a month alone is sufficient enough to mark a physician for life.

Doreen Smith, of course, was disappointed. "Except for the suspension, he got nothing at all." She couldn't possibly understand what a suspension does to your career. Nor could the board, after all most of them were not actively practicing physicians. With a history of licensure-board action, one is now a medical refugee, treated like a leper. An internist or family medicine doctor is not impacted as much, but a surgeon in an overcrowded field like orthopedics? Forget it. Your career is toast, and your personal life will be forever disrupted. I could never again secure a stable job. I have seen other doctors with lots of issues, but continued to be able to practice. The one factor that really made the difference: They had no history of licensure board suspension or probation.

As time progressed, my hours were increasingly consumed by fruitless and costly searches, having to fill out endless preliminary application / screening summaries, talking to hundreds of recruiters but to no avail as my rejection list, at least those who were kind enough to even get back to me with the bad news, grew longer.

Fast forward to the present. When I did get the third job toward the end of my orthopedic career, I could never contemplate selling my old house purchased at my second job. I never knew after leaving that job when I would have to move back when my third job fell through. The hospital was in that kind of financial difficulty. This added a new twist to the rent-versus-buy decision. I had to do both. How many belongings to take with me? I didn't know. In this third orthopedic job, the hospital paid some moving expenses to go there, but I had to be careful and think how much it would cost me to move back once the job ended. I could not even determine how long an apartment lease to take out. Six months or a year? All of my hobbies, my drums, reef aquarium and so on were put forever on hold. Then, of course, the address changes and all the nagging little details that occur with moving. There were duplicate utility bills for the house and the new apartment. Returning home only meant assessing what repairs from disuse would be needed. I could never again call a place home. You don't know the feeling until you have been placed in my situation. There were mid school year conflicts. Did my wife and daughter stay at our home while I worked at another location until the school year ended, or did I pull her after the start of her school year?

Because the fourth orthopedic job for which I had been recruited and a contract signed was suddenly rescinded late in the summer, my daughter had to go to school back at my hometown while I spent several additional months finding the wound-care job. I had to relocate to the other end of the state for wound care. Thus, my family has been divided. The salary I was making with wound care was less than that of an RN, and I didn't have any vacations or benefits. My family went on vacation without me. Nice life. Thank you, medical board.

Even in the military, at least one is put on notice that he is going to be stationed at a certain place for X number of years, and the government pays for and does your moving. I didn't know whether my wound care job would last for weeks, months, or years. It, too, was over promised, this time fifty percent below even my most pessimistic assumptions. I got the termination without cause notice just ten days after renewing my one -year apartment lease and four months into my daughter's new school year. The company did not even give me the required 60 days' notice, as it quietly transitioned a new doctor to replace me. The doctor had to take my facilities because she reportedly did not have enough patients either. Meanwhile my wife had stayed back at our home. More strain on the marriage. This is the life of a medical refugee. You cannot pick where, when, whether, and for how long you will be able to continue to practice. Your life plans are thrown into chaos. Do you get out of medicine early in time to retrain for a new career?

The Weather Report and Board Follow up

The next week after the board's sentencing, the board's orthopedic ex-pert who had exonerated me called. "Bryce? Hi. This is Dr. X. I was calling you to let you know that you really got screwed."

"I know I did," I responded. Thanks for the weather report, I thought. Not much more to the phone call. I had also written him ahead of the board sentencing to ask him to reaffirm his opinion that I was being railroaded. I wondered why he had even bothered calling me. I wondered why I had no support from any members of my profession. This case was unprecedented and should have been a call to arms. The board had now established a precedent for being able to suspend, probate or revoke a physician's license for a single isolated unintentional event on a whim.

So, what was the purpose of probation? It wasn't like the board was checking up on me to be sure that I wasn't injecting medications into patients without checking what was in the syringe was it? A probation made no sense whatsoever.

But wait! Actually, they *did* send a medical investigator to my house months later. He had no idea what he was supposed to do, but he came with a specimen container to do a urine sample for drugs, because the board typically uses probation to be sure a doctor is not a relapsing alcoholic or drug addict. I told the investigator what my act and punishment were, showed him the board's sentence, orders, my canceled check, copy of the apology letter.

"Obviously, you see I am not practicing, I have paid the fine, and I certainly do not appear to be under the influence of drugs or alcohol, nor was I required to participate in any therapy. I have written the apology to the family. Do you still wish to take a urine sample?"

The investigator looked totally befuddled.

"Well, I guess pay the fine and write the letter ..."

"I've already done that," I reminded him.

He just left my house without doing anything.

"Ole Ten Percent" and the
Medical-Licensure-Board Appeal

I appealed the medical board's opinion. Burned by the incompetence of my previous counsel in the divorce and medical board actions, I wrote the petition *pro se*. It was unquestionably more concise and distilled the salient points better and more comprehensively than what Goerbing or my attorneys had done at the hearing or since. Most of these have been clarified by me and have been presented here.

I advanced for the first time the broad legal argument/standard that the board had to have substantial evidence, termed "clear and convincing evidence," to support its action. The orthopedic standard, initially recognized by the board, had clearly and convincingly had exonerated me. Thus, the requirement for substantial evidence to discipline me could not possibly have been met. It had been crowded out by the orthopedic standard of care.

The board's attorney, Sal McCliven, argued that this was a new legal argument and could not be introduced on appeal. I also argued that when there was a more specific standard or law available, the court could not rely on a more general one, in this case, outside my specialty, as medical malpractice specifies what a like person in the same specialty, an orthopedist, would have done in the same set of circumstances. It was not whether the court agreed with the standard; it is whether I fell below the standard. The court had arbitrarily selected a different standard that arguably was a double standard, as the board's anesthesiology expert, Dr. Stockli, testified he could rely on the RN *totally* to carry out his verbal order, both selecting and injecting the medication without him even being there.

Finally, the facts certainly indicated, that the RN's act was a *deliberate, premeditated act*, not simply a *mistake*. She knew allowing the tech to get the medication was *prohibited*, would potentially place the patient's life in jeopardy if the wrong drug was drawn up, and admitted as much in her deposition when she answered the question posed to her: "Nurse, what was your first thought when you realized you had given Dr. Sterling the wrong medication?"

Her answer: "There goes my nursing license." It was as if she were getting behind the wheel intoxicated, knowing her intoxicated state would pose a threat to other drivers.

The lawyer who represented me during oral argument for my appeal of the board's action argued that my *pro se* appeal certainly was "sufficient to be addressed by the court, as no magical words or phrases" were needed, and my appeal "certainly stated the basis for that."

There was a concurrent article in the state newspaper about the ten judges in this city where my appeal was filed. All of them had been recently rated by attorneys, presumably for competence. All had been rated above fifty percent, except for mine, the one who presided over the amusement park lawsuit mentioned earlier. His had only a ten percent approval rating in an article in the state newspaper.

Why did my case wind up in his court? I suspect that any case that needed to be disposed of or had been filed *pro se,* found their way to the least competent wastebasket judge who could get away with just flushing the case and snow-jobbing the appellant. In my case, the board could rely on him to deliver the necessary opinion, reaffirming the board's ruling, full of glaring omissions, inconsistencies, with poor grasp of the statutes, and most of all, not squarely addressing the argument of standard of care within a like specialty. It was the same reason, it seemed, for the board having selected my hearing officer: They wanted someone who would not disagree with them.

I still would like to know how a particular hearing officer or judge is really selected to preside in a particular case. Is it really random selection? I don't believe it. On one medical blog, I read a response from a physician who was also an attorney expert in medical litigation. She stated: "Based on the facts as you state them, you should not have been suspended."

As I sat in "Ole Ten Percent's" court hearing for my appeal, my suspicions were confirmed. This judge could only analyze the case at a layman's level of understanding. He had no understanding of the legal doctrine of standard of care. After oral arguments had been presented, all of which had flown right over his head, he asked, "I jist wants t' knooow, who'z 'spons'ble fo' checkin' da druhhhg?"

Again, in the context of an orthopedist in the operating room having made a verbal request for a medication to be handed to him by the nurse who has read back the order, written it on her scrubs, and was obligated to select and draw it up herself, it was the nurse.

"The nurse," my attorney responded.

Sal McCliven's written argument rebuttal/response had been boiled down to that I "simply blamed the nurse." This implies that blaming or holding someone else responsible is in violation of the standards or laws. Very vague. No legal basis. No argument why the standard of care could be switched to anesthesia. McCliven then hypocritically introduced his new argument, that I was "captain of the ship" and therefore responsible.

Ole Ten Percent's written opinion evaded the entire issue of traditional medical-malpractice standard of care. He dodged the whole issue of anesthesia versus orthopedic standards as controlling and redefined the case on the grounds that "begged the question: to what standard of care is the patient entitled?"

This was the equivalent of saying that any traditional specialty specific standard of care was no longer applicable. The case had been reduced to the layman situation. If someone is baking a cake, he should know what ingredients he is putting into the cake to be sure none of them are poisonous. But what goes on in an operating room where strict rules and protocol established by the medical profession about who may order, select, and administer drugs are far different than in a kitchen. In a sense, the trial court threw the issue of standard of care deeper into the waste basket by now nullifying both anesthesia and orthopedic standards. I wonder if Ole Ten Percent even wrote that opinion himself. It was almost as if he directed one of his paralegals to write an opinion that would reaffirm the board's suspension. I would like to know how much of this work is subbed out?

On one hand, the board wanted to hold me to anesthesia standards, thus introduced and argued anesthesia standards as controlling, meaning anesthesia standards would now establish the rules/basis for determining whether my act was malpractice. On the other hand, if anesthesia standards were to be recognized, why was Dr. Abulencia *not* disciplined by the board? After all, he was an anesthesiologist, and there was undisputed testimony by Dr. Stockli that his act was tantamount to abandoning the patient once he had arrived in the operating room in violation of American Society of Anesthesiology standards. He should have been disciplined, or at least reprimanded, but was not.

In his conclusions and findings, this hearing officer stated that Dr. Abulencia committed no act of negligence. "He merely turned the case over to Dr. Sterling." The board had therefore validated this anesthesiologist who determined that the case did not require the anesthesiology specialty. This act of turning over the case to me nullified any need for anesthesia or its standard and left the orthopedic standard as controlling. The board and the courts however wanted to pick and choose and have it both ways within the single anesthesiology specialty.

On to the Court of Appeals

I appealed Ole Ten Percent's decision to the state court of appeals. One judge, the brother of my divorce lawyer, was one of the three judges who unanimously reaffirmed Ole Ten Percent's ruling. A closer examination of the opinion showed that it was simply rammed through.

The court of appeals clearly identified my arguments in the opening paragraph of its opinion.

1. The medical board had held me to the wrong standard of care.
2. The verdict was not supported by the evidence.

The appellate court then stated succinctly: "We disagree."

My second argument was just a follow up to the first. Again, the case was really very simple. I had been held to the wrong standard of care, and by definition, the board had no evidence since their own orthopedic surgeon, my specialty, had exonerated me. However, the court of appeals never squarely addressed this critical issue of *competing* standards of care. It ignored my first argument and just *assumed* that the anesthesia standard was the correct one, and rambled on how I had failed to specifically follow this anesthesia standard of care until the very end of its opinion, when it cited two medical malpractice cases, neither involving a medical board action, and neither of which had anything to do with the central issue of competing standards of care.

In the first of these cited cases, the issue was whether an anesthesiologist had fallen below the anesthesia standard of care when he failed to monitor the patient's vital signs during a gall bladder operation and failed to act on a drop in the patient's blood pressure, resulting in brain injury from oxygen deprivation. There was no issue of whether the surgeon was at fault or had fallen below either the surgical or anesthesia specialty standard of care.

In the second case, a general surgeon had biopsied a suspicious mass in a patient. The wound was routinely closed and the patient was awakened with no sequela from the operation. The patient was then informed by the surgeon that his mass appeared to be cancerous. Later, however, pathology determined it was non-cancerous. Yep. Sue for emotional distress. That was it! Again, there was no issue of competing standards of care between the surgeon and the pathologist. These two cases were dumped by the appeals court to make it appear that my issue of competing standard of care had been addressed. It had not. In fact, I don't even think the court read these cases! This act reeked of deliberate disinformation that bordered on deception, just as the medical board's attorney had wildly accused me of trying to deceive the cardiologist into thinking that I had injected xylocaine, and then accused me of being a party to Dr. Abulencia's conspiracy to conceal the cause of death as a "severe allergic reaction" when all the facts and testimony clearly established I wasn't even present during solicitation of that conspiracy and in fact had loudly announced from the outset to all present in the operating room that the wrong drug had been given.

Finally, the court of appeals erroneously introduced a third case based only on an inferred argument of *Respondeat Superior*, but did not identify as conforming to either doctrine of "captain of the ship" or *Respondeat Superior.* The appeals court dodged this distinction. At least Sal McCliven, at the trial court appeal, had actually correctly identified the "captain of the ship" as the proper legal doctrine, in contrast to *Respondeat Superior*.

In this third case erroneously cited by the court of appeals, the orthopedist's office staff failed to follow up on a carpal tunnel electrodiagnostic study test result. The surgeon, as head of the corporation and employer of his office staff, was legally responsible under the doctrine of *Respondeat Superior* for his employee's act which delayed the patient's surgery and compromised the outcome. In contrast, the applicable legal doctrine to my case was "captain of the ship." In the "captain of the ship" argument, the nurse and the tech were employed by the hospital, not me. However, once in the operating room, the hospital no longer controlled them. Instead it was I who was acting as the "boss" and therefore as if I were their employer. The old legal term was that they had become my "borrowed servants." I was responsible for them, even though I did not employ them. I was just "borrowing" them from the hospital for the case. In the above case cited by the court of appeals, the orthopedist clearly employed his staff who worked in his office. Thus, the court of appeals had cited the wrong case and the wrong doctrine. Because the hospital employed both the nurse and the tech, the doctrine of *Respondeat Superior* applied to the hospital and its agents, but not to me. It was below the standard of nursing care to delegate a medication order to a tech.

At issue is whether this new argument, even if correctly identified as "captain of the ship" could be entered on appeal or supersede standard of care. The "legal" justification of this has been called the "Gorilla Law." It comes from an old joke:

Where does an eight-hundred pound gorilla sleep? Answer: Wherever it wants.

In the same way, when can an appellate court introduce a new argument into a case? The answer is: "Whenever it wants." Remember the Supreme Court of the United States' introduced a new argument to allow passage of Obamacare? It was now a tax, therefore it was legal.

To cop out of the ruling on medical care issues, the trial and appellate courts generally have stated that "great deference" be made to medical boards in weighing evidence since the boards are best qualified to address the practice of medicine. However, my appeal was not based on the practice of medicine within each specialty *per se*. It narrowly focused on a purely legal argument beyond the purview of the medical board: Given two standards of care, what *legally* determines the correct standard? The appellate court failed to address the board's deviation from the statutes which had required the "same specialty standard." It just checked off my arguments and ignored them, just as a physician who was supposed to check a patient for rectal bleeding, but then fudged his records stating that he had performed a rectal exam when he did not. Believe me, this happens in medicine all too frequently and a more serious rectal cancer diagnosis is missed. (Speaking of rectal exams, another comment to my license suspension story came from a You Tube reader, accusing me of "doing a prostate exam with both hands on the patient's shoulders." The public does not like doctors. I get it.)

Another analogy to these Court of Appeals case law citations is the car dealership that "pencils in" maintenance, stating that the tires have been rotated and balanced, the radiator and brake fluids checked, but have never been done. The appeals court merely "checked off" that it had answered the issue of competing standards of care by citing these three cases.

In retrospect, all of my attorneys failed me in that they did not hold the appellate courts' feet to the fire, but rather, allowed this "controversy" to remain hidden in plain sight. This case was screaming for appeal to the state supreme court in order to get a definitive published opinion on what constitutes the proper standard of care when a medical board is presented with two conflicting standards, especially when the statutes expressly state that the malpractice standard has to be in the same specialty as the accused doctor.

In the alternative, another state provided the doctor with the defense by the doctrine of "Two Schools of Thought." Even if a physician failed to follow the standard of care in one specialty, if there was another group or specialty that regularly and in sufficient numbers followed a different standard of accepted care, the Defendant physician had a defense. This second school of thought standard might not be sufficient to defeat the "substantial evidence" requirement for Board to discipline a doctor. Indeed, I have asked the question: What constitutes "substantial evidence?" I don't know.

Finally, at the very end of the opinion, to demonize me, the appellate court declared "It is ignoble of Dr. Sterling to blame the nurse."

My attorney said that a final appeal to the Supreme Court was probably a lost cause. I had to agree at the time, but looking back at the devastation that this suspension has caused my career, I probably should have appealed it to the bitter end and certainly would have appealed it based on my better understanding of the issues as they are presented here. As mentioned above, specific arguments of "Dr. Abulenica's validation as an expert to surrender the case entirely to me, and therefore, define the case as a global orthopedic one," the nurse's act being "premeditated misconduct" and not just a "mistake," the lack of "substantial evidence," and my being punished for the result, not the act were never articulated by Goerbing.

Insurance? What insurance?

At the time my incident occurred, the statutes stated that the board would secure insurance, presumably in case it was sued. Why was this law written in the first place? It would seem that this was tantamount to acknowledgment that the board could abuse its authority and destroy a doctor's career, for which the doctor would be entitled to recover economic damages. The requirement was struck from the statutes in 1994, just months before my hearing. The significance was that the board now had sovereign immunity and therefore could no longer be sued. The board, on motion by this psychiatrist who probably hadn't been in the operating room for decades, clearly fired off the lawsuit without first thoroughly reviewing the case. Sal McCliven was clearly acting as an all-out advocate for the family in violation of the board's mandate for his impartiality as an arbiter of justice. These were not honest mistakes. This was intentional.

In this case, it would be interesting to see if legal precedent would have allowed me to sue the board and/or the hospital for economic damages, which have totaled millions in lost income over the span of my career. Goerbing emphatically told me I could *not* sue the hospital and later advised me, in writing, "in the strongest terms possible, not to sue the hospital." Why? In view of the global incompetence and ignorance of my lawyers up to that point, I now wonder if this was still more wrong advice, or worse, part of a secret deal between my insurance carrier and the other parties to seal the deal to protect the hospital from a high-profile countersuit. This is indeed a very convoluted theory, and it will never be answered. The bottom line, assuming that he can get competent lawyers, a doctor should always hire his personal attorney in a potentially complex medical malpractice case. You cannot, I repeat, *cannot*, ever totally rely upon or trust the counsel provided by your insurance company. They pay their attorney, not you.

Goerbing only vaguely argued at the hearing and in his exceptions to the hearing officer's findings that "I had a right to expect competent" help to be provided by the hospital. But he fell well short of the mark on his arguments, most of which have been refined here by me and spelled out. I had a right to expect not only competent help, but help that was knowingly following known established hospital and nursing rules and regulations. In retrospect, he probably would not have argued my case very well had it gone to trial, or on to the court of appeals. I cannot win my case if my lawyer doesn't make the proper arguments.

In a case from another state supreme court, the surgeon had asked the RN for the correct drug for a bunion procedure but was handed the wrong drug containing epinephrine, causing loss of blood flow to the toe, which became gangrenous and eventually had to be amputated. Unless I had been given the bottle and drawn the medicine up myself, there was as no way to have been absolutely sure of what was in the syringe because both drugs, Marcaine and Xylocaine, are clear and colorless. Even if I had been shown the bottle from which the medicine had supposedly been drawn according to the anesthesia standard by the board's medical expert testimony, there was no way I could have been absolutely sure what was in the syringe unless I had drawn up the medication myself from that bottle. In this foreign state supreme court opinion, which reversed the trial court decision that the physician was liable, the state supreme court argued that "the doctor had a right to expect competent help." But again, per the nurse's admission, the nurse's act in my case went beyond incompetence. It was a premeditated act. It was misconduct.

What Legal Argument Might Convince Me the Board's Decision Was Correct?

I didn't stumble upon this doctrine until recently, nor do I know if has ever superseded the doctrine of standard of care in a case. It is called something like "the doctrine of the patient's last best chance." As the last person to handle the drug, I was Arthur Smith's last chance. It was up to me to save him from dying. It certainly does tug on my sense of not being there for someone when they really were depending on me.

I have not researched this doctrine, but I think it would have to presume that I had *anticipated* getting the wrong drug or that there was a possibility that I might have been handed the wrong drug, which was the furthest thought from my mind at the time. Needless to say, I would have thought that the courts would have at least written a scholarly explanation of why the traditional time-honored specialty-specific standard of care no longer applied in my case.

Rogue Agencies Everywhere

In my opinion, medical boards are nothing less than rogue agencies with no oversight by elected government or effective legal protections/remedies afforded a doctor against random, capricious, arbitrary, or unusually harsh punishment. The medical-practice act statutes should be struck. They are simply meaningless. Doctors would at least be put on notice that they can *never* expect or rely on justice.

This sets up a dangerous precedent for any agency that has been deputized by state and or federal lawmakers. The horses have long left the barn on this one. Witness the rogue agencies we now have with CIA, NSA, IRS, ESF (Exchange Stabilization Fund), and so on. Even Trump's temporary immigration ban, clearly constitutionally legal, regardless whether you agree or disagree with his order, was temporarily reversed by federal appeals judges, one of whom was Obama's Harvard Law classmate. Trump's executive order had to (needlessly) be appealed all the way to the Supreme Court of the Unites States before it could be enacted.

I started to realize this blatant disregard for rule of law in the lowly trial courts during my divorce and these medical-board actions. Statutes apply only when they serve the legal collective or special interests. Whether the public is actually served by the legal system is irrelevant. It only matters if the legal system profits. We have now clearly entered a blatant "without rule of law" (WROL) era.

Without a doubt, the biggest rogue agency of which most people are thoroughly unaware, and whose mention usually causes their eyes to roll if you talk about it, is the Federal Reserve Bank (The FED). It is a nongovernmental, unelected, cartel of private bankers who, through their charter in 1913, have the power to conjure up, out of nothingness, currency. From there, like most central banks, it can influence politicians, industries, world commerce, and even enable wars.

Currency is not real money like gold or silver as required by the Constitution. Originally, it was the Treasury who had been charged with issuing this money as coinage. Instead, we now have fiat (meaning, "so be it, by government decree or legal tender laws") paper currency with no backing. This allows the bankers/moneychangers to create fiat out of nothingness, loan it to the government and collect interest. Not a bad gig.

So how does the government get the money to pay the principal plus the interest back to the FED? The income tax was also enacted in 1913 to pay for this, but the bulk is repaid by more borrowing and, therefore, even more debt. More insidiously, this debt cycle snowballs and causes the currency to devalue over time from inflation. Inflation is indeed the second tax foisted on productive American taxpayers. These bankers had it all figured out over one hundred years ago. Remember: Amschiel Rothschild said in 1896, "Let me control a nation's money supply, and I care not who makes its laws."

In contrast, most people must perform productive work and expend time and energy to earn their money, which is not real money, but rather only paper fiat currency which ultimately becomes inherently worthless through inflation, but not before the bankers have used it to acquire their wealth. Banks literally loan currency they don't have and earn interest/profits on it. It is a racket called *fractional reserve lending*. If your bank receives a dollar deposit, by its charter it can loan out nine dollars and collect a higher rate of interest than it pays to you the depositor. I hate to digress, but these opinions took root twenty-five years ago when I had to deal with the legal system and the absence of rule of law. The monetary, legal, and political systems are corrupt and rotten to the core.

What factors might have influenced the board to act out of public relations concerns? Could it have been that the public was outraged when it learned that the president of the state medical association, a family practitioner in my town, had raped his baby sitter and had been sexually molesting patients in his office for decades? Was it because an OB-GYN had been making headlines for leaving his patients in stirrups in the labor and delivery room while he was out enjoying drinks at a fast-food chain? Was it because the state had been ranked thirty-seventh in disciplinary actions against physicians? Was it because there was a Medicaid-funding shortfall for which the doctors were to blame? But you know, everyone wants to make a lot of money. Everyone wants to enjoy cruising in their new Corvette, fishing in their new bass boat, enjoy their bowling nights, movies, ball games, and so on, but not spending the best years of their lives and hundreds of thousands of dollars it costs for medical training. Everyone wants to practice medicine, but no one wants to go to medical school. Now, how would you like to go through all that and then get it all trashed in an instant because you didn't check a drug? Log on to a state medical board web site and you can see all the doctors who get disciplined by their medical board. The reasons are numerous: drug or alcohol abuse, diverting hospital drugs for personal use or for sale to the public or even to buy sexual favors, soliciting prostitution, inappropriate sexual relations with patients, sometimes even when they are under anesthesia, Medicare and other insurance fraud, other criminal acts of assault, DUI or reckless driving, a pattern of repeated malpractice or acts of premeditated gross negligence, fraudulent advertising, accepting bribes from drug companies, disruptive behavior, falsifying license, hospital or insurance applications, falsifying medical or hospital records, practicing with an inactive license, refusing to comply with board directives, writing prescriptions for family members or friends, especially if that patient has not been seen by the physician and a medical record created, sham operations or drug treatments, and so on. But never, ever, to my knowledge, for a single inadvertent drug mix-up.

Finally, did the board succumb to the negative publicity of this case being sensationalized all over the state newspapers and on national television? Of course. This board had egg all over its face. I was the first in the state, and probably the country, to ever get suspended for an isolated unintentional "malpractice" event like this. The focus was only on the horrific result, not the act.

The Long Wait—October 1994 to 1995

I had publicly vowed to the state newspaper reporter never to practice in my state again. I complied with the board's requirements and then allowed my license to lapse. I could not find another position for well over a year. I knew I would have to apply for multiple licenses and cast my net widely, as I expected half my applications to be rejected. My dilemma was that to get a hospital to consider me I would first have to get a license. However, a board could turn the argument around and say why should we give you a license if you don't have a definite practice opportunity in our state? Finally, even if I could get a license, I would still need medical-malpractice insurance. All three things had to come together: medical license, malpractice insurance, and hospital privileges (credentialing).

A supposedly physician-friendly state denied me because I was still serving a probation. It did not matter whether on justifiable grounds. It was not going to retry the medical-board case. Another state denied me for the same reason.

I had argued the "two schools of thought doctrine," which afforded a physician an absolute defense in my case because there was a school of thought (my orthopedic specialty) that said I was not required to check the medication if I had given the order to an operating room nurse.

Another state had a different twist. It stated on its application that once an application was submitted, it could not be withdrawn, yet I never received an answer to my application. They swallowed my application fee, though. Another state wanted me to first produce two years of operative and fracture-care records for review before they would consider giving me a license. That would require showing up with a U-Haul in tow. But I was suspended for failure to check a medication, not because of bad operative or nonoperative orthopedic fracture care. Talk about making me have to stand on my head. This board's attorney could not help but agree with me—off the record—that I was getting the run around.

Finally, one state gave me a license. No interview required. Then my state where I'd done my residency reactivated my license. No interview. Another state required an interview. A righteous, possibly mildly senile, retired general surgeon, who had no voting input on my license decision, tried to challenge me on the issue of the conspiracy to cover up the cause of death.

Not only was the press there, but also there was a public advocate who did background research on physicians. In one hilariously pathetic case, the advocate produced reports where one of the applicants had diverted thousands of narcotics for his use and the doctor was fumbling with how to explain this.

My case was different. I explained the event, the sequence of discovery, the role of the nurse and tech, and how it was nearly impossible that I could have been part of a conspiracy and that the family was clearly lying. Suddenly, no questioning of my explanation by anyone in the room, not even the surgeon. Not a word. Silence. They gave me a license on the spot.

The Scarlet Letter

From one of the newsletters years ago, I found this excellent article writ-ten by Michael J. Schoppman, Esq., at mschoppmann@drlaw.com, entitled "Physicians as Targets." He offered five insights after seeing how a doctor who had failed to list a malpractice claim on his hospital application form had it snowball. The hospital denied his application on the basis of this omission, then reported this denial to the NPDB, who then notified his medical board, who gave him a reprimand, which was then reported to his other licensure boards, who in turn suspended those licenses, which were reported back to the NPDB and from there, insurance companies withdrew his participation. His career was consumed by this snowballing chain of events.

The insights:

1. Everyone is watching—medical boards, insurance companies, consumer protection agencies and so on.
2. Everyone talks to each other.
3. It's happening more every day.
4. The snowball effect.
5. Beware the scarlet letter. Physicians who are labeled disruptive, impaired, or outliers must realize that these scarlet letter labels are permanent and can be potentially career-ending accusations. To manage this risk, physicians should not expect that there is, or will be, a day in court that exonerates them or provides them with justice. Regardless of the environment (medical malpractice, licensing authority, hospital quality-assurance review, health-care audits, and so on) initial conclusions are binding, virtually irremovable, and devastating.

The Search Begins

Finally, in 1995 I drove to my final state for an interview with their licensure board. I explained my situation and what had happened to me. A senior member was chairman. He asked me who my headmaster was at my prep school. It was a newer one at my graduation, but it had been a venerable one for the previous years, and because I figured he would know the latter by the way he asked and his age, I replied, "Chris Markham."

His face lit up as if he personally knew him. Then he noticed the college I went to and he said something like "not too shabby there either." He stepped back into his room with a few of the board members. They discussed it for fifteen minutes, and they came out with the good news that they could give me a provisional license, meaning I would be officially on probation for a year, and that at renewal, I would revisit the board, and if everything was going well they would give me a permanent license.

This meant yet another (third) hit on the data bank for the same event. I had already been reported because of the malpractice civil case payment by my insurance company for $200,000. I was reported again for the medical-board suspension. Now I was being reported again for a probation as a condition for my new state license.

But it didn't end there. When I showed up a year later, clean, the board extended the probation for a year, and then another year, and another. It wasn't until 1999, four years (and four more hits on the data bank), that I finally got an unrestricted license. All because I hadn't checked a drug eight years ago back in 1991.

I was very grateful for that chance offered by this medical board at the time and thanked the chairman, as tears welled up in my eyes. Equally good news was that when medical board gave me a provisional license, it automatically qualified me for malpractice-insurance coverage by the state's medical mutual insurance company. In contrast to a private insurance company, the doctors owned shares in the company.

I will go on record stating that this insurance company always represented me vigorously, zealously, *and at great cost.* It is a good company, but the expenses really underscored my perception of the attitudes of the public: "We want the best care with no expense spared and use of the most advanced technology. We shouldn't have to pay for it. We shouldn't have to wait, and if the doctor or other health-care delivery system screws up, we want to be able to sue them for everything they've got. All our excessive drinking, smoking, obesity, and not getting enough exercise are no excuse." A huge money trough has been created by these expectations from which lawyers and other nonproductive parasites of society feed.

This brings up a point about medical-malpractice insurance. In a way, the medical-malpractice insurance companies are essentially able to make a decision that determines whether you can practice or not, just as a medical board can. If you do not get a license, you cannot practice. If you cannot get insurance, you cannot practice. Issuance of malpractice-insurance coverage is based on risk factors, specialty, and past claims history and is made in part by bean counters, and other physicians who review applicants before writing insurance.

I really liked the fact that this medical mutual insurance company basically was taking a stance that if an applicant was good enough to get a license, then he was good enough to insure, even if at a surcharge. (I did not face a surcharge.) Why subject a doctor to two different standards?

The NPDB keeps track of all physicians who have been disciplined, successfully sued, or who have settled malpractice cases at a certain $10,000 threshold amount. The medical boards have access to this just as malpractice-insurance carriers do. I am aware many will disagree with me on this one as my opinion is clearly self-serving and counter to my more libertarian philosophy, but I think malpractice reform should socialize the costs of medical-malpractice insurance if they are going to socialize the doctors' Medicare and Medicaid reimbursements- especially for those physicians who are trying to maintain an independent practice. However, once a physician joins a healthcare corporation, the issue becomes moot. The corporation and its malpractice insurer are joined as one. The corporation has to deny automatically deny a physician a job if its insurer refuses to insure him, even if the physician can get insured by an outside company. It has happened to me. It is an interesting concept that I have not seen addressed (i.e., if I qualify for a license, then it also means I am automatically insured). This is what is in effect at the VA Hospitals, although I am reluctant to justify my argument using this example because of the perceived guilt by association, i.e., the perceived abysmal care provided by VA hospitals and their doctors.

Furthermore, when I apply for privileges at a hospital, a group of doctors sits on the credentialing committee and decides whether you can work at that hospital. This offers the community yet another layer of protection against bad doctors. There is no need to subject doctors to additional scrutiny for malpractice insurability. If I am judged to be an incompetent or impaired physician, then don't issue me a license in the first place! But, even if I have a license and insurance, a hospital credentialing committee should always have the prerogative of rejecting me.

The standard for medical malpractice should be universalized across the states and a higher standard of proof should be required. In civil law, including medical malpractice the standard is 51 to 49, i.e., a medical malpractice event is more likely to have occurred than not. This borderline "flip of the coin" standard allows frivolous cases to slip in, including some won based on junk science. This standard should be revised substantially higher than the current fifty percent threshold. In other words, did the doctor obviously screw up and is a risk to the public, or has the doctor been unfairly tagged with a number of marginal or even frivolous lawsuits?

Abulencia's stroke and Goerbing's lying to me about severing my case with the medical board cost me many idle months. I mapped out each and every hospital in this state. I was rejected everywhere, just like an unwelcome refugee, until finally I got a call from the recruiter at what became my second practice where I would stay for sixteen long, bitter, and embattled years.

About the time I was negotiating with the hospital, I was informed that I had the option of joining Dr. Felix, the orthopedist who had been there for years. He seemed initially to be presented as the preferred option. I was *immediately* concerned that this small-town hospital had gone through five orthopedists in the last six years, four of whom had gone through Dr. Felix's office. So obviously this was not a stable position, and this would explain why they were willing to look at me. They couldn't get anyone else. Really made me feel special.

Dr. Felix informed me that he and Dr. Sylvester, an orthopedist in the neighboring town thirty-plus miles away, just happened to be in the process of forming a regional group to cover both towns. On the surface, it might appear they wanted me to join their group. That intention may or not have been true if one examined his contract. This one-year contract identified Dr. Felix as the employer and me as the employee, and that the employer shall assign patients to the employee. My payment (for one year at least) would be determined by how much I *collected* from my patient encounters, surgical and nonsurgical care, office visits, consults, hospital visits, emergency room visits, and so on.

From this amount collected, expenses would be deducted based on the number and cost of these encounters, regardless whether I was paid for them or not. The glaring problem is that Dr. Felix could assign me low-paying or nonpaying (indigent) patients. I could do a lot of assigned work but not get paid, and yet I would wind up paying a lot of overhead, essentially subsidizing him. Of course, he assured me it wouldn't happen.

This actually was not a big obstacle itself, because the hospital was guaranteeing me a modest income and did not want to be subsidizing Dr. Felix. However, it was a sign of bad faith in my opinion and might explain the revolving door of dissatisfied orthopedists who'd come and left his practice.

The real kicker was that later, if I decided I did not want to remain in his group and wished to strike out on my own in the five surrounding counties, I would be subject to a penalty of 15 percent of my residual collections as an expense charge. The problem is that in collecting this money I had already paid for this expense and overhead. Now I would be charged again.

The fact that so many orthopods (orthopedic surgeons) had already come and gone had to give one pause. There was absolutely no goodwill in his practice. Dr. Sylvester could afford to join Dr. Felix because Dr. Sylvester essentially had his own practice in the neighboring town. In contrast, being in the same town with Dr. Felix would have potentially more impact on me. In fact, I was decreasing my chances by associating with him—guilt by association. I rejected his contact.

The Clubs

I suspect Dr. Felix's group was also formed to prevent me from establish-ing an independent competing practice. I was, in a sense, being welcomed, or enticed, to join this club with the above contract in one hand but threatened by a join-or-else club in the other. If I didn't join them, Drs. Felix and Sylvester would refuse to work with me, cross cover, and so on. Even the call schedule would not be altered. It would be regularly scheduled: on call every third day, and holidays scheduled every third anniversary, for years down the road, all in attempt to deny me any flexibility. Pure control.

This guy Felix was an asshole. I cannot emphasize that strongly enough—no kids, but a big forty-foot boat, a miserly tightwad. His partner, Dr. Sylvester, wasn't much better.

This arrangement between Felix and Sylvester quietly slipped by the medical staff by-laws for years. These had required a physician who was on full-active staff take emergency room (ER) call and, therefore, had to live within a thirty-minute response time, unless he had someone close by covering for him in the same specialty. This was termed *call radius*.

Dr. Sylvester's home, his office, and the hospital he primarily worked out of were all more than thirty minutes away. When Dr. Sylvester or Dr. Felix were on call, their schedule stated that one would be on call for both hospitals. This immediately resulted in two violations of the call-radius bylaws. Whenever Dr. Sylvester was on call, he was automatically in violation because he lived and worked at his primary location, which was beyond the call radius. When Dr. Felix was on call, if he had a case over in Dr. Sylvester's town, he could not cover the home hospital as he was now outside the call radius. I was, in fact, called by my hospital at least one time to cover when Dr. Felix ran into this conflict.

Ask any physician and he or she will tell you that physicians hate taking call. Light or no on-call responsibility is used as a sales pitch when hospitals recruit. However, this town was different—orthopedic volume so low that an orthopedist had to take as much call as possible. We orthopedists, therefore, were fighting over call like hyenas fighting over a dead carcass.

There were some basic reasons why fewer than the projected number of orthopedists could be supported based on the population. For starters, although competent and a good surgeon, Dr. Felix had a bad reputation based on his personality. The constant turnover of orthopedists had also poisoned the well for future orthopedists. The public perceived that the orthopedic specialty was not stable and would automatically leave town.

It made no sense to me for the hospital to rescue Dr. Felix by allowing an outside orthopedist, Dr. Sylvester, to join him for the purpose of competing against the orthopedist they had just hired, yet these simpleton hospital administrators could only figure that the more orthopedists on staff, the more money the hospital would bring in. The administrators' analysis was always "this town had a population of 18,000 and a drawing area of 60,000 and, therefore, should support three orthopedists"—except that it didn't.

The hospital administrator quietly convinced me not to joint Dr. Felix. Then Dr. Krutch, one of the orthopods who had previously left, showed up at my door. He was literally knocking on the front door of my house. I had heard through Dr. Felix that he had been wanting to come back and practice at the beach. (My town was inland and served as a stepping stone.) Well, here he was.

Krutch gave me his canned spiel of how he had bopped from place to place, couldn't even work with his own brother or father who were also orthopedists, and had been to about nine locations. I had just rejected Dr. Felix's contract but had nowhere to go and now had to suddenly set up an office, hire staff, and so on. Plus, it was two against one: Felix and Sylvester against me.

The fact that I had to throw my lot in with Dr. Krutch shows you how desperate and pathetic my situation was. Call would be further diluted from thirty-three to twenty-five percent, but so would expenses, and in theory I could get some flexibility with call and vacation. Plus, the hospital guaranteed me a glorious one-year salary guarantee of $188,000 after expenses. What could go wrong?

Dr. Krutch had returned to my town after having left the previous year. He told me that the hospital had tried to recruit him back and had offered him a guarantee—even as they were recruiting me. I was unaware that the hospital had been in contact with Dr. Krutch. When we both met in conference with the hospital administration to discuss our partnership, Dr. Marvin Mace, a urologist, suddenly rescinded the guarantee for Dr. Krutch.

I said to myself, "This Mace guy is one weird fuck." That was the only description that came to mind. He seemed to be ready to cry as he rejected Krutch's reminder that he had been promised a guarantee if he returned.

The administrator joined in, saying, "Dr. Krutch, your star has fallen." That phrase would later apply to me in spades. Dr. Krutch basically had no money and went from bank to bank. They all refused him a loan. That's why he had to come to me. It was only when I came with him to the bank and declared that we were going to be partners, and that I had a guarantee from the hospital was he able to "get some dough" from the bank headed by this bank president whose bank was eventually bailed out by the federal emergency Troubled Asset Relief Program (TARP) funds. This bank president reportedly received a huge bonus on the sale of the bank.

Krutch and I agreed to try to set up our home office in town and a satellite office at the beach. Krutch wanted to practice at the beach, but his brazenness, selfishness, and unreasonableness were shocking for someone who didn't have a pot to piss in. It was true that my girlfriend, Tessie, as the office manager, was a conflict of interest, but she was able to get the practice up and running very quickly. To balance this, I proposed that only Dr. Krutch could sign the checks that Tessie printed and that Dr. Krutch would keep his own daily computer backup. We even flipped for whose name would go first on our sign. I lost the coin toss.

We would both see patients in the main office, and one day per week, travel to the beach satellite office. Things got problematic when I would fit in an occasional patient on the days Dr. Krutch was supposed to be in the office. The volume was still so low that it really didn't detract from his ability to timely see any and all of his patients, but he did express some displeasure at this, which I suppose could be justified. My position was that we had to see any and all patients we could whenever we could to get market share from Drs. Felix and Sylvester. Also problematic for Dr. Krutch was that he purchased a home at the beach nearly an hour away. Taking call required him to camp out in the office to satisfy the hospital thirty-minute call-radius requirement. He wanted it both ways.

Krutch started telling the beach doctors to refer patients only to him because he was the designated "beach doctor." Great, so here I am, like a dutiful spouse, supporting him at our home-base office, doing the billing, purchasing, medical records, and so on, while he is relying on it to have an affair with the beach, planning his own office and quietly, almost secretly, building up his practice, and telling the doctors there to refer exclusively to him.

In fact, he was in such dependent financial straits that at one point I had to advance him $16,000 to pay for his share of the overhead. He was a pathetic little twerp. This was the price I figured I had to pay to keep Felix and Sylvester at bay. Nice practice.

It wasn't long before his beach practice had built up enough on the side, and we split up. He was given his share of the buyout, which he acknowledged was an amount greater than he had figured. Even still, he was asking if he could use the billing codes to set up his own office? Can you believe it? Here was this guy whom I had rescued who had literally been living in a roach motel with his wife and two daughters, had been secretly screwing me behind my back, had been paid a generous buyout, and now wanted to mooch still more from me?

I suggested he take his money received from his buyout and set up his own computer and billing.

"Well, you don't have to be such an asshole about it," he yelled at me over the phone.

But the one thing I could count on was his wimpy, pathetic response to every accusation: "That's not true." Oh yes, it was, Krutch. It most certainly was. I had confirmation from one of his former partners from another state who swore that he would never have another partner after having dealt with Dr. Krutch.

We still needed to work together to a limited extent. He needed me to vouch for him to be credentialed as a Fellow of the American Academy of Orthopedic Surgeons (FAAOS). He needed me to take his call at my hospital to remain on full-active staff, even though he was wanting to transition completely to the beach. I needed his call slot to offset Felix and Sylvester's share of the call.

When yet another orthopedist, Dr. Jones, was recruited, he too had eyes on practicing at the beach and joining Krutch, and wanted to maintain full-active staff privileges at my hospital. Both of them would need to do cases on occasion, and at the time, the beach hospital and my hospital were under the same ownership/management. If I took Krutch and Jones's call, then I was in effect turning the tables on Felix and Sylvester by capturing 60 percent of the call. Again, this was very unusual because it is unheard of for doctors to fight for more call. But in this town, it was necessary because there was so little elective patient load, and the administrator could only see more orthopedists meaning more money for the hospital, even if they starved. Your practice depended on taking call. However, historically, when the previous orthopedists saw that the town could not support them, they promptly left soon after their guarantees ran out. In contrast, I was stranded.

It wasn't long before Drs. Felix and Sylvester cried foul. But again, they had started it. They tried to get Krutch and Jones off the call list because they lived outside the thirty-minute call radius. But, if Drs. Krutch and Jones had someone (me) taking call for them and I was exclusively practicing at this hospital and available all the time, then this allowed them to live at the beach, have their share of call covered, and maintain full-active staff privileges.

In contrast, as mentioned before, Drs. Felix and Sylvester were trying to cover *two* hospitals at the same time with only one of their group on call, and Dr. Sylvester actually lived beyond the call radius.

The funniest thing occurred when both Drs. Felix and Sylvester had a conflict and neither could cover their rigid, cast-in-stone, scheduled call. Remember: they had insisted on a regular and rigid schedule for years in advance (for the objective of denying me any flexibility through trading of call days or vacation coverage). They could not suddenly ask me if I would suddenly agree to trade call days after they had been screwing me over for years.

No. Instead, they called Drs. Jones and Krutch to see if either would agree to take call for those days. But Jones or Krutch would then have to spend the night in town on those days/night(s). They didn't want to do that unless it was I who was taking a vacation, and they declined. Plus, they already had an arrangement with me. But you get the idea. This is what assholes Felix and

Sylvester were. They had to hire a *locums*. As urologist Dr. Marvin Mace, who later became my major antagonist, said, "Doctors are not nice people."

Eventually, Dr. Krutch terminated Dr. Jones. Remember: Dr. Krutch could not work with anyone. Anyone. Part of the problem I suspect was his wife was a domineering, rip-roaring, ruddy-faced, never-without-a-drink-in-her-hand alcoholic.

The rumor was that Dr. Jones came back from vacation one day and was suddenly informed through his child's classmate that he was being fired by Dr. Krutch. I guess Dr. Krutch figured Dr. Jones would pack up and leave, but he figured wrong. It was Jones who persevered, started a new practice, added two partners, and finally drove Krutch out, an act Krutch swore would never happen. Krutch relocated ironically to a position I had applied to and been rejected.

Visit from the FBI

I was so angry and frustrated with my former divorce lawyers, judge, and commissioner that I wrote them all really nasty notes. I wrote Salazar that "if I could get away with it, I would crush your skull." I wrote the commissioner and judge that they were the judicial equivalent of "Dumb and Dumber," that they could not apply even the most fundamental laws concerning divorce, and that the lawyers Salazar and Mitchell knew "you were incompetent and made fools out of you. How did I know? Because Salazar and Johnston told me so as they groaned when they learned my divorce case had landed in your court."

Someone contacted the FBI. I suspect it was Skyler because she was so anal about appearances and protecting her reputation, what little of it she deserved, but it might have been Salazar in view of such a gruesome comment I made to him. Skyler wrote as a warning after my criticisms of her prior to filing my lawsuit against her: "But be warned, Bryce: we will avail ourselves of all measures to protect the reputation of this firm." (She later broke up with her errand-boy associate and now has two young handmaidens in her firm.)

In yet another coincidence, this FBI agent, who had lived in the same town where my divorce occurred had recently moved to my new town where I started my second practice. He now lived only about six houses from me on the same street. His wife had all these gaudy flowers in the front yard. This G-man, a lawyer, was sent to talk to me or issue a warning.

He acknowledged, "Your lawyers certainly didn't do you any favors." He tacitly agreed that my lawyers and judge had screwed me over and admitted that my letters trashing them were actually humorous in a way.

When I replied that based on what they had done they deserved to be strung up because they had lied, stolen a small fortune through fraud and misrepresentation, deceived me, and incredibly were still insisting they had done nothing wrong, this twerp FBI giggled as he warned me, "Now you are making a statement."

This guy was such a twerp. I can't believe that I didn't punch him out in my office. A total twerp, and my taxes pay for his government job. As he left my office, he said, "Just don't send them any more Christmas cards, and maybe sometime you might stop over at the house for some lemonade."

And Now Problems with Tessie

Tessie initially did a good job as office manager, especially getting the practice up and running. We had started living together while I was still fighting my divorce and medical-board action, and she relocated with me to my second job.

Dr. Krutch had at one point accused her of not crediting him with work he had done. He was obsessed with his production being credited as work done at the beach. Tessie showed him that the work indeed had been credited as work being done at the main office instead of the satellite office. This was similar to the Medicare issue that had occurred at my first practice. We had not overcharged; we had simply charged at the wrong facility.

Selena had been our office manager at my first practice. She was convicted of embezzling from our office, a felony, and ordered by, you guessed it, Judge Lattimer, the same judge who had presided over my divorce and the Smith family's medical-malpractice civil case to make restitution only. She never went to jail. She never made any restitution.

True to a woman's scorn, Selena then reported to Medicare that our office had been engaged in fraudulent billing. This accusation, again based on a convicted felon, was front-page news in our town's newspaper. We had to go back and review a whole bunch of charts that Medicare had selected for audit. When we were done, we had actually undercharged Medicare, and discrepancies were due to patients being simply charged at the wrong office or hospital.

The newspaper later printed the shortest, yet most convoluted and bizarrely worded retraction in the corner of the back page. It is amazing and quite the double standard that any lawyer who gets sued seldom gets his name in the paper. Lawyers may get reported for criminal wrongdoing, whereas I have never heard of a newspaper writing an article about a lawyer getting sued, even if successfully sued, for legal malpractice. In contrast, articles about doctors getting sued are routinely reported.

Another rule for doctors, particularly those who are still in or contemplating solo or small private group practice: your office is being embezzled until proven otherwise. Doctors are the easiest targets. They often don't want to press charges even when they discover they are being embezzled, because it makes them look like greedy tyrants punishing their poor underpaid working single moms. Both of my practices were embezzled. The doctor to whom I had recently rented my building was embezzled.

Tessie became the town party girl, got to socially mingle with the mayor and a few other people who hit the bar scene. Pretty soon she got hooked up with the wrong crowd, and I suspect started getting on meth. We split up, and she had to get her own place, although I still let her work at the office. Latently, I was trying to avoid the hassles of firing someone and having to deal with workman's comp. *Big mistake!*

Unbelievable how the phone company tried to get me to pay for Tessie's delinquent bill at her new residence because her name had been on the bill at my residence. I explained we were not married, I had not signed for her new phone at her new address, and that my signature applied only to my current home phone. I finally had to contact the state attorney general to get the matter dropped.

I then learned Tessie was probably bisexual. (My new office manager discovered them.) She was seen with another office worker whom Tessie had hired. Dolly was absolutely "butt ugly," as my friend so aptly put it. Left alone in the office for ten minutes, Dolly stole seven hundred dollars out of the opened safe. Couldn't prove it though. In contrast, the other workers had worked there for years without ever a problem with missing money. She was briefly married, got into her husband's bank account, cleaned him out, and left him.

Tessie's work deteriorated. On our planned trip abroad, she couldn't even get her tickets in order, had misplaced them, and was left fumbling in the airport with obvious signs of total decompensation from drug overdose. I was so pissed I abandoned her at the airport. What did she do next? She sent for my other office worker to drive her back home and get the tickets.

Even then, Tessie was so strung out, so decompensated, they would not let her board the plane. Tessie later booked new tickets for the next day at incredible cost on my orthopedic office credit card and finally rejoined me overseas, claiming she had found the tickets.

I didn't find out about these duplicate ticket purchases until after she'd fled to Canada when I saw all the other credit charges ($15,000) she had piled on the orthopedic practice to pay for shipping her things to Toronto in preparation to join her boyfriend whom she had met on a trip she'd taken earlier to the Caribbean with Dolly, who could not afford such a trip (unless she stole money from the office). Tessie had also given herself an unauthorized pay raise.

I recently learned Tessie ultimately suffered a stroke and got divorced from this guy. Just this year, she showed up at my house while I was away. She met my wife, Vangie, who didn't know what to do. Vangie handed me the phone. Tessie tried to act as if nothing had happened years ago and, incredibly, wanted to be sure we were on the same page.

I said, "No, we are not on the same page, you lying, drugging, embezzling piece of shit. Get off my property." She handed the phone back to Vangie and went back to her home state.

Again, my office embezzlement occurred while Tessie had been living at her own residence, months after we had stopped cohabitating. This was pure embezzlement. We got in an argument at her house because she refused to take me to the airport. I told her she was fired. Her mother drove up the next day and helped get her things. She immediately applied for unemployment insurance, even before I could give her official written notice, and fled the country.

Even though I was able to show with the office business credit cards that she had clearly been embezzling the office, making charges for items to be shipped to her Canadian address well in advance of her termination, which demonstrated *immediate* plans to quit her job and leave the states for Toronto, Canada, the unemployment insurance adjudicator, a lawyer, said I had unfairly terminated her (without cause) and was required to pay her unemployment because at the time I fired her, I had been unaware of the ongoing embezzlement and her intentions of already leaving.

Can you believe this? I may not have been aware of the embezzlement until I saw the credit card statement, but Tessie was certainly aware of it and showed clear premeditation to leave town and join her Canadian boyfriend. You cannot get justice. Yet another reason why I would never start a business. There is so much parasitic drag. Not only am I supporting a felonious-grand-theft drug user, I am supporting through the unemployment insurance agency bureaucracy another useless incompetent lawyer. There is just no end to them.

I went to the police to file criminal charges for embezzlement. An acquaintance of mine on the police force, Sergeant Dick Pall, said he would not be able to prosecute Tessie because we had lived together. I could only file civil charges. Wait a minute! This embezzlement as registered on the orthopedic practice credit card had occurred well *after* Tessie and I had stopped cohabitating. Tessie had her own mailing address, phone, checking account, credit card for months. She had long since moved all of her things out of my house. My state did not recognize common law marriage. The evidence that she had been making these charges on the office credit card was undisputed. They were clearly not business related.

That "fucking" Dick Pall (his police colleague had overheard me calling him that derogatory term at the gym) was simply *too* damn lazy to pursue the case. They only police for profit: ticketing law-abiding citizens for isolated speeding or moving violations or, even worse, confiscating property through a process called civil asset forfeiture: no charges, no due process, just taking or seizing your personal property on merely on suspicion or claim that it was somehow involved in drug trafficking.

I went to the district attorney twice and asked him why he would not press criminal charges. He just sat there like a box of rocks and gave no answer. Again, incompetence and refusal to apply the statutes no better than commissioner or judge from my previous state. These god damn lawyers and judges! What are we going to do with them all?

On the phone conference with the unemployment agency concerning Tessie's termination, Dick Pall, whom I had requested as a witness to verify that indeed I had gone to the police over this embezzlement, whined, "Do I have to stay on the line? I have a murder investigation." He was just using that as an excuse and would do nothing to support me. In contrast, I had helped the Assistant DA with an attempted murder investigation to the point that my forensic analysis of bullet placement resulted in the criminal changing his plea to guilty. Pall was the laziest cop I have ever known. And he knew what I thought of him, and everyone in town knew him and thought the same. He had even tried to hit on my office assistant when she was underage. I absolutely despise this guy.

Misdemeanor Assault on a Female

When my wife, Vangie (married February 2000), charged me with domes-tic violence in 2002, Pall, in his capacity as a police officer, instructed her to call his brother who was an attorney and my next-door neighbor to get help with a divorce. This Dick "the Prick" Pall necessarily had issued a warrant for my arrest, and but was now presuming to act as a marriage counselor.

Sometime afterward, he was demoted. I don't know the reasons for that or for how long. Ultimately, it was he who was divorced by his wife, a nurse at my hospital and daughter of the magistrate who'd performed Vangie's and my marriage at the courthouse. Because Vangie had come from the Philippines on a fiancée visa, we had to marry within three months; otherwise she would have to return to the Philippines. Our marriage was, therefore, rushed, especially with me working and decidedly not the special day a bride normally dreams of.

After two years of marriage, Vangie still could not discern the reason for my anxiety (with the hospital and my career). She thought I was having an affair and suddenly launched a physical attack on me the night before we were to depart for our trip to Antarctica December 2001. I pushed her back. She got injured and sensing the need to protect herself from deportation, pressed charges of domestic violence against me.

All her Filipino friends in town rushed to her side and urged her to get as much money out of my account as she could and press charges. She did not, unlike Mindy. If I were convicted of domestic violence, then Vangie could not be deported. Of course, there was never any infidelity. I had been literally sitting at the desk the night before our departure getting our tickets and documents arranged when she physically attacked me.

I went to Antarctica alone, almost missing the trip, but I finally caught up with the group in Santiago, Chile. The price of Vangie's ticket's? Over $10,000. Wasted. Police Sgt. Dick Pall did let me escape to Antarctica and return to face formal arrest and perp walk with handcuffing in front of the same magistrate who had performed our marriage ceremony. I was escorted across the street to the court for arraignment.

I showed up at trial. Pall was there and asked if I had sought any counseling. Not only was he recommending a divorce attorney, now he was an expert on recommending psychologic evaluation. I said it was irrelevant. I was convicted at trial for assault on a female, which was a misdemeanor. I was on probation for a year, after which the record could be expunged, except of course if you are doctor, it can never be expunged.

Any medical-related applications licenses, hospital privileges, insurances, and so on specifically state that even if the record has officially been expunged, you must list it. And one more thing, the word *ever* always appears. Have you *ever* been arrested? Has your license *ever* been suspended, revoked, limited, and so on? Even if the record has been formally expunged.

The judge, black, looked at the photos of Vangie's face with her black cheek, made a look of disgust, and put them down. He politely gave me a chance to tell my side of the story for the record, which was not disputed. He nevertheless found me guilty and sentenced me to a year of probation and mandatory psychological evaluation.

I later went to that evaluator, and he quickly cleared me. The assistant district attorney who'd represented Vangie was the same one who had represented Tessie earlier in support of her claims for unemployment benefits. She was black and dumb as hell. Years later, I think she ran for election to the bench—and I think might have even won. Actually, I should have reported Vangie for domestic violence because she started it. But that was trivialized by this assistant DA attorney at trial. "But she didn't hurt you, did she?"

So Vangie's act was forgiven by this double standard. This assault on a female charge automatically disqualified me from getting credentialed for a *locums* temporary service (Weatherby *locums*). It had to be the ultimate confirmation that I was indeed a problem physician. Malpractice suits, licensure-board suspension, assault on a female—now what hospital, licensure board, or malpractice-insurance carrier would ever consider me?

Years, Vangie admitted to her Filipina friends that she had started the whole thing. Of course, they never approached me to apologize for their behavior on Vangie's behalf. The difference between Vangie and Mindy, of course, was that Vangie's concerns were genuine, even if they were wrong, and, therefore, forgivable. There was no manipulation or premediated treachery as there had been with Mindy.

The Struggle to Keep My Second Practice

I was very concerned that my second location would not support four orthopedists, but I had little other choice but to try to make it there, as I had no other alternative, although in retrospect I may have been better off toughing it out at my first position.

The fact that so many orthopedists, five in six years, had cycled through this second location hospital obviously tells you that something was very wrong. Remember: it would be a different matter if five had cycled through a big city like Los Angeles, Chicago, or New York, where they have dozens of orthopedists and one might expect that kind of turnover due to retirement and relocation for family reasons.

"Family reasons" or "desire to be closer to one's family," are the excuses hospitals give for the previous physician leaving when they are trying to recruit another. They don't want to admit that the previous doctor couldn't stand the place, the administrator, or the doctors on the staff, or that doctors would not refer to him. For example, Dr. Felix told me Dr. Ely had to leave because he would not complete his medical records and had charts all piled up in the medical-records department. I suspect that Dr. Ely, like all the others except Dr. Sylvester who had his own office in the neighboring town, couldn't stand Dr. Felix. Sure, Dr. Ely may have been delinquent on his medical records, but that wasn't the real reason.

My situation was different than these other doctors, who, if they didn't like the place, could simply leave after they found another position, especially when they had short-term, two- to three-year contracts with salary guarantees and no commitment to closing their office. They just shuttled in and out of Dr. Felix's office.

There was only one exception, an orthopedist who had set up, sold his office, and left within two years before I arrived. These orthopedists had no record of licensure-board suspension. Jobs were plentiful, especially since they were young physicians, and they easily moved on. In striking contrast, I could not simply leave because I didn't know if I could *ever* find a new position due to my suspension, and if I did, it would likely not be a very stable one and no better than where I was currently. This new second location would have to be really bad for me to have to leave. It was.

As expected, there was never enough patient volume for two orthopedists, namely Dr. Felix and me. Felix had a group of old cronies. It seemed that if you owned a big boat, that made you a member.

The administrator who'd brought me on, was terminated about two years after I arrived. The next one got caught in the middle of the conflict between Dr. Felix and me, which essentially rekindled the previous conflict of trying to take each other's call. For a while the arrangement was allowed to stand. I would take Dr. Krutch's and Dr. Jones's call and, thus, three-out-of-five nights. Drs. Felix and Sylvester took the other two.

Dr. Felix, as far as I can tell, was not motivated to build his practice but rather to drive me out. His arrangement with Dr. Sylvester still violated the bylaws. When I turned the tables on him by using Dr. Krutch and Dr. Jones to claim a share of the majority of call and he saw that I was not going to be worn down by the call, Dr. Felix cried foul. Eventually, after about two years, this second administrator left. For a year, the hospital went without an administrator, and things seemed to stabilize. The bills were paid, and operations were maintained by the chief financial officer. Eventually a new administrator was hired around 2001—Shirley Tate. It was then things started to slowly unravel.

Shirley Tate was, in my opinion, what I could only describe as a fat, arrogant pig. She had already screwed up a hospital in a neighboring state. I can't believe how stupid the local politicians and hospital board members were for not vetting her. The local politicians really made some bonehead decisions. The most notable was the signing of a fifteen-year contract with a power company that left people having to pay exorbitant utility rates because a provision had not been made for a boondoggled nuclear power plant that never got on line. No matter. Once the contract ended, the city renegotiated new lower rates, but did not pass these savings on to the customers. It kept the difference for itself.

Government is guaranteed to become lazy and non-productive because they form a collective, who as individuals, don't have skin in the game. It explains the eventual guaranteed futility of government, especially as it becomes larger and more centralized. Government produces nothing. Government always gets bigger. Government always requires more money. It is a breeding ground for corruption and waste. There simply is never enough money for the government. They take it from productive people no matter what. It is a testament to the productivity of the working class that they have been able to support such a parasitic load for so long.

Tate was, like most other hospital administrators, sophomoric in her understanding of the medical community. By the numbers, she was convinced that the town should support more orthopedists. She really didn't understand why so many had already left. She would continue the pattern of hiring more orthopedists, who like those before, would stay two to three years until their guarantees ran out, and then, realizing that they could not maintain a viable practice without a hospital subsidy, would leave. A hospital typically loses money on this kind of rapid turnover.

As a solo private practitioner, I had to pay overhead. In contrast, these employed carpetbaggers just walked into an office that had already been set up by the hospital and took patient load away from me. As Tate increased the hospital employment to other specialties, internal referral patterns were established for elective patients, and I was slowly starved. Taking extra call had allowed me to mitigate some of this.

I felt pressured to try to capture as much business as possible and stretched myself too thin at times. I would try to do cases during my lunch break so I would not have to interrupt my office hours. I ran into problems with anesthesiology once again, especially with Dr. Bart Clarke, who would repeatedly call my office in the morning and nag my staff to see if I could come in early and do my emergency/or semi-elective case so anesthesia could leave early that afternoon instead of having to wait until after I had finished my afternoon office.

Of course, practically every time I made a special effort to show up early during lunch, they did not have the patient ready. They figured that, once I had showed up, there was no need to rush to get my case started. There was absolutely no consideration for me getting back to my office on time.

One time, Dr. Clarke and I got in an argument over this. He had been harassing my office all morning: "When can Dr. Sterling come over and do his case? When can he come over? Is Dr. Sterling done yet?" My office was exasperated.

When I finally did show up, the patient wasn't even in the holding room, nor had anyone started the spinal block. No one was around. I checked to be sure there wasn't another emergency case which could have caused my case to be delayed. Nope. I couldn't believe it. It was just complete, total selfish inconsideration toward me. Dr. Clarke's only concern was his getting out early, not whether I would be late for afternoon my office or that I was working through my lunch break.

No good deed went unpunished at this hospital. Dr. Clarke was a self-centered, spoiled brat, with the same temperament as Mindy's brother, and he had the most unbelievably clingy girlfriend to boot. Unbelievable how she would never let another woman approach him, even in social-group settings. Her jealousy and insecurity were the most pathetic public display I have ever seen. She hovered over him like a presidential bodyguard.

The Registration Worker and My First Suspension

I finally got caught in another double pincher when I had a scheduled hip injection under fluoroscopy (in the x-ray department) during my lunch break. This procedure was to follow a case in the operating room that I had added on, again at anesthesia's request so they and the patient would not have to stay late.

Again, the operating room was late, even though they had assured me that they would be ready if I could just come over early. Just like Charlie Brown who kept getting assured by Lucy that she would hold the football, I was tricked again. The case was delayed. I finally finished it and then went to the x-ray department to perform the injection. I figured the patient would be ready and waiting. She wasn't there.

Where was she? "She is still up in registration." I figured she was probably late also. When I arrived, she was in tears complaining of her arthritic hip pain and very upset because the registration worker would not register her. The clerk claimed the necessary registration paperwork had not been done.

I could not believe it. I went back to the office and talked with my manager who was also very upset because she had indeed not only completed all the hospital required paperwork, but also had sent our office records and permission forms. This worker was too lazy or too dumb to find them, but *not* to spend a lot of time arguing with my office manager.

I approached the registration desk where three people were working. I did not know who was responsible, so I cussed them all out loudly in public, saying that they didn't care about doing their jobs, because a case canceled is a case done, and after 4:00 they can leave and don't care about anyone else being inconvenienced. They were "just a bunch of lazy asses."

The head of registration tried to defuse the situation by having me continue my tirade in the back office. There I learned who the culprit was. It was Marleen Maloney. She was the classic lazy-ass black who had been hired because she was black but should have been fired because she was useless. She would chant, "Praise Jesus," every time I used the *goddamn* or *lazy-ass* description (but not the N word or gutter profanity).

She took a lot more time and effort to write a grievance to the hospital, demanding action to be taken, than she had trying to get that patient registered. She signed her name *Min. Marleen Maloney*, the prefix an abbreviation for "minister." She could do no wrong because God was on her side. Her father was also a minister in town. On the basis of this incident, I am now absolutely against any more affirmative action for minorities. I am tired of blacks' excuses. While in high school, I spent two summers teaching remedial math at a prep school in upstate NY to the kids from the boys' clubs from the Bronx, Manhattan, Lower East side for Project Broad Jump. Unfortunately, my attitudes have changed.

I finally agreed to discuss this outburst, my first ever, in front of the hospital medical executive committee (MEC). My neighbor, Roland Powers, MD, a grumpy, old family practitioner was chief. Dr. Clarke was also a member. The director of human resources was there, and said he wanted to hear this. A few weeks later, he left the hospital.

Dr. Powers opened the meeting, informing me he was pissed that he had to be at the meeting, and that "we (the MEC) are the only friends you got." I explained to the committee what had happened, and that this was a glaring case where this registration worker should have been summarily fired. Not only was she not doing her job, but she was arguing with and obstructing my office manager. In fact, it was later confirmed that the paperwork had been done. Even Dr. Dan Canton, one of the general surgeons on the MEC, chimed in and admitted that he had had problems with her too.

But did that help me? No. It was classic reverse discrimination. Marleen was transferred from that position (but not fired) and sent for some kind of patient/doctor relations training, but admittedly, I do not know if it was specifically for her. I do know this kind of training is generally mandatory for all employees these days.

No one on the committee openly supported me. I guess I did not have any friends after all, contrary to Dr. Power's opening snide remark. The medical executive committee issued an *unprecedented* seven-day suspension for this first-time incident to appease Minister Marleen Maloney who demanded I be reported to the medical board.

According to the medical board guidelines, a seven-day suspension did not meet the ten-day threshold requirement for being reported to the board. The board also stated on its website that all reported incidents were first referred for screening/review by the Physicians Health Program (PHP). I had a several hours long discussion with the head of PHP Dr. Mark Williamson, who simply concluded three things: (1) I got a raw deal with my former license suspension; (2) the seven-day suspension by my hospital was harsh, especially for a first-time incident; and (3) I should leave. (Easy to say, but hard to do with my license suspension/malpractice history.)

I thought that this PHP meeting would be the end of it, but this was the classic case of "not so fast, buster." You see, it was 2003 and medical boards were starting their politically correct crusade against the "disruptive physician." I was the poster child for their new cause, and they were, oh, so righteous. A seven-day, not ten-day, suspension suddenly would be enough for the board to launch an investigation. The board's medical investigator merely confirmed that I had been suspended for seven days over the phone. She didn't talk to me, the members of the MEC, or even Minister Maloney. I knew this investigation would be the start of another quagmire.

Going on Courtesy Staff and Second Suspension

I was getting so stressed with the hospital, the new pending medi-cal-board review of this latest incident, and Dr. Felix that I realized I had needed to step down from active staff and go on courtesy staff and get a breather. Some would call this burnout. Switching status to courtesy meant that I would no longer have to take emergency room call, nor Drs. Jones and Krutch's call. My call, currently on a three-out-of-five cycle night cycle, would be uncovered for any new patients who had not previously seen an orthopedist. Drs. Felix and Sylvester would now each take one out of three nights' call, since no physician was required to take more than one night out of three call. The third night would go uncovered. Of course, patients recently seen, treated, or recently operated on by us physicians would have to be seen no matter who was on call, even if no physician was on call.

I had performed a total hip replacement on a very affable but alcoholic man for avascular necrosis (alcohol abuse had caused his hip joint to disintegrate and, therefore, required replacement) a few months earlier. He turned out to be a chronic hip replacement dislocator. (It was suggested that he was deliberately dislocating in order to come into the hospital for narcotics and so on, and he was noncompliant with the usual total hip precautions to avoid dislocation.) He was a recurrent dislocator, not a first-time postop dislocator, the latter which could be argued would have been a more relative "urgency", but not a true emergency. Thus, he would come into the emergency room arguably not for a new emergency but an old problem.

As any orthopedic surgeon will attest, this condition can be a very stressful situation, as oftentimes there is no good solution (e.g., revising the hip), especially if the components are in good position and the patient is an alcoholic, smoker, and so on. I had informed the patient earlier that I was going off staff for six months and that if his hip dislocated again, Dr. Felix or Dr. Sylvester would have to pop it back in. In the past, whenever I was on call, I had always been willing to pop back in ("reduce") dislocated total hips, even those done by other surgeons. It was no big deal.

I had been on courtesy call for almost a month when I got a call around midnight from the emergency room, informing me that my patient was back with his hip out. I replied that I was scheduled for an early morning trip out of state, that I was now on courtesy staff, and that the other two doctors would have to attend to it; otherwise if neither was on scheduled roster call that night, the patient would have to be transferred to another hospital.

When I returned from my trip three days later, I saw my patient sitting in the hospital parking lot in his wheelchair, smoking. I was surprised that he was still there, because usually these patients were discharged the following morning or a day later at the latest. He informed me that Dr. Felix had done nothing to pop his hip back in. It was still out! Instead, Dr. Felix had taken the time to file a grievance against me to his crony urologist, Marvin Mace, MD, the chief of surgery at that time.

Dr. Felix was accusing me of patient abandonment, yet here my patient had been in the hospital for three days, and Dr. Felix had done nothing for him. Isn't this patient abandonment? Quite the double standard. Dr. Mace combed through the medical staff bylaws line by line, searching for any violations that could be used against me. Never had the bylaws been so carefully reviewed as they were for this incident. After all, Dr. Felix was his boat buddy (Mace owned a boat also). I was accused of having placed the patient in "critical danger" and so on. Of course, if this were all true, how critical could this patient's problem have been if Dr. Felix saw fit to do nothing for three days and even let him go outside to smoke until I returned?

In unprecedented fashion, I was suspended for thirty days. I was already on courtesy staff, so this second suspension didn't immediately impact me. This suspension would have ended before my elective six-month courtesy staff status was up. The problem was, I was then denied return to full-active staff when the original six-month courtesy period ended. I was trapped. I was being punished twice. Once with the thirty-day suspension, which I had already served, and then again by being denied return to active status.

Meanwhile, the hospital had recruited two orthopedists, Dr. Knight and one supposedly from Maine. Theoretically, the hospital no longer needed me. Arguably, my return would only detract from these new physicians from building up their practices. However, a bigger problem lurked. Because this suspension was for thirty days, it automatically had to be reported to the board. It should also have been reported to the NPDB, but it never was. Why not? I wonder if the suspension was later determined to have been such a blatant double standard and abuse of the hospital and board's discretion that the whole thing was hushed up in the end, as might be suggested when it came time to applying for a state license for my third and final job seven years later.

When applying for a state license, a physician is required to have his previous hospital send a letter of verification that the physician had worked at that hospital and indicate whether he had encountered any problems.

When I applied for my last state medical license for my third practice—poof!—everything had vanished from this hospital and board records. No record of any of these hospital suspensions on the verification or data bank. Even the additional three yearly follow-up probations from the medical board had just disappeared.

Center for Professionals Evaluation

The medical board was still on my tail for this first suspension. They re-quested that my wife and I submit to an in-state professional clinic for evaluation by Dr. Polomy, PhD (former anthropologist who didn't want to elaborate on his background in response to my question), and Askew JD, MD, at my $2,500 expense.

I was immediately skeptical of this whole setup. In my opinion, a thirty-day suspension for refusal to present to the emergency room for a nonemergent problem when already on courtesy staff is hardly classic disruptive behavior. The board was using this incident as a vehicle to advance its disruptive physician crusade. Obviously, Dr. Askew may have practiced in the emergency room for a few years, couldn't hack it, may have gone to law school either before or after, couldn't hack it there either and so wound up in one of these opportunistic physician fleecing operations, usually under the guise of marketing, practice management, or personal relationship/interactions training.

At the end of the day, Dr. Polomy sat me down and informed me he was going to ask me to read a book, *Anger Kills*, and he was even going to give it to me. Without further ado, he verbally prefaced his remarks, "Now for my findings and recommendations to you, Bryce." He paused, looking squarely at me. "Bryce, what in hell are you still doing in that town? Get out of there, man. Go to the Philippines. Anywhere. Get out of medicine."

Again, he like the others, could not appreciate how difficult it was to do this. He already had a nice cushy job, fleecing other doctors and professionals, while I was fighting the war in the trenches. This only served to inflame my anger even more. It was like the movie preview for *Anger Management*, starring Jack Nicholson and Adam Sandler. "Adam used to never have an anger problem. But he's got one now."

He defined my problem as my tendency for avoidant behavior. I didn't want to confront issues as a general rule, tried to be accommodative, but in doing so let things build up so long that I would suddenly erupt. He made the analogy of a dormant volcano that suddenly erupts.

I later received a copy of Dr. Askew's formal legal correspondence to the board. She "could not determine whether I could practice medicine with reasonable skill or safety." This had been her charge by the board, requested in legal context. Of course, it was all totally misdirected because I, an orthopedic surgeon, was in a different specialty. Psychologically, she could draw no conclusions either, as she was not a psychologist/psychiatrist and had done no testing. Her primary function appeared to officially communicate Dr. Polomy's findings to the medical board in a legalese context.

Again, as with Dr. Williamson's findings from PHP, I saw no other reports or findings. No written records or findings were generated from this evaluation other than the Dr. Askew's legal report. Specifically, I am unaware of PHP or the center *ever* addressing any personality, emotional, or behavioral issues. I had only Dr. Polomy's implied verbal communication that I was getting screwed. This evaluation had been a waste of my time and $2,500, and only invited further evaluation.

In short, the medical board sent me for an evaluation to this center because the act of requesting me to go there would give the appearance that the board was performing its politically correct duties in getting me evaluated when, in fact, it was not an evaluation. It was nothing more than a feel-good directive. I don't even know if the board was even aware of the center's capabilities for evaluation, goals, or provisions for implementing any treatment plans or recommendations. If the board received no negative reports from Drs. Williamson from PHP or Polomy from the center, that should have been it, right?

Oh no. Another "Not so fast, buster!" Here we go again. The board now wanted me to submit for a psychiatric interview, and this time they were trying to appear accommodating and impartial, by allowing me to go to a psychiatrist of my own choosing. Had the board now recognized they had sent me to the center for a useless evaluation, or had they not gotten the findings they wanted?

I refused to go a psychiatrist of my own choosing because I was sure that if my own expert cleared me, the board would send me to yet another expert of their own choosing. The board was overtly witness shopping and, from my standpoint and my accountant's opinion (he was also a lawyer), harassing me. This witness shopping by this board was similar to what the previous medical board had done when it had searched out different experts as they sought to dispose of the orthopedic standard in my anesthetic death case. Initially, I was held to orthopedic standards by the board. When that opinion exonerated me, they looked at cardiology standards briefly and reviewed the cardiologist's deposition (the cardiologist who was called in to try to resuscitate Arthur Smith), but seeing that his, a neutral specialty, also supported my case, passed over his deposition and finally held me to anesthesia standards.

The board sent me to Drs. Calvin Hardy, MD (psychiatrist), and Jeffery Caster, PhD (psychologist). These were the board's forensic experts to whom the board referred "problem" physicians.

I was greeted by Dr. Hardy, whose first remark was not the usual whether I had any questions before proceeding, but, "Why are you being evaluated so many times? This is very unusual."

His question opened up my line of questioning. I asked him to confirm that he received a number of referrals from the board, and he replied, "Yes." I pointed out that he had just asked me why I was getting so many evaluations. I then politely concluded that it would, therefore, not be unreasonable to assume that the board wanted him to say something that no one else would. He promptly denied the inference that his evaluation would be biased to accommodate a referral source.

I claimed I was being harassed by the board, which was on a crusade to find a poster child for their nascent crusade against the so-called disruptive physician. Dr. Hardy would later write in his opinion that I was "righteous." I told him that, my concerns about the whole process notwithstanding, I would cooperate with his and Dr. Caster's evaluations/testing, and that I had been through these before during my divorce.

Not much came out of the evaluation. It was a sort of hedge. In his written report, Dr. Hardy identified some behavior issues of anger, sulking, blaming others, and so on, but that these did not require in-house or even outpatient counseling or behavioral or drug therapy, but that if future disruptions occurred then he would recommend it. Specifically, he did not opine that I was unfit to practice medicine.

He handed me a little post-it note of things to do:

- Exercise.
- Get more rest.
- Let go of past hurts.
- Avoid the use of profanity.
- Be less combative with the MEC.
- Leave.

After Dr. Knight arrived at my hospital, I could only watch on the sidelines, my active-staff practice privileges still not restored at the six-month mark, as his patient load built up. Dr. Felix had all but retired. Dr. Sylvester had pulled back to his home base. Dr. Knight was now in charge. The second orthopedist from Maine for some reason was not coming.

Kayla "Big Butt" Bailey and My Third Suspension

I occasionally went to the hospital to see what was going on. I was on courtesy staff and, therefore, allowed in the hospital but not allowed active-staff privileges. One afternoon, I went up to the operating room after hours to look at the schedule to see how many cases were being done. There was really no other earthly reason for me or any doctor to go there at that time.

Kayla Bailey, RN, the surgical nurse director and wife of the former hospital administrator who had recruited me to the hospital, was sitting at her desk. She asked me what I was doing. I kidded her and told her I was "snooping." I then unloaded on her about how Shirley Tate, the current administrator, was screwing things up at the hospital, had sabotaged my practice by unfairly cooperating with Dr. Felix, had harshly punished me with these suspensions because of politics, and so on. I think the word *scumbag* was used as well. A security guard walked by and looked through the door window, thought nothing of our conversation and walked on. (I got along well with security. In fact, one of them and I would have friendly arm wrestling matches, even practice wrestling takedowns in the halls—just horsing around.)

To my disbelief, Kayla reported me. And you don't think nurses are not out to take down doctors? How things have changed in medicine. She implied my kidding remark about snooping constituted nefarious activity. I still have a copy of her letter. I was then summarily suspended indefinitely from the hospital. For this, a conversation in private about our administrator? Doctors are always criticizing administrators. Why was this any different? Unbelievable, especially when my comments about this administrator turned out to be very prescient. Later, Tate was terminated and escorted out by the police. A YouTube video emerged with all of the OR staff, nurses, and techs all lined-up River Dance-style, singing, "Ding Dong the Witch Is Gone." I would have loved to provide the link here, but that would violate the fiction restrictions.

To rub salt in the wound, within a few months Kayla left the hospital. I don't know whether it was to join her former administrator husband who had originally recruited me, whether she was fired, let go, or what. I don't know. But it was a classic "she screwed me and then she left me." I thought Kayla and I had gotten along well over the years. I was totally and utterly blind-sided by her tattletale treachery, and for what purpose? (Was Tate offering her a reward for such information? See what happened to Dr. Ballance later if you think my suspicions are far-fetched.) Now Dr. Mace, chief of surgery, was back on my tail. I appealed this third suspension but was denied by my fellow physicians.

Who was signing all my suspensions? Why it was Dr. Roy Bospy, the ER physician who was acting chief of staff. He had physically assaulted a nurse in the ER—twice. I know, because she happened to have been my patient and confided this to me. At one of the hearings, Dr. Bospy brought up my assault on my wife, Vangie. So now activities outside the hospital were being used to build a case against me.

According to the bylaws, I was entitled to further appeal. This time my appeal was successful contingent on agreeing to go back to PHP and Dr. Williamson for reevaluation. Oh, another thing I forgot: Dr. Mace, the urologist who was chief of surgery and who had launched my second suspension for thirty days on behalf of his crony Dr. Felix, had also physically assaulted a nurse a few years earlier, except that "back then, it didn't matter," he said.

Dr. Felix sold his practice to the hospital when he retired. In contrast, I received no offers from the hospital for my building when I left. Dr. Knight joined Dr. Felix and took over his office when Dr. Felix retired. Then Dr. Thompson joined Dr. Knight. When both Knight and Thompson eventually left, they didn't have to sell the practice or office building. They just packed up a few books and left.

I wonder if the hospital suddenly softened its stance because the other orthopedist from Maine was not coming, and with me gone, Knight was by himself. Dr. Felix had retired (finally) by this time. Things should have gotten better, but the hospital did not realize that with the noxious Dr. Felix gone, things from my standpoint might have actually improved on their own. But the Tate had big plans for me. I was soon to go on a "vacation."

Dr. Knight was a nice guy, quiet, soft spoken, and a good surgeon, but he had gutted my practice while I was pinned down with this third suspension. I remember only two physicians stood by me and voted in my favor on my second appeal. One of them was a longtime emergency physician who knew me well and acknowledged that I had always been very prompt and responsive, in fact more than any other doctor when requested to appear in the emergency room.

In contrast, the hospital attorney made sure to criticize me on record: "It is amazing that Dr. Sterling doesn't even recognize his anger and the disruption it causes. Dr. Sterling reported that he has had several evaluations, all of which he claimed had given him 'glowing reports' which is simply not the case … Dr. Sterling is experiencing situational anxiety."

Of course, I was anxious, and of course, I was having difficulty controlling my temper. I *never* said or implied I had received glowing recommendations, rather the serial evaluators saw my issues in context and could not justify intervention. They simply were not going to come out and state the obvious: Shirley Tate and the hospital were royally screwing me over. I should have taken legal action and sued the hospital, but based on my experience with attorneys, I would have gotten screwed by them even worse and gotten even more upset. I had to accept that I had landed in a shit hole and there was nothing I could do about it short of quitting medicine.

Indeed, I was in trouble but the hospital kept aggravating the situation. I was punished far more severely than other physicians through a blatant double standard. Bylaws were ignored when they applied to Drs. Felix and Sylvester. When I challenged Dr. Sylvester's eligibility to be on full-active staff in view of living outside the thirty-minute call radius, Tate had the hospital attorney review the bylaws to see if he was in violation. When I asked to see the opinion, Tate would not let me see it, nor would she verbally indicate the content, citing attorney-client privilege.

When I challenged Dr. Bospy on this glaring issue of call radius violation through the bylaws committee, his response was simply, "You do not interpret the bylaws." The bylaws were then suddenly changed to accommodate Drs. Felix and Sylvester. "Doctors will live within a distance judged to be adequate for presentation to the ER as may be required by the ER physician"—or something vague like that. This relationship with Dr. Sylvester had allowed Dr. Felix to keep control for seven years, even though at one point I garnered 60 percent of the call due to my relationship with Drs. Krutch and Jones at the beach.

No one could appreciate my predicament because no one else ever had to walk in my shoes. I was trapped in this doormat town with no ability to leave and find another position, yet I was being squeezed financially by an incompetent, pugnacious, and arrogant administrator who could look only at numbers in her office and was convinced that the town should support three full-time orthopedists.

I had tried to tell her she should first try to understand why the town would not support more than one and a half orthopedists: They'd had this bad apple, Dr. Felix, for decades, and he had pissed off a lot of people. They had gone through a series of orthopedists (six) in the last ten years, a phenomenal number that does not build public confidence.

When I am upset, distressed, constantly getting suspended, and so on, my ability to settle down and build a practice is derailed. It is not a formal recognized diagnosis, but in a way, I became an impaired physician—almost as if I were bipolar or alcoholic. My anger was quite manageable under reasonable normal circumstances. The correct thing to have done is to let my anger simmer down by eliminating some of my stressors, but instead the hospital MEC, Tate, and the board kept pouring more gas on the fire.

The simple fact was that never once did Tate or anyone else ever sit down and talk to me over a cup of coffee about what was bugging me, or what I was hoping to do in my practice, or what my goals were. I think I saw Tate about once or twice in the hospital outside the obligatory quarterly medical staff meetings or the monthly/bimonthly surgical staff meetings. I suppose I could have asked for a meeting, but she was so hostile, untrustworthy, and arrogant that it was pointless.

Back to the Medical Board and Alfred the Asshole

My third suspension had to be reported to the board. It was a summary or emergency suspension and of indefinite duration. Sure enough, I was recalled to appear in front of the board again. The board's investigation had started with my first seven-day suspension and had never been closed. Generally, the board on this appearance seemed like a pretty reasonable bunch and was doing its job, except for one. There is always at least one in the group.

The director was pretty conscientious about digging into my long-forgotten past evaluation by a psychiatrist whom I had gone to concerning my anxiety attack during flying. She had started me on Elavil. I was scheduled for follow up to have some blood-levels drawn, but I realized that under the circumstances I was too emotionally stressed and financially strapped to be flying, and therefore, the whole issue was moot, and I did not follow up.

But there is usually one righteous member in a medical board, and this one sat directly across the table. When I complained about being subjected to all these evaluations, Alfred (I don't recall if he was a doctor or not) lit up and scolded me. "Doctor, do you ever stop and look into the mirror to see the problem? We are sending you for evaluations, and we are going to keep sending you for evaluations because you have an anger problem."

It was the classic teapot-kettle exchange, as the rest of the board members sat quietly during his tirade. I told them that I was scheduled for a follow-up visit to Dr. Williamson at Physicians Health Program (PHP). I guess they felt that this appointment would keep me sufficiently in the loop, and so I left with no formal action against my license. It was still active and unrestricted, but I remained under investigation and still under full hospital suspension.

Back to PHP and Dr. Williamson

How Dr. Williamson had changed since I'd last seen him, or rather, his interviewing. He was much more animated, not hostile, not critical, but more hurried and pressured with a sense of urgency. He was amazed that I had been through so many evaluations and said he "had never seen anything like it." He immediately declared, without any further questioning or discussion that I needed further evaluation for in-house therapy and mentioned something like "You keep your side of the street clean, and we'll keep our side clean." I don't know what that was supposed to mean, other than his attempt to reconcile with my perceived bitterness at being harassed by all these evaluations. I don't even know if he remembered anything from our previous meeting. He had clearly jumped on the bandwagon.

It was summer 1993 when I traveled to an out-of-state rehabilitation and recovery center for formal evaluation—again. There I was met by the nurse who gave me all this applesauce (trying to justify her job and the center's purpose?) about how "I had a right to be happy." *Puhleeze*!

I went through several evaluations, the most interesting one by this doctor who caught me on the memory test. He interrupted our conversation and asked me to remember three things, for example: fender, insight, boutique. He then continued our conversation, until suddenly interrupting me ten minutes later to ask me repeat those three things. I could remember only one. He was concerned that I had suffered some traumatic brain damage in the past.

"Have you ever been knocked out?"

"Yes," I said. "When I slammed into an opening door at the ice rink. I skated full speed right into it, and I was also almost knocked out in college when I went just one round against a Golden Gloves fighter, forty pounds lighter than I. I had a headache for a month."

I met a cardiologist there who had also been sent for evaluation by his hospital. He was an interesting guy, openly much more defiant, hostile, and argumentative than I was, but he had not been tagged with any medical-board suspension, malpractice, hospital disciplinary action, or other black marks. I immediately clued him in about my stormy course and that his best bet was to lie low and play the game. He later confided to me that he got so pissed off at the evaluator that he told him, "I have learned more from talking to Sterling during lunch than you guys all day."

A week later I think, I heard the results of my evaluation. No written report, though, and that was no surprise. I sensed anyone who presented to this center for evaluation automatically received a recommendation for in-house therapy. You never met a life insurance agent who said you didn't need life insurance, did you? Strangely, though, the center said they didn't have space or a program for in-house anger management and referred me to another place. Was this yet more accommodation and agreement with a referral source?

Off to the Funny Farm

Off I went to the funny farm, September 1, 2003, for three months of in-house anger management therapy. (Sorry, psychiatry, only psychiatrists are allowed to use this slang term. It is demeaning when used by other specialties.) Vangie was now four months pregnant and alone with our cat, Bebe. My office was still open, but in hibernation. Fortunately, BCBS paid for most, if not all of this treatment. It was already bad enough being out of work and having to keep the office open.

I guess the only good thing about the funny farm was I got away from my town for a while and connected with some distant family members on my father's side. The program director kept me on my Zoloft. I had been taking it for about two years because I again had tried to go back to flying. I had asked our neurologist back around 2001 if there was any new medication besides Elavil that could be used to treat anxiety attacks. He said yes and started me on Zoloft. As a side note, this neurologist's outbursts and anger were legendary, greater and more numerous than my single event with the minister. He never had action taken against him. He soon left for a VA position.

I still did not get back into much flying, as I'd even started developing some transfer anxiety when I drove on high bridges over open water, but I'd noticed serendipitously that I'd felt better and had not been as anxious or angry. Interesting, so I stayed on it. The side effects were ten to twenty pounds of weight gain, and, of course, decreased libido.

The funny farm medical director added Abilify. Now that I am writing this, I recall that I had indeed been on a ten-day Zoloft holiday when my incident with the hospital registration worker-minister leading to my first suspension occurred in 2003. The evaluation center doctor who was concerned about my head injury used the term *holiday*, and I remember that now.

I learned to never, ever, go off any of these selective serotonin reuptake inhibitors (SSRIs) (like Prozac or Zoloft) cold turkey. If I ever had to go back on these, I would only do so under an agreement that I would also be issued a sufficient extra number to taper off if for some reason I was ever cut off from refills.

I finally did go off the medication completely in 2011 when trying to get a position as a medical officer with the US Army. I have continued functioning to this day without it.

What *really* happened at the funny farm in 2003? To make a long story short, I received no treatment, counseling, or therapy for anger management, but I sure got to see a lot of impaired doctors. Due to confidentiality established at the facility, no names or locations here. One or two seemed like pretty competent guys, not impaired, but they had just gone through rough patches. A surgeon who had attempted suicide was clearly the leader while he was there, seemed very level-headed, and I could not identify anything wrong with him—smart fellow, nice guy, lovely wife. He was discharged by the third week after my arrival. There was an orthopedic surgeon who came there under the impression he was there for evaluation, but then *snap* went the rat trap. He got hooked there for three months. He seemed pretty reasonable, no drugs. I wondered why he had been sent there.

But, whoo, baby, there were some doozies. My first roommate was a medical student, referred for drugs, alcohol, and soliciting prostitution—very quiet, almost cold or aloof (schizoid) personality, no empathy. He got kicked out of the program after a few weeks for sneaking out drinking, drugging, and whoring. My next roommate was an anesthesiology resident, referred for alcoholism. A somewhat aloof guy, he too got in trouble for drinking and having sexual relations with another patient, a medical student who had been a very good athlete in college, but also an alcoholic. She was visibly very angry, bitter, and unhappy. Neither of them got kicked out.

Then there was this gastroenterologist who had been referred because of some patient deaths from complicated endoscopy surgeries according to him. But he had a cocaine addiction, had been burning through $1,000 a day, would go picking up chicks in his van and enticing them with coke for sex. There was an elderly ophthalmologist who had a challenged coke habit, would invite girls over to his place for negligee/coke parties. He could not give up the nude pictures of his party girl friends that he brought with him. Then my next roommate, well, he was just an average guy, he claimed with a false modesty, because he could not take credit for his daughter's IQ being 170 when his was only 150. He described how he'd rolled his Porsche on the way to the hospital one morning for a semi urgent case and had to be extricated by the wrecker. He was taken to the hospital where he performed this C-section in fifteen minutes, skin to skin, no problem. It was a different story of pathetic desperation when I overheard him on the phone lamenting to his former partner that he was broke, with no job, and that his partner was cold and ruthless for kicking him out of the office practice.

Finally, my other roommate, a lawyer, who referred to his other treatment place as "five star," was so gorked out (okay, sedated or obtunded) on prescribed meds when I first saw him that I didn't see how he could ever participate in therapy. But to my surprise, he cleared up and made some very interesting comments about news anchors and politicians on TV, specifically that they should speak in simpler sentences. He was actually quite bright and articulate. Claimed, too, that he had an IQ of 150.

So, what did I have to do? Well, I sat around the circle with these impaired physicians most of the day. Some of them insisted I had to have a drug problem simply "because I was there." Of course, the facility chased me around with the specimen cup a few times in the wee hours of the night. But I was clean. Drugs or alcohol had never even been an issue. Never!

When asked how much alcohol I drank, I said a glass or two of wine or beer when I am out socially once or twice a month. Sometimes I kept a six pack of beer at home if I remembered to buy it during the summer, and on occasion it had been brought home as a leftover after a social event with my wife's friends. They jumped all over that and accused me of being an alcoholic. They rejected my explanation of anger management and accused me of being an alcoholic because I had an anger problem. Alcoholism was a comorbidity of anger they claimed. But the one thing I heard over and over again was that "I always blamed everyone else for my own problems."

This was part of the repertoire of canned responses these doctors learned while they were there. Same thing when I attended the Caduceus meetings for impaired health-care workers: doctors, nurses, pharmacists, and so on. As part of my introduction to the group I told my brief story with the anesthetic death, licensure-board disciplinary action, and my subsequent career derailment and having being sent to the funny farm for anger management. I hadn't stopped for even one second when this guy parroted out. "You blame everyone else for your troubles."

I then made the mistake of admitting that for one year after my divorce I had subscribed to *Playboy* magazine. Now I was suddenly a sex addict and had to not only participate in the twelve-step program for alcoholism and attend the AA meetings, but now had to go to sex therapy. I was told to read *Man Enough*, a book about philandering men, even though I have never cheated on my ex or current wife, nor had rumors ever circulated about town or the hospital of any romantic interests or gossipy misconduct. I was accused by this counselor of wanting to go to the mall to see if I could pick up any young girls.

"Oh, come off it, man. I am over fifty years old, married with a child on the way. I have been to the mall only twice in two months and even then, with several members of this group," I snapped back, stunned that he would make that kind of remark. Unbelievable.

There was a young psychiatry resident who arrived later during the end of my stay. He was sent there for alcoholism, DTs, and other withdrawal symptoms. He denied it, but it was so obvious he was impaired. He had tremors and was clearly agitated. Then there was this young female pediatrician who admitted she raided every medical cabinet she could open trying to find narcotics from cough syrup or other over-the-counter drugs. She is the one I would have never suspected as being impaired. She was pretty forthright about her addiction.

Then there were a few who were just not quite right, almost like zombies. One medical student zombie and I made a ritual of taking our afternoon walk around the campus. How they practiced or make it through the first day of medical school or residency was beyond me. Although there is a current opioid/heroin epidemic, narcotics did not seem to be the pervasive drug of choice back then. It was cocaine and alcohol.

What really pissed me off was this issue of advocacy. If a physician agreed to go to therapy, then his misconduct or drug and/or alcohol issues would not be formally reported to the medical boards or the NPDB. Ostensibly, medical boards want to encourage physicians to get help before they get into trouble. Fair enough, I suppose. But I was the only one there, to my knowledge, who did *not* have advocacy. I had already been reported to the board, subjected to three psychiatric evaluations, and suspended by the hospital three times.

Actually, only my first offense, publicly chewing out the registration worker, was clear-cut disruptive behavior. My second offense, not showing up in the emergency room to see a nonemergent patient condition, was hardly in the category of being disruptive, although I suppose if one wants to be a purist about it, you could call that technically disruptive behavior. But I got suspended for it, my one and only offense. No one else ever did, not even repeat offenders.

Then finally, my third suspension, a summary suspension because I told the surgical nurse in private what I thought of our administrator Shirley Tate who was trying to get rid of me to make way for an "orthopedic renaissance," especially since she had already hired one orthopedist and was trying to hire another. No, I was not paranoid. That hospital simply wanted to get rid of me. Of course, this endless harassment only made things worse. Sending me to the funny farm in my opinion was simply a method of exiling me.

The second orthopedist never came, and no other recruitment had been successful. I think Tate realized she had to get some relief for Dr. Knight. Suddenly, after my return from the funny farm, all was forgiven. My nemesis, Dr. Marvin Mace, said that I had changed. Bullshit! He sent me his grandson for treatment of his broken wrist. He came to my office once weekly per the follow-up contract requirements from the funny farm and asked me how my practice and caseload were doing.

"Nothing," I said. "It's gone."

"Well, how many cases did you do last week?"

"None."

"Well how many do you have this week?"

"One."

"Well, at least it's a case," he said as he tried to squirm out of the carnage he had wreaked upon my life and career as a favor to his buddy, Dr. Felix. My career destruction was so blatant that it was painful for him to make that weekly follow-up visit. I soon put an end to his embarrassing and awkward situation when I finally called up the new director of PHP who was responsible for my follow-up after the funny farm. This follow-up involved enforcing my monitoring contract and payments. I chewed him out on the phone, told him exactly what had gone on there at the funny farm, how I had been harassed by the licensure board, the hospital, and now Dr. Mace was trying to act as if nothing ever happened.

This new PHP director's *only* response over that phone was "I'll let you off that contract." No explanation, no apology, no follow-up letter, no acknowledgment or record that I had completed the course at the funny farm, no record that I had fulfilled my requirements. No acknowledgment by the medical board that it was calling off the dogs and finally closing its investigation of me, only a two-sentence generic notification a few months later that their investigation was closed. *Nothing!*

The only acknowledgment came from the new chief of surgery at my hospital, Dr. Canton, who complimented me on having shown great improvement or something politically correct like that and that I was now reinstated to full-active medical staff.

It was really hard to tell why the hospital seemingly did an about-face on letting me back on staff. I hadn't threatened to sue them. Soon, the next orthopedist on the two- to three-year cycle, Dr. Thompson, had signed on. Life was a lot less stressful in many ways with Dr. Felix gone. Knight and Thompson weren't out to control/corral me. They just went about their quiet ways.

In theory, the hospital could now be designated as a level III trauma center, since it now had the full complement of three general surgeons and three orthopedic surgeons taking call every third night to achieve seamless, round-the-clock coverage. A level-three designation allowed the hospital to bill higher than a level-four designation hospital where there was not seamless coverage every day/night, or at least that was what I was led to believe.

I knew that since Knight and Thompson were together, and a growing number of other doctors being recruited into the organization, these new doctors would refer patients to these two orthopods within the network. I could still get cases out of the emergency room, but I was going to be gradually frozen out.

I cannot help but believe that Tate was still trying to recruit yet a fourth orthopedist to drive the final stake in my heart. However, until the fourth one came, I guess I was useful for maintaining the seamless three orthopedic call coverage and level-three trauma center designation for the hospital. The physician hospital recruiter denied this motive, and even seemed all too willing to help find me another job. He gave me contacts from Delta and Medicus, medical recruiting firms he had used in the past. He told me getting a job was a numbers game. He was right; just like the lottery is a numbers game—one chance out of twenty million. None of those ever panned out, not even a return phone call or email. My situational anxiety was always present. I did not want to stay in town at this hospital because there was not enough work, and yet I could not just find another job and leave. I was trapped—for the remainder of my career it seemed. My colleagues just couldn't understand that because they didn't have to walk in my shoes.

Horse Latitudes 2004–2011

I don't know what happened to these years. It was just slow, steady anx-iety. I saw that the housing bubble of 2006 was building, and I tried to sell the house, but I could not find another orthopedic position. I was stuck. Every two or three years, I would restart a job search, but to no avail. I just muddled along.

Dr. Thompson was, according to the one nurse, an ass. Probably my most memorable moment confirming this was when I had a patient on the operating room table and was preparing to start a partial hip replacement for a broken hip. Anesthesia was already placing the epidural. Dr. Thompson suddenly walked into the surgeons' lounge and announced that he had an emergency open-wrist fracture on an elderly patient and that he was going to have to bump me. This type of wrist fracture was *not* an emergency. Thompson just didn't want to wait, and he would have wheeled my patient out of the operating room if possible. My orthopedic rep, who was one of the nicest, most decent people I have ever known, was sitting with me in the surgeons' lounge to witness the event. He could not believe it.

I then struck back, saying, "Arnold, here you have four times the amount of elective morning OR start time, and still you are trying to bump me."

"Bullshit," Dr. Thompson replied to my numbers, cutting me off.

"No, Arnold. You have a Monday and a Thursday 7:30 a.m. start time every week, and I have only a Friday every other week. Go check the schedule." Thompson had no idea about my schedule. He only considered himself. He eventually left the hospital after having an affair with one of the techs, who in turn was let go by the hospital because of that and the fact that she had swung the overhead operating room light into the new widescreen operating room TV twice in about a month, cracking the screen each time (actually, lousy design in the newly remodeled operating room suites). This tech's husband reportedly even stormed into Dr. Thompson's office and told him to stay away from his wife.

Speaking of OR scheduling. There was the time I took a vacation to Ecuador around 1997. The week before my vacation, we surgeons had attended a meeting about operating room scheduling. Surgeons like to get a guaranteed 07:30 start time (block time) for their elective schedules. If you have to follow another surgeon, it can be very difficult to plan your surgery and your office because you don't know when the surgeon booked ahead of you will actually finish his case and the room turn over.

My nemesis, Dr. Felix, chaired the meeting and said that a surgeon's allotment of OR block time (and thus guaranteed start morning start time) "was based on a simple principle: You use it or you lose it." Fair enough, I thought. However, when I returned two weeks later from Ecuador, I got a call from Dr. Jason Kemper (the "Piggy Two" surgeon who claimed to have performed an appendectomy on that girl but hadn't, confounding the diagnosis of recurrent abdominal pain when she returned, cut the vocal cord nerve in our mutual patient during a thyroidectomy, and worse, watched as a young man who should have been operated on for a serious problem, but was not, and after having spent several days in the hospital, wound up dying.) Dr. Kemper left the hospital while he still could according to one of his partners.

Dr. Kemper told me that I had lost one of my two OR start days. Guess who was doing fewer cases than I but who somehow did *not* lose one of his two days? Yep. Dr. Felix. Now, who took my coveted OR morning start block time? Dr. Joseph Wall, an ENT (ear, nose and throat) surgeon, who also lived about two doors down from me across the street. (Next to Dr. Roland Powers, the Med Executive Committee Chairman.) Dr. Wall essentially did two types of cases as an ENT surgeon: tubes and tonsils on kids. Placing tubes in the ears takes about two minutes, and tonsillectomies maybe a little longer, but they are some of the easiest, quickest cases to do. The surgeon doesn't even have to scrub, all outpatient.

It seemed that Dr. Wall needed more elective time to do his kiddie cases and wanted to offload his Friday surgical caseload, and so he took my Tuesday, which meant my bigger, higher risk, more complicated, equipment- and personnel-intensive cases would have to be done later in the day. I wound up having to do big femur fractures with the OB-GYN crew after hours. (I later got sued on one, which is why I remember so well.) This schedule change was slipped in while I was away in Ecuador.

Dr. Kemper said that I would only be held up a short while on Tuesday. What eventually happened was that Dr. Wall started unloading more of his Friday cases on Tuesday so he could get out earlier on Friday for the weekend. My Tuesday wait became longer and longer. But think of the children. Actually, Dr. Wall was doing a lot of tubes and tonsils—*a lot!* I suspect these two surgeries were over 95 percent of his practice, which was way in excess of any other typical ENT surgeon's practice profile, especially in a such a small town How did he do it? His wife was a pediatrician and, thus, referred kids with sore throats and ear infections left and right. It was a classic mill. I am surprised he did not get a Medicaid audit.

A Tale of Two Fingers

When Dr. Wall divorced his pediatrician wife, his referral source dried up. She too believed she shouldn't have to work, especially with four kids but who were all older than seven. He didn't want to pay his ex-wife, a doctor, alimony or child support, I guess, especially when his referral source was gone and practice revenue was about to take a hit. Reportedly she showed up at the hospital parking lot with a shotgun. Don't know if that part was true.

What I do know is that Dr. Wall then "accidentally" shot off his thumb with a black-powder handgun, long barrel, revolver, not a semiautomatic, not a double action, but rather a single-action trigger. You have to cock the hammer to fire it. He shot off his thumb. How do you manage that? I have seen lots of accidentally self-inflicted gunshot wounds, but those wind up in the foot or leg, not the hand. You almost have to intentionally want to do it to get the barrel to point to the base of your thumb.

No matter, it was good enough for Dr. Wall. He reportedly got disability, whose payments are legally protected from his ex-wife. He and his new girlfriend could enjoy their drinking together. His girlfriend, a nurse, got terminated by the hospital for drugs. She reportedly left her car door open and the engine running one day at work and appeared impaired, which tipped the hospital off. Dr. Wall's ex-wife had accused him of being an alcoholic. I must admit I never saw a bit of it or suspected, but that was before my visit to the funny farm and becoming an "expert" at diagnosis.

Speaking of the funny farm, my other neighbor down the street, a surgeon, had flunked out of drug rehab and AA rehab three times, had at least one suspension, and so I made the grave mistake of having once prescribed him narcotics. Last time I saw, he was employed as an "addictionologist." Glad he was able to turn his life around. No doubt he had his license suspended but this did not seem to impact his career as my suspension did mine. He is considered a former impaired physician for which there is less stigma. By "turning his life around" and overcoming drugs, he was rewarded by becoming a medical expert in treating other impaired physicians, whereas I am forever labeled a disruptive physician who carelessly executed a patient in the operating room and beat his wife. I don't qualify to treat drug-addicted doctors. I would first have to have been an addict. The medical boards, and even the public in my opinion, don't look at impaired physicians as bad doctors. They consider alcoholism a disease which if treated, restores the doctor to good standing, even if he has had a license suspension or probation.

I got a call from an emergency room physician in the emergency room early one morning. He told me Dr. Knight (the hospital-employed orthopedic surgeon) had just chopped off his nondominant left index finger at the base.

"You're not serious," I said.

"Serious like a heart attack," he replied. "He claims he did it cutting cheese."

I came in to the emergency room within twenty minutes, but by the time I arrived, the vascular and general surgeons already had him up in the operating room under anesthesia and were aimlessly picking away on his index finger amputation site.

"Now what in the hell are they trying to do?" I thought. "Reattach it? They had no experience or expertise in doing that." I didn't have anything to offer at that point other than suggesting to close the wound, but not before first doing a ray resection of the second metacarpal for cosmesis, which is what I would have requested to be performed by either a hand, plastic, or orthopedic surgeon before being put to sleep had it been my hand, but they didn't even wait for me to give my evaluation or recommendation. It shows you how low in regard I was held at that hospital. You don't reattach a single amputated digit in a fifty-six-year-old man. He was transferred to another hospital where they finalized/formalized the ray resection/amputation.

I suspect, but cannot prove, that Dr. Knight was drunk, depressed, and may have wildly chopped off his finger, maybe while trying to cut cheese. Surprisingly (for a simple finger amputation), I guess he'd lost a lot of blood and had delayed presenting to the emergency room until he had sobered up by morning. I never knew if they took a blood alcohol level on him. He was going through a divorce, financially strapped, and secretly seeing one of our anesthesiologists whom I had complained to about my situation: "Knight's a nice guy, a good surgeon, and I get along well with him. There's only one thing. While I was away at the funny farm for anger management *cum* drug/alcohol rehab, he devastated my practice, and I have never recovered."

In one way, he was like my other partner, Dr. Krutch, who had practiced at many locations, traveling from place to place. I had even called his old partner to get a better assessment on whether Dr. Knight would stay, and he'd told me that he'd tried to invite Dr. Knight and his wife over for dinner, and every time, he'd made an excuse not to come.

"He won't stay there long," he assured me. I was close to having to shut down my practice by that time because of Dr. Knight.

Dr. Knight's old partner was right. He didn't stay long. One day out of the blue in the surgeons' lounge Dr. Thompson announced simply, "Knight's leaving." I don't know why Dr. Thompson seemed upset, probably because he wouldn't have any coverage. But it could have merely confirmed what a dead-end the town was and planted the seeds in Dr. Thompson's mind of leaving too. It was learned that Dr. Knight had some DUIs and the medical board had issued a letter of concern. I don't know what treatment plan he was required to attend, but he sure wasn't exiled for in-house therapy at some distant place like I had been. Again, drug or alcohol abuse does not have the same stigma as a "disruptive physician."

But let me get this straight. I was exiled to the funny farm for anger management but instead was misdiagnosed and treated as an alcoholic, while Dr. Knight, my replacement, turned out to be the alcoholic. And you wonder why I am pissed?

The groundskeeper at my hospital broke his leg, and I had to fix it (same operation for which I was sued in my third job). On the final follow-up visit, he told me about how many bottles were in Dr. Knight's garbage can every Monday morning and yet had not been aware of his problems with alcohol. He was amazed that Dr. Knight had still been allowed to practice. I discussed my conflicted opinions about this because Dr. Knight was indeed a very good surgeon, easy to get along with, and showed no visible signs of any impairment. Dr. Knight and his girlfriend (an anesthesiologist) left and moved to a nearby state. I later met up with another orthopedic surgeon from Canada, who was doing *locums* temporary work and still had a big million-dollar house where Dr. Knight was relocating, but had to leave years ago because not enough work there. Small world. I was interviewing for that position he was leaving after leaving my third and final position in the South. I had been accepted, signed a contract, but it was rescinded as will be seen later.

Dr. Thompson and I coexisted for a year or so after that, had only the spat where he tried to bump me that evening. My practice recovered a little bit. The hospital was hiring other doctors, who automatically steered referrals to Dr. Thompson. But the damage had been done. My reputation was shot. Then I got the news that Dr. Thompson was leaving and going to the place where I eventually got my total hips replaced by an excellent surgeon on the recommendation of my good friend, the orthopedic rep. My total hips were a godsend. I had gotten the nickname "Bryzilla" because of my stilted lurching Godzilla gait due to the severe pain from arthritis. Now after the replacements, I don't even know they're there.

For a while, as the only orthopedist in town I was doing okay. Even my accountant noticed how dramatically my practice had picked up in those few months. It was like I had a regular orthopedic practice. My mood was more upbeat. Of course, the eternal question was how long before the administrator, Shirley Tate, hired two more replacements to start my starvation cycle all over again? She was spending money like a drunken sailor, employing physicians.

She had taken out $40 million in debt to build brand-new operating rooms and the most unwieldly, impractical, poorly designed emergency room I have ever seen. The operating rooms were indeed very nice, don't get me wrong, but totally unnecessary for a community that size.

No sooner had the last brick been laid when the census started dropping. People were convinced that since the two-lane highway to the neighboring state had been expanded to four lanes, more people would move to my town to escape higher costs of living and would also get their health care locally. I explained that it was literally a two-way street. It was easier for people to travel *back* to the neighboring state where they worked for their health care.

The hospital's numbers started dropping. My predictions were totally disregarded and forgotten. The old saying rang so true: "When I am right, nobody remembers. When I am wrong, nobody forgets."

And Now Dr. Paul Stine

Right on cue, Dr. Stine was recruited a few months after Thompson de-parted. He showed up in my office to introduce himself. At least he showed me that courtesy I had not seen from others. He seemed odd, probably because of his speech quirk. Every sentence ended with a volley of okays. Okay? Okay? Okay? He had been around, and at age fifty-nine, this was his eighth or ninth position. The hospital just wanted a body and hired these guys right off the street for salaries four to five times what I was making.

Fortunately, he was not an eager beaver as far as doing cases as Dr. Knight had been, so he didn't hurt me too badly as a competitor. The hospital bought him a ninety-thousand-dollar fracture table. (I never got even a doormat.) It was so big, complex, and cumbersome that it was difficult to move. The operating room crew dreaded having to use it. I used it just once. A total waste of money.

Around this time, in my opinion, the hospital may have realized that maybe they didn't want to get rid of me, because they couldn't attract or keep a good surgeon long enough to drive me out. I am not saying I was great or even good, but I guess I could be termed "adequate." The hospital physician recruiter approached me offering hospital employment and leasing of my office. I cut to the chase and asked point blank whether I would get the same salary that the other recruits were being offered. He said no—it would be based on my production history. This was my eternal catch-22. As long as the hospital kept recruiting orthopedists, the competition starved my production, which in turn allowed the hospital to lowball me on an employment contract based on my low-production history. I think in the end it would have amounted to renting my office to my competition. In fact, an orthopedist in another neighboring town had inquired about leasing my office for a half day or a day per week. That was rich. Leasing my office under my circumstances to a competitor?

Dr. Stine did very few cases, so I wasn't impacted as much by him as I was the steady decline in overall patient census at the hospital. This didn't stop the hospital from recruiting another traveler. Dr. Melvin Kurtis at age fifty, had been to about five other practices. His wife reportedly said that he always left just before the hospital ran into difficulty, and that this was going to be the final one. He bought the ER doctor's $500,000 custom-built house—lucky for the ER doctor. This house reportedly had problems with sinking foundation due to the fact that it was on the waterfront.

Dr. Kurtis was also maybe a little weird, I guess, because he was so quiet. I hadn't seen someone so quiet since Mindy's husband, Ben Holcomb. I guess the nice thing was that since these orthopedists were employed by the hospital, they weren't out to control me, use me to defray overhead, or take over my practice like that asshole Dr. Felix. The problem was that the overall numbers were declining. Dr. Kurtis would hurt me more than Dr. Stine.

One night, Dr. Stine was called in to the emergency room to see a patient. He was on call, on full-active medical staff, and refused. The emergency room, therefore, called me, because they knew I could be counted on as a last resort. The patient was admitted to me.

About an hour later, Dr. Stine reconsidered, came in to the emergency room, and insisted on admitting the patient, who had already gone up to the floor. He got into a verbal argument—I guess what might be described as "disruptive behavior"—and had to be led out of the hospital by security. The chief medical officer, Dr. Doug Tannenbaum (later involved in running a car off the road and punching the driver in the face and threatening to murder him, and who was the son of the police officer who heard about my fight with Marty Montgomery) was called to settle the dispute, and directed the patient to stay on my service.

Dr. Stine was terminated within a week. In my opinion, the hospital probably felt it was no big loss since he was down to one or two cases a week. To my knowledge he did not get written up or reported to the board, unlike me! A deal apparently was made whereby if he just voluntarily resigned and left, the hospital would not report him. My impression is that a lot of these kinds of cases go unreported because hospitals don't want to get bogged down in potential lawsuits. It is easier to kick the doctor out the door by just threatening to report him. I was never so lucky. There was nowhere I could have gone because I had been reported and suspended for everything I did. Those who had not been reported or suspended in contrast could leave and start right back up again.

I believe that there was a similar case at my third location where a mutual agreement out of convenience versus threat was reached. The doctor, who had accumulated a fair number of lawsuits, had his contract terminated and his renewal for privileges denied. He agreed to leave without legal action if no report to the board was made by the hospital. Dr. Stine wound up a few states away in the mountains. When I called him for a phone number where he could be reached by a hospital recruiter for a position I was seeking, he told the nurse in his office to tell me "he didn't have the time." This guy, too, really turned out to be an asshole.

As a side note, interestingly, when I was rehab director in 2015 at my third and final position as an orthopedic surgeon, I noted that he had done a case out of a distant hospital as a *locums*. He could not have been tagged with this latest disruptive behavior incident, since he had been able to promptly get new permanent and temporary positions.

Finally, after losing my third and final orthopedic job after four years, I called my old hospital (second job location) about being considered for the employed position for which they were advertising. I knew it would never happen. The recruiter snubbed me (because of my credentials) and laughingly mentioned that Dr. Stine also had the nerve calling her trying to get his old job back there too.

Dr. Melvin Kurtis

Dr. Kurtis arrived suddenly and without notice. That was to be expected. Tate never notified or consulted me when a new candidate was being considered, hired, or visiting. Dr. Kurtis told me Tate had even instructed him *not* to talk to me.

Dr. Kurtis seemed like a nice guy, but he was quiet, very quiet, and only announced his presence by his cologne bomb. Quite tragically, I learned a few years after I left that his son had committed suicide. I think he may have been rejected for a sales rep position by several orthopedic firms. Dr. Kurtis soon left the hospital. Normally, hospitals explain away a doctor's departure from a hospital due to a "desire to be closer to family" or for "family reasons" rather than admit the doctor was dissatisfied with the hospital. In Dr. Kurtis' case, this tragedy must have understandably made it very difficult for him to stay.

Another False Alarm

I thought I had a position in the neighboring town maybe a hundred miles from my home on a tip by my good friend, the orthopedic rep. The orthopod there and I hit it off famously. I was interviewed, had a meet-and-greet with members of the medical staff, and a dinner banquet that the rep also attended. My wife and daughter visited the excellent private school there. I thought that at last I was going to be able to dig myself out of this perpetual pit. I met with the CEO, who looked like the dad from *The Munsters*. He suddenly nixed the whole thing a few days later. I remember getting the call from the in-house recruiter, who said that his hospital had to decided they were "going to go in a different direction," meaning the offer had been rescinded. They took instead a female hand fellow orthopod who didn't last there but two years and did not get along with this orthopod. As my sales rep so astutely summarized, "Oh, what might have been."

My First Veterans Hospital Interview

I applied at the Veterans Hospital near the coast in 2011 and even got an interview. I met first with an ophthalmologist whom I liked right from the outset. She was very frank, open, and honest. She said based on her impressions, my background notwithstanding especially when taken in context, I was the best candidate. However, she warned me that the current chief of staff, Dr. A, would not accept me. He had a history of never accepting a candidate who had a history of licensure-board disciplinary action. I was to later learn why.

Nevertheless, I was introduced to him in his office for just a few minutes. I think I understood through his thick Middle Eastern accent that "he just wanted to see my face." I was there less than two minutes and excused. Practically no questions that I can recall, just "Hi, Dr. Sterlim, nice meet you," and that was it. The ophthalmologist walked with me out the building, said goodbye in the parking lot, and wished me luck. I must admit she was one of the nicest doctors I have ever met. Several months later, the candidate ultimately selected was in the paper for a series of wound infections and other complications and had been dismissed.

The US Army and Back to Where I Grew Up

I decided to try the US Army. The navy and the air force said they were well staffed. At my age of fifty-five, and two total hips, I would need some waivers. The US Army recruiter drove to my house, took chest and abdomen measurements, told me I had to get off the Zoloft and, based on my waist measurements, had to lose some weight. I filled out a lengthy application process, tapered off the Zoloft, which to this day have never restarted and started getting my weight down. Much of my weight gain I attributed to the Zoloft. I never heard back from the army.

In the meantime, I applied for the VA position in my childhood hometown. The chief of orthopedics was the older brother of one of my junior residents, who was female. I don't think she was treated well by the other residents in the program. I remember one day in the hospital parking lot, changing her flat tire for her. We got along fine. Anyway, that must have been a feather in my cap because her brother called me, discussed the position, and told me his sister had put in a good word for me. I was very hopeful, but I kept waiting and waiting. The word never came. I eventually learned years later that it would not have mattered. I could never get a position with the VA system. My licensure-board suspension automatically triggered a denial that could only be overturned by a regional review board, which was very unlikely due to my malpractice history.

Dr. Seymour

Now here was a real gem and a former neurosurgeon to boot. He appar-ently was rumored to have had a medical train wreck up north, came down to my town probably like me, as a sort of medical refugee according the surgeon Dr. Canton. Dr. Seymour would never talk to me. (Tate instructions, I am sure.) Then out of the blue he came in one day to observe me doing a vertebral biopsy with the C-arm (x-ray guided). I guess he had never done one before? Later he became an expert on the technique and its application in a procedure called *kyphoplasty* used to treat osteoporotic vertebral fractures in elderly whereby instead of biopsying the bone, a balloon was inserted to expand the collapsed vertebra, and then the cavity injected with bone cement to stabilize it.

I saw him at the YMCA on occasion. He did not seem physically impaired in any fashion whatsoever, either in the hospital or at the Y. Suddenly he had to close his practice. I did not know why. Next thing I knew, Shirley Tate in the hospital monthly newsletter wrote she was "pleased and proud" to announce Dr. Seymour as the new chief medical officer (CMO) and vice president of quality. This newly created position reportedly paid a salary of $275,000, which was a hell of a lot more than I could ever make. (Dr. Seymour was one of her lapdog yes men.)

People were scratching their heads, wondering why this position was needed in the first place, especially in such a small hospital. Dr. Thompson said it succinctly. "I don't see what Dr. Seymour adds to the equation." When I later developed some MRSA infections spontaneously, I had them cultured after performing some incision and drainages of these on myself, "Rambo style." (I had also repaired my left index finger extensor tendon lacerations I sustained in the jungle of Ecuador from a machete injury back in my hotel room in Quitos back in 1997. It took a while as I had to wait for my girlfriend Tessie to recover enough from nearly passing out each time to hold one end of the suture to allow me to tie the knots.)

Dr. Seymour got a hold of my culture results and, full of self-importance as always, said I had to go to an infectious disease (ID) specialist. This specialist started me on Bactrim. By the tenth day, everything had cleared. I have never had another recurrence since. Strange that it just disappeared just as mysteriously as it appeared, and in the nick of time. On day ten, I developed a total body rash. I had become allergic to the sulfa antibiotic.

Of course, Dr. Seymour was going to pounce, looking to dig up any case where I may have infected a patient. He had to justify his newly created position. However, there were no infections in any of my patients.

The incident reminds me of my general surgery internship. The first outbreak of this new superbug methicillin resistant staph aureus (MRSA) occurred around 1983 during my internship. To get a handle on the source and transmission/spread of this new superbug, all the residents had our nares (nasal passages) cultured, as that is where these bacteria concentrate in the human body. Of all the residents, I was the only one who cultured positive.

This cigarette-smoking vascular surgeon (took smoke breaks in the surgeons' lounge in the middle of long cases) chewed me out, told me to get the hell out, go on the prescribed antibiotic regimen and not to come back for at least ten days until I was cleaned up. The funny thing was that on follow-up, I was the only intern/resident with no infected surgically operated patients. I may have been rubbing my index finger up and down the halls and tables and picking my nose at every moment, but I washed my hands, gloved and gowned sterilely. No patient I had scrubbed in on ever got MRSA—an incredible statistical impossibility. Of course, there was no apology or explanation. The other explanation of course would be if they mixed up swabs to protect another resident. "Come on, you might say. Would they really do that?" Yeah, they would.

One day around the time I got the rejection news about the orthopedic opportunity from the town close by, Dr. Canton was yakking away, and I finally learned the reason Dr. Seymour had closed his practice and landed this newly created position of CMO. According to Dr. Canton, Dr. Seymour had performed a lumbar laminectomy/discectomy (back surgery) on a nurse's mother. It got infected and reportedly developed an acute postoperative epidural abscess (infection around the outside of the spinal cord sheath), which is truly a life-threatening and surgical emergency. Dr. Seymour had refused to come in to evaluate the patient in the emergency room.

The internist or family practice doctor admitted the patient and frantically arranged for transfer to any accepting neurosurgeon. The patient subsequently died a few days later. Why hadn't I heard about this when it happened a year or two earlier? My second suspension for failing to come in to see that

Bryce Sterling

nonemergent total hip dislocator was all over the hospital, and I was hounded and suspended for it.

Dr. Seymour, in contrast, had his incident all hushed up. No inquiry that I am aware of. He wasn't suspended. No, he was *rescued* by creation of this new job of CMO and vice president of quality position by this administrator, Shirley Tate. Now it made sense why he had to close his practice. His act of patient abandonment was so egregious that he probably was no longer insurable as a neurosurgeon. Only later did he make a special point of telling me that he had to quit his neurosurgical practice because of an old horseback riding injury/fall that was now causing him so much back pain, he could no longer stand long enough to do surgical procedures. *Fucking liar!*

Even worse, Dr. Knight reportedly had given him disability, so he was presumably collecting disability and collecting on his $275,000 a year CMO job. When Dr. Knight left, Dr. Thompson, to his credit, reportedly denied his disability renewal. Dr. Seymour had to travel out of state to see Dr. Knight.

Dr. Ballance Mics Herself

While Tate made a point of building up the bureaucracy (and expense) of maintaining her lap dogs like Dr. Seymour, she also showed no hesitation in scuttling certain physicians' practices. The next event that leaked out, again I think from general surgeon Dr. Dan Canton, was how the radiation oncologist Dr. Christine Ballance was being set up by a false accusation by one of the workers at the radiation oncology facility.

My understanding and impression was that Dr. Ballance was a competent, compassionate and dedicated physician/radiation oncologist. She never appeared confrontational (unlike yours truly at times). Nevertheless, she allegedly was being falsely accused for something by this worker at the facility at Tate's behest.

Dr. Ballance had the presence of mind to finally mic herself and record this worker's admission that his accusations were false and that he was being goaded or even threatened with his job by this administrator, Tate.

Dr. Ballance later married one of the family practitioners in town whom I always liked and respected. I used his attorney brother to draw up my trust (one of the few lawyers whom I trust and respect if you can believe that). These two doctors relocated. I cannot give any more details of this story other than reportedly a sum of money was paid to Dr. Ballance. There was a gag order on the terms of the settlement.

General Surgeons vs. Shirley Tate and "the Secret Deal"

It is well known in the medical field, of all the medical specialties, general surgeons and OB-GYNs are more likely to get called in and have to present to the emergency room in the middle of the night. Orthopedists, in contrast, especially in a small town, rarely get major trauma that requires immediate emergency surgery, for example, for a broken leg where the bone is sticking out. Most of the time, orthopedic injuries are broken hips or wrists that can be admitted or splinted without the orthopedic doctor having to actually come in. Such was the case for the dislocated total hip that I did not come in to see while I was on courtesy staff which had prompted my second hospital suspension.

The general surgeons, however, were grumbling about all the hours they were having to spend covering the emergency room at night and wanted reimbursement. There was an emerging national trend for doctors to receive pay for call.

Shirley Tate could not get her way all the time, no matter how much she surrounded herself with bureaucratic yes men. This time, however, she had to give in.

It was quite hypocritical when Dr. Roland Powers, the chief of the medical executive committee, disseminated a memorandum about how active-staff on-call doctors were not responding to the emergency room requests to come in to see those unassigned (roster) patients and in some cases their own patients. I approached Dr. Powers on the second floor and asked quite directly as I showed him his memorandum:

"Hey, Roland! How come I got suspended for not coming in to the emergency room on my first and only incident with my patient's dislocated total hip, even when it was clearly a nonemergency (as confirmed by Dr. Felix's decision to do nothing for four days for this patient until I got back) and my courtesy staff status at the time did not even require me to take call, and yet nothing happens to these doctors who are on active staff, on call, and still refuse on multiple occasions to come in? How come they never get suspended? Why was I the only one?"

Dr. Power's answer: "Oh, I'll be so glad when I am no longer chief of the medical executive committee."

Yep. That was it. And to rub salt in the wound, at the bottom of my second suspension for my hip patient was the admonishment to all doctors: "This action serves as a precedent for future acts of this nature." In context, this is tantamount to saying that I was singled out, to the exclusion of all others. Was my suspension merely random, capricious, or arbitrary? No. More than that, it was as purely political as it could get. The ultimate in a double standard.

The general surgeons threatened to leave the hospital if they did not get a subsidy or pay for call. I knew something was up when Dr. Tom Romando, the senior partner, approached me in the surgeon's lounge about buying his office, which was next to mine. "Come on, Sterly. Make me an offer."

The general surgeons were finally able to extract a deal to be paid for taking call. This offer was kept secret from all other doctors. In fairness, I don't think that a dermatologist or ophthalmologist should get paid for call, or certainly very little compared to a general surgeon or OB-GYN. In fact, in my sixteen years, I think I saw an ophthalmologist once in the ER at night. I never saw a dermatologist. Even a pathologist gets called in if he had to do a frozen section on an emergency surgery case where for example, a bowel obstruction caused by cancer is encountered, and the surgeon needed confirmation that the specimen is cancer and not infectious abscess before he resected additional bowel. So even the pathologist can get put on the spot in the middle of the night.

The surgeons were paid for call and no one else. Like most secrets, this didn't remain secret forever. Tate, I think in this situation, had no choice but to pay the surgeons, as a general surgeon really is the heart of the hospital. Lose your general surgery service and you become a shell of a hospital. I think the fact that pissed everyone off was that Tate hid this subsidy from the rest of the medical staff, a deception that was well within her comfort zone and her operative level of lying and screwing people over. When a new hospital corporation took over running the hospital three years later in 2013, the general surgeons did finally leave, so I don't think they were bluffing back then when Tate caved in and gave them a subsidy.

Justice Is Hard to Find in a Small Town: Hicks vs. Sterling

One thing did not change between my two states, and that was prevalence of legal incompetence. I was in an uneasy situation where I had for years been hiring my office worker's father Rodney and mother to remodel the upstairs of my house and my office. They had done a good job on both. I also had removed a melanoma off Rodney's hand but never got paid for that.

But then something started happening. We had a verbal agreement that I would pay Rodney and his crew per man by hour worked to add a sunroom foundation and floor on the back of my house. Finally, one of his men took off the whole day (actually to deliver some medical equipment for which he made double compared to his hourly wage), but I was still billed. They started showing up later and later each morning and extended their morning coffee breaks, but continued charging me for hours not worked. It got so bad I had to put my foot down and not pay him for those hours he was not working. He then filed a claim in small claims court.

I filed a counter claim, stating that I had not been paid for my surgery on his hand. Rodney wrote me a check for $5.00 so that I wouldn't turn him in to collections. This is tantamount to admission that he recognized the service I'd performed and his obligation to pay—undisputed evidence.

We appeared in front of this magistrate. Rodney did not dispute my claims that we had a verbal agreement for an hourly wage per man and that he had not been working all the hours had billed me, especially when his worker had skipped a day to deliver medical supplies. His only testimony was that he had been working for thirty years and deserved to get paid what he was owed for his work.

There was no dispute that I had paid him the agreed amount based on the number of man-hours that he and his crew actually worked. The dispute was that I had not paid him the amount for what he was fraudulently billing me. This difference was for $500.00.

In summary, my evidence and testimony were undisputed at the hearing in front of this idiot magistrate. The payment for the medical procedure on Rodney's hand and the note accompanying it explaining reasons for paying such a pathetic initial payment for fear of being sent to collections were un-disputed. Five dollars didn't even cover the cost of the xylocaine needed to numb his hand, much less the other medical supplies, drapes, scalpel, suture, and so on.

Rodney had no evidence, no proof to support his claim. He did not, could not, dispute any of the facts or my testimony. His only testimony was that he "deserved to get paid for what he is owed." Sounds more of my ex-wife Mindy's claim that she expected the court to respect her right to be a full-time mother. There is absolutely no rule of law, no justice. The legal-judicial system is a farce. And here we are supporting these useless idiots through our taxes: district attorneys and police officers who won't investigate/prosecute crimes, worker's comp attorneys who defend employee fraud and theft and then turn right around and award unemployment benefits to these same criminals.

Are you ready for the decision? First of all, this magistrate accused me of being an "educated yet vindictive man", insinuating that I should not be filling this counter claim or refusing to pay Rodney the disputed five hundred dollars.

"I don't think Rodney really owes you for that medical procedure. But I think he has to pay half of the court costs, and you owe him the five hundred dollars." Huh? Not only is this ruling erroneous in that it violates the most fundamental rule of law, it was completely off the wall. We clearly established and it was undisputed that his demand for the five hundred dollars was based on fraudulent billing. If one party has no evidence and does not dispute the evidence of the opposing party, the court cannot rule in favor of the party who has no evidence. If Rodney won the case, why is he paying half the court costs? Quite the inconsistency. You cannot make this stuff up.

This magistrate, like my divorce commissioner, was a complete moron. Rodney never paid another dime of his medical bill.

The Final Months at My Second Position

The federal government (Medicare and Medicaid) forced the use of elec-tronic medical records upon me (as well as other doctors) unless I was willing to accept a penalty in the future for *not* using it. That is the problem when you accept Medicare/Medicaid payment. You are dependent on the government for your income, but then you have to run your practice the way they dictate.

My office had been using software called Lytec for scheduling and billing, and we had been doing fine with that, but now the government wanted to know everything about the patient, what meds, what medical problems, allergies, and even reportedly whether the patient owned any guns. (I never asked or cared.) I figured I would have to get a whole new electronic medical software program if I was planning to stay. The problem was that I really could not make a decision, because I never knew how long I was going to be able to stay in private practice or whether it would be worth it to make the upgrade.

My "trusted" office manager, Amy Hasley, had been mooching raises off me for years and I had treated her very well. Very well. So what did she do? She recommended what turned out to be the most expensive, most useless electronic medical records (EMR) system out there. A five-year lease for $60,000. How do these software sales people work this? A major digression is in order. My opinions are, well, rather unique. Follow closely. The following supplements my remarks about the FED and rogue agencies.

First of all, the politicians (former lawyers) have one goal, and that is to get re-elected so they are protected from having to work in the real word of private, productive enterprise (assuming they are not on the take through no-bid government contracts). Politicians, if they are enterprising enough, can amass their fortunes from government service or bribes. To get re-elected, they have to offer, or appear to offer, free lunches to the voters. Medicare, Medicaid, EBT cards, cell phones, Section 8 housing, government-sponsored school loans, and so on.

The problem is later paying for it. A young demographic and a post–World War II industrial boom, plentiful cheap energy and raw materials, and most of all, world-reserve-currency status standard allowed rapid economic growth. These freebie programs could easily be funded at that time. Soon, spending had grown, especially with the Vietnam war and LBJ's programs.

In 1971 Nixon went off the "honest money" gold standard, which was the clarion call that health-care costs, entitlements, military expenditures, interest on government borrowing, imported oil, and so on, were starting to act as a drag on future growth needed to sustain this Ponzi. For a while the US could make up the difference by borrowing money from China and Japan and getting the OPEC countries to agree to sell oil in dollars in return for US military protection (the petrodollar). OPEC then loaned these dollars back to us by buying our treasuries. Not a bad gig.

If Japan buys oil, they have to make cars, TVs, and sell them to raise cash and in turn exchange the cash for US dollars in order to buy oil, whereas the US could buy oil without having to make anything. We just printed up dollars and bought the oil. This worked for a while, but now these countries are saying no. We want to be paid in gold or hard assets, no more US paper.

So where does the United States get the money now? They (the FED) print it. In short, the baby boomers are getting older and need more health (sick) care. New advances in health-care technology do not decrease health-care expense; they increase it by allowing people to live longer and consume even more health-care. Countries are slowly abandoning the US dollar as the world reserve currency and arranging to do trade with their own currencies. It is only a matter of time when they stop buying US Treasuries. Bottom line, the government can't pay for all this health care.

So now what are the politicians going to do if they have to renege on their promises of "free" health care, especially when the public feels so entitled? The politicians are not going to come out and tell the people, "Sorry, but we have run out of money, and your health care will have to be rationed."

No, they'll say we are going to "cut costs" through, among other things, better management of payments, which can be achieved through electronic medical records (EMR) and electronic hospital records (EHR). This will decrease waste, fraud, and abuse they claim. Pure smoke screen. Never ask if certain legislation will benefit the people. Never. Always ask first: Who in Washington or which big corporations benefit? That is how Washington works.

These EMR and EHR companies have no doubt lobbied Congress to pass these EMR/EHR requirements. It also allows Big Brother to dig into people's personal lives. I am stuck with a financial gun to my head, saying that I have to buy this useless EMR crap. It is junk that no doctor would ever purchase because it theoretically was practical or made "good business sense." It makes practicing medicine a pain in the ass.

The EMR salesman will first work the front office on the easy aspects of the software: the things that your current software already does. Once he has them hooked, then you, the busy doctor, are the last to find out what a piece of crap it is when they start training you for the medical-records-data-entry part. Doctors, never let your office staff near a new software program, or the salesman, until you personally have evaluated the electronic medical record system first. Especially the medical data entry. Most, if not all of them, are complete crap.

No sooner had I signed the contract than the software company sold it to another an investment bank who didn't even know what they had purchased.

They harassed me constantly for payment of property taxes. I tried to explain that since I leased the software, there was no property tax—unlike my computers, x-ray machine, cast saw, and so on. Within a few months, the practice was declining so rapidly, I realized that I had made a huge mistake in buying this software. Amy's salary was approaching mine. It was academic. I had to close the practice and possibly sell or rent the building.

Amy added insult to injury when she later went to work for this company that had sold me this EMR. Later, when I was in my third and final practice, I was contacted by a pediatrics group office manager who was suing this practice management company who'd sold this EMR. I don't know how she got my name. Her group eventually lost the suit in arbitration. She said arbitration would not give any reason for its decision. Of course not. There is no rule of law, only the "necessary" or "convenient" ruling. Attorneys on both sides of this dispute made their money. No health care, patient, or doctor benefit was realized.

Final Quarterly Staff Meeting, June 29, 2011

I finally realized that I had to shut down the practice. As a last desperate measure to get rid of Shirley Tate, I stood up at the end of the meeting. Ordinarily, she was asked to leave at this time so that the staff and board members could speak freely. I asked Tate to stay and listen to what I had to say because I didn't want to talk behind her back.

I stood up and said, "Shirley Tate, you should resign immediately."

She replied, quite Hillary Clintonesquely and condescendingly, "I know you feel that way, Bryce. But that's all right if you want to be angry with me."

I then recited my opinions about how sophomoric was her understanding of the hospital environment, private physicians' practices, her misguided grandiose building spree, and reckless costly recruitment of doctors who came, collected, and left, which had saddled the hospital with enormous debt to the point that it could not be sold and had undermined doctors like me who could not compete against this subsidized competition. I mentioned how our highly regarded neurosurgeon had just resigned. I cited her blatant double standard rescue of Dr. Seymour with creation of a CMO officer position whereas I had been suspended and even exiled for 3 months to the funny farm for far less serious transgressions, and how I had been suspended for a single chewing out a useless registration worker who should have been fired, yet Drs. Mace and Bospy, chiefs of surgery and medical staff respectively, had physically assaulted nurses and yet quite hypocritically signed my suspensions. I went on how she'd tried to frame Dr. Ballance, that she had made secret deals behind the medical staff to pay general surgeons for call and not a penny for anyone else, and so on. Dr. Ballance's husband was sitting beside me and winked with a smile and a subtle nod when I brought up Tate's failed extortion plot.

When I remarked how a properly run hospital nearby (the one I had applied for but was rejected by the Munster CEO) had built up a $90 million reserve to weather the forthcoming storm in contrast to Tate's reckless profligate spending spree, a female board member, who ran an outpatient homecare service for one of the potential bidders, merely responded, "Good."

No discussion about the fact that Tate had financially compromised the hospital with her mismanagement. The board members had been outright enabling Tate through their indifference, incompetence, and ignorance.

Not a single physician at this meeting came to my rescue. They all sat there stone silent like deer in the headlights until finally the chief ER physician, also employed by this administrator, said, "Bryce, I think you have made your point," implying I should stop and sit down. The doctor who later rented my office later stated that I'd stood there and poured gasoline all over myself.

It is unbelievable how the doctors have caved in to the government and corporations. Doctors try to defend our passive tendency by saying that we doctors are too independent to unite against administrators and CEOs who have but a fraction of our training yet have taken control of our livelihoods. Having observed animal behavior on the Serengeti in Africa, I am reminded that doctors act like a herd of wildebeests who continue to graze, oblivious to the fact that a predator has just killed one of their herd, basically, as if to say, glad it wasn't me. Just as the wildebeest is the staple prey for lions, hyenas, wild dogs, and leopards, doctors are the staple prey for the legal profession and big health corporations. In contrast, Cape buffalo will come to the rescue of one of their members, even when attacked by an entire pride of lions.

No. Doctors have lost their profession, not because of their independent spirit and inability to organize, but because they are simply spineless. They are the most insecure, self-centered people out there. They are so afraid of losing a dollar that they will surrender at the drop of a hat. "Physicians have given away their profession," one of my favorite doctors in at my third practice put it succinctly.

I go one step further. I have posted multiple times on medical blogs that doctors have given away their profession just as if they had given away their completely paid-for homes to total strangers, simply because they were asked or threatened, and now have to turn around and rent their homes back. On a more ominous scale, politicians, in their endless quest to preserve their useless, parasitic government jobs, have given away our country to illegal aliens and freeloaders—just for votes. One of my wife's Filipina friends, Leanna, who now works as a house sitter for a hedge fund manager in East Hampton, New York, voted for Clinton because "she allowed her to get her green card and citizenship."

Leanna, Clinton made you think that she was the reason you got into the country. But the truth is the only reason she got you into the country is for the very thing you did: you voted for her. Now that you have voted, she couldn't care less about you—or the country.

A year after I left, my predictions about Tate were realized. The hospital could not be sold, as it had too much debt incurred by a $40 million building project for a new emergency room and surgical suite and the massive financial hemorrhage from employing doctors who would collect and then leave. When Tate started out as CEO, the hospital was reportedly about 40 million dollars in the black. When she was terminated twelve years later, the hospital was reportedly 100 million dollars in the red. This debt had been used in part to subsidize my competition. The news reached me a year after I left that she and the CFO had been suddenly terminated and led out of the hospital under police escort. Scuttlebutt had it that Tate had been trying to hide some of these losses. The hospital reportedly was finally leased with a forty-year contract. I still don't know if this hospital has since broken even. I suppose it might have if it can cost shift to its main hospital, but I don't believe what I read in the papers anymore, so I leave it at that.

Blast from the Past

About one year after leaving this second practice, I was notified by my friends that the new CMO who had replaced Dr. Seymour had been charged with forcing a car off the road and punching the driver in the face. Dr. Tannenbaum did not approve of this guy and threatened to murder him if he didn't stop dating his daughter. Dr. Tannenbaum kept his CMO job at this hospital. I am unaware if he got exiled for three months for anger management as I had been for my trivial offenses, and I don't know anything about the criminal charges. I figure he reached some settlement out of court. There is no report on any action by medical licensure board or entry into the NPDB.

So, let me see: my chewing out a registration worker versus Tannenbaum's reckless endangerment with a vehicle and assault. My failure to come in for a nonemergent recurrent total hip dislocator versus Dr. Seymour's failure to come in for a life-threatening postop epidural abscess. Dare I say double standard? The bottom line: All three of my suspensions had been absolutely unprecedented in this hospital, and probably in any hospital's history, and the severity of which has never been duplicated since. Just like my suspension by the medical board. Unbelievable. But I digress. I am just a disgruntled surgeon.

Sean and Sherri—Whatever Happened to My Children I Gave Up for Adoption?

I had to adjust to life after giving up my children. Their bedrooms in my "more valuable residence" became memorials. They had visited only once from between the time the divorce had been finalized until I finally gave them up for adoption. Ironically, the stress of having to fight the medical-malpractice suit and the licensure-board action drowned out any emotional ties, or at least a lot more than I expected. No formal goodbyes, the last time they visited me. They were about five and three, so psychologically not much impact on them.

I heard a few bits and pieces about Sean. One of Tessie's relatives was a teacher in the public-school system and said Sean was good at math. It was gossiped about how Mindy had managed to screw her ex-husband over so badly that she didn't have to work, even though she was a doctor. Mindy was viewed as an "alimony queen." This "bush hog" commissioner who had replaced the idiot who recused himself had, in my opinion, already determined my sentence and was ready to give everything to Mindy. I had nothing to work with, and I threw up my hands and said, "I'm done."

Again, Skyler had implied through her drafting of the divorce settlement terms, I could get this high level of child support modified after two years. Wrong. Once a level of child support was established, it would be very difficult to get modified without substantial material change in the children's requirements or incomes of the parents. Several thousand dollars in private school tuitions alone would not be sufficient for the court to change the child support payments. In my opinion, Skyler sold me out. She tried to make it palatable by saying that after two years, I could renegotiate to get the amount reduced. But by then, Skyler and Salazar would be long gone.

It could be argued that Mindy had already anticipated a substantial change in my ability to pay for child support at the settlement amount of $2,800 a month. My medical malpractice case and board action rulings were imminent. She may have pressured or tricked Skyler into this "front end load" of higher child support in exchange for a lower more realistic level afterward. It was a can't-lose proposition for Mindy. If I miraculously recovered and continued to earn a high income, I would have been locked in at these high established levels. But, if my income crashed, then I would be able to renegotiate a lower amount anyway. In the meantime, Mindy would have received two years of higher amounts no matter what.

Were Skyler and Salazar aware of these impending medical licensure board and malpractice suit actions to the point that they had actually taken these into account at settlement? It's hard to believe that they were not, but it is glaringly obvious that no provisions for them were made at settlement. In fact, none of my attorneys I used as experts against Skyler and Salazar had even been aware the divorce had been bifurcated. I still don't know whether this sudden ambush settlement was to hide consequences of Salazar's ill-advised bifurcation which may have made these provisions for the malpractice and license board actions moot points. Were they trying to hide these catastrophic consequences of the bifurcation before this issue blew up in the middle of the trial? Mindy and Mitchell sure would have pressed the issue: My practice had already been valued at $630,000 with goodwill that had been assessed and time stamped *before* the bifurcation. The anesthesia event had occurred after the fact. That's too bad if Dr. Sterling's practice is worthless because of something he did after the divorce decree.

All my experts were in disbelief that these issues had not been addressed. As it was, Mindy had been negotiating for child support of $6,000, the same nominal amount I was paying in combined child support ($1,500) and alimony ($4,500). The catch had been, child support was nontaxable to Mindy, so she knew if she could collect this amount, then it would be a full $6,000 a month or $72,000 tax-free, whereas earlier under temporary orders, $4,500 of her temporary alimony was taxable to her, but even at $4,500/month x 12 = $54,000 a year plus declaring two dependents, the tax bill was small, and still covered more than our marital expenses—again, because we had no debt, mortgage, school loan, or car payments and she wasn't working.

The child support was negotiated down to $2,800 a month and no alimony in the final settlement, which was a hell of a lot of money and which Mindy was obviously not spending on the children or paying taxes on. She had argued for higher child support levels based on increased costs of private school tuition. Mindy soon pulled the children from private school and diverted even more money to herself.

I must admit that the public schools where she and her husband lived were good, so a strong argument for not sending them to private school could also be made. But why would Mindy give up all that child support and agree to adoption when she already had total custody control? Again, I think she knew that I was in trouble and that I wouldn't be paying that amount much longer when the two-year obligation was up.

You have to really know Mindy to understand the complexity in her motivation. Mindy is very histrionic, manipulative, and opportunistic. She wants to portray herself as mother and wife of one big happy family, but, on the darker side, she wants to make sure she has her new husband hooked. Obviously, Mindy would have liked to keep the child support payments coming in *and* have another baby, but not because Ben might have wanted his own child. No, Mindy didn't care about Ben's wishes. Having another baby would allow her to reactivate her old ploy: not having to work because she was a full-time mother. The longer Mindy delayed, the more resistant, and wiser, Ben might get.

I wonder if Ben was a little reluctant to have a child of his own so soon. Actually, according to Sherri (a liar, so take it with a grain of salt), Mindy even wanted a fourth but "Ben wouldn't give her one." So maybe Ben was a little hesitant in giving Mindy her third.

The problem was Ben's income was far lower than mine, so there were limits to Mindy's strategy. According to his deposition, Ben had been only coaching the high school cross-country team and drawing on his savings. Mindy's divorce settlement afforded a huge reserve, but eventually someone would have to work.

If Mindy's plan to get pregnant was stalled by Ben's indecision, then she would have to try plan B: get Ben to adopt the children first, lock him in the "father mode" so that having a third child was not such a shock to him, and maybe force him into going back to work, even as I suspect Ben eventually made Mindy realize she would have to go back to work, especially since they would no longer be collecting $2,800 child support.

Ben did not have the earnings capability that would make him vulnerable in a divorce like me, so he had some leverage over Mindy, who clearly had the greater earnings capability. Finally, I think Ben increasingly liked Sean. In contrast, my impression was that he really did not care about Sherri.

It shames me to have to spell out this scenario. Of course, I look like the cold, calculating, selfish father who is only looking to avoid having to pay child support and wanting to give up his children. I argue to look back at all the things I did for our marriage. Every concession, at every step of the way was made by me. Mindy, in contrast, manipulated, lied, and deceived even before we were married.

How are the children supposed to feel if they find out that they are being played as nothing more than financial pawns in a divorce? "Dad doesn't want us because he has to pay money. Mom wants us only because she gets money and doesn't have to work." I hate to admit it, but it was probably better they grew up not hearing me curse their mother for her lying, manipulation, and treachery. I did not handle the divorce well and did not and could not follow the time-honored rule of never disparaging your ex in front of your children.

Sean turned out to be a trophy son. Ben Holcomb, no doubt, was enthused that he was able to convince his stepson to quit soccer and take up track and cross-country, as he and Mindy were runners. My daughter Sherri later related that Sean had been a good soccer player until he switched. Sean's running career was overshadowed by a superb runner from a Catholic private school who, as Sean described, "was in a class all by himself."

However, similarly to how the stars lined up for me for my regional championship wrestling tournament my senior year at college that I won (because other better wrestlers had moved up a weight class 190 pounds and I had moved down to 177 pounds due to weight loss from sickness) Sean won the state cross-country championship his senior year because this top runner did not show up.

Sean went on to run in college, where he got a full academic scholarship but never made it as a top runner, although I quickly add, he was running in NCAA Division I, which is much more competitive than my wrestling at a Division III level. Sean was a national merit finalist. He busted the no-one-gets-a-100-percent-in-organic-chemistry rule at college. He was best speaker/

orator at Duke law school's national moot court competition as a senior in high school. The dean of the law school approached him and asked if he was going to apply to Duke law school. Sean declined, saying he was going into medicine.

Most of this I leaned either online or from my father, who still maintained a little contact. Sean came up to visit him one time. My dad took him to see the movie *Apollo 13*. Mindy and Ben showed up to attend Sean's receiving a $10,000 scholarship award at college. I saw the picture showing the check being awarded. Of course, Mindy would attend that. She would never miss an opportunity to bask in the publicity. She had arranged for the local press (the same newspaper that would later trash me) to feature her in an article about Sherri's birth using epidural anesthesia and her obstetrical anesthesiology specialty as a vehicle to make her the centerpiece of this article, even though childbirth has only happened only about eight billion times before. "Look at me! I'm having a baby. Isn't that amazing?"

Mother of the Year

The most nauseating public display of Mindy's histrionics was her inter-view by the town newspaper shortly after our separation. It was entitled "Women's Career Choices." Everyone cynically called it the "Mother-of-the-Year" article.

The newspaper featured Mindy with her picture of her all dolled up with the kids on either side. The article drew howls from most of the working women I knew at the hospital but especially from my office staff and my partner's wife. Mindy made sure to proclaim, as she had done in court, that "only she could be a mother to her children" and "that she had to be there" for her children (except when she wasn't) because "you never knew when you might miss opportunities for learning, whether it was in the morning, fixing cereal, or after school when they have had a bad day."

She acknowledged that we were separated and that "luckily he gave me some child support/maintenance, as I couldn't have done it all by myself." Then she reiterated that "the children are just extremely important to me." Of course, the father was not important, and I was not mentioned other than I was paying her some maintenance and child support. She didn't admit I was paying for all of it—all-out total support to allow her and the children a higher standard of living than they ever had enjoyed during the marriage while she sat home and did nothing expect train for her newfound running career and date her fellow runners.

She mentioned the concerns that others might think she was wasting her career. But she did not look at it that way. The problem got sticky because it still begged the question: if you have always felt that way, then why did you go through all that training for a career that would preclude you from being a "full time mother"? If you want to spend your time and energy going to medical school, fine, but don't forget: it is also at taxpayers' (including single working mothers) and your ex-husband's expense.

Sean brought home a girlfriend from college whom Mindy did not like. Personally, I thought his high school classmate, who later attended the US Military Academy at West Point, was hot stuff—smart, extremely good looking, vibrant. I told Sean, now there is someone I think you should really check out. Sean responded as if to discard the subject. "She was my prom date," and no other discussion about that.

But I guess nothing clicked, except they reunited in some old barn with other high school classmates in the middle of winter. I saw some of those pictures and others of her skiing out west and on patrol in Afghanistan on Facebook. I think she was interested in Sean, even emailed him out of the blue (this was during the brief time I had a Facebook account), asking how he was doing. He gave a surprisingly curt, almost rude, answer, "Same as always," which surprised me. I never met her, so I can't say anything more.

Sean got accepted into a private prestigious Midwestern medical school, having just missed out on an acceptance, according to him, at Stanford because he did not answer a question in the politically correct way. Sean did well in medical school, got a top-notch residency in diagnostic radiology at another prestigious university, where he just completed his final year there in some kind of fellowship. He seemed to connect with an Indian medical student during medical school, whom he also brought home, and of course whom Mindy disliked, especially that red dot on her forehead, according to Sherri. I guess they maintained their relationship throughout separate residencies, even though they were separated geographically for six years. I heard Sean is going to join her when he finishes residency and fellowship.

I had only two personal contacts with Sean after the divorce. The first was when he visited my home for a weekend his senior year at college. We then visited him in Washington, DC, after he had graduated from college during a summer medical PAC internship before starting medical school. In retrospect, and as I told my wife, I was surprised by his sudden email saying that he wanted to see me after all these years. I figured for once, he must not have had a single other thing to do that weekend.

I flew him to my home. Not much clicked between us, I guess. After Washington, I made one more mention of a possible visit at medical school. He said he would make time for me if I came to visit him. "Make time for me?" Sorry to be such an imposition, Sean. Not much follow-up except very super-ficially via email. He emailed me the link to the video of his graduating class residency choices, where he announced his as diagnostic radiology.

The only other time he emailed me occurred an hour after Mindy, after twenty years, suddenly called me up out of the blue.

"Bryce. This is Mindy. I am sorry to bother you." To which I responded, "I'll bet you are." I hung up. Mindy would *never* call me unless she wanted something. It had been a marriage of incessant manipulation and treachery. What in hell could she possibly want now? Actually, I already knew. When visiting him in Washington, DC, Sean had informed me that Sherri was in trouble.

I asked, "Is Sherri pregnant?"

Sean answered with a smile, almost a laugh. "Yes."

About an hour later after Mindy's call, Sean emailed me, warning me about Sherri and not to help her. Mindy had contacted Sean to tell me not to help Sherri financially, and Sean was carrying every drop of Mindy's water. I could no longer trust him, and I think he too has been poisoned by Mindy. There has been no further contact between us. It has now been over ten years.

Sherri's boyfriend, Steve, was in jail. Mindy had him arrested for stealing her jewelry. They needed money for bail. Sherri hadn't contacted me for all these years. Now suddenly she needed money. Problem is, whom do you trust? Was Mindy trying to control Sherri, or was Sherri lying? I had already sent the money before Mindy or Sean contacted me. Bailing out Steve had at least thwarted Mindy's revenge.

Basically, Sherri had been stealing her mother's jewelry and giving it to her boyfriend to pawn, classic drug-addict behavior. During the divorce, Mindy started buying and hoarding clothes. Now Mindy had become a full-fledged jewelry hoarder. There was not a single piece of jewelry in all the stores in the city or for sale on eBay that she wouldn't buy. She would even buy multiples of the same thing, according to Sherri and Steve. Steve probably had a better inventory of what Mindy had purchased than Mindy. On one of Mindy's eBay accounts that Steve emailed me, she had spent $10,000 in one month on jewelry. Mindy had not guarded her passwords very well.

Mindy was making the rounds at the jewelry stores and pawn shops and suddenly recognized a piece of jewelry she had purchased was back on the store shelf. She had not first realized it was missing from her collection at home. In fact, according to Sherri, between her clothes and jewelry, Ben had to build an addition onto their house.

This sudden explosion in clothes and jewelry purchases was the behavior I had noticed immediately after Mindy and I separated. When I snuck back into our marital residence one evening, the closet was stuffed full of new clothes with the price tags dripping from them. I videotaped it for the divorce. Mindy was now a certifiable hoarder, and her bank-account burn rate confirmed this.

Even my child-custody LCSW expert admitted she saw Mindy in action one day at a clothing store, gravitating toward the most expensive item on the racks. Mindy wouldn't even wait for the sales price. Sherri informed me that Mindy would buy an item on the spot and then later return it with the price tag still attached and reacquire it at the new lower price. She had to have it now, even if she did not intend to wear it.

Mindy proceeded to file charges against Steve for felony theft, and later against Sherri as accessory to felony theft. Sherri claims she was imprisoned pregnant and with morning sickness. Sherri is such a liar I don't know if she was telling the truth.

Sherri and Steve drove to visit me with their three-year-old daughter. It was basically a ploy to weasel more money out of me. Steve was a pathetic piece of shit loser, a heavy smoker with a chronic hacking cough already, an OxyContin addiction, a little twerp about five three. Of course, they promised they would pay me back because they were going to sue Mindy for false arrest and so on. Their lawyer dropped them as soon as I stopped paying his bills.

I had given Sherri explicit instructions that if I helped her, she would promise *not* to get pregnant again. She had to go back to school for her nursing degree, and Steve would finish his tech degree. (BTW, these are bogus degrees issued by bogus schools.) I knew how treacherous and controlling Mindy could be, and a lot of things Sherri mentioned were very consistent with what I knew about Mindy. I felt that I should give them a chance, even if it was very risky. I had shut down my office and was not working, so I would have to raid my retirement funds. In the end, I expended $200,000 trying to help them. Every week, Steve and Sherri would have some new crisis for which they needed more money—lawyer's bills, their apartment broken in, their dogs injured and needed money for vet bills, money to buy back their laptop they had pawned because not only did it have sensitive data they claimed that could be used against them, but also because they needed money. Then suddenly Sherri needed money to get her teeth fixed (probably from all the crystal meth). When Steve emailed me, he texted, "Hey Bryce, give me a call." That was the last straw.

Can you believe the disrespect this little shit had? "Hey, Bryce"? Not "Hi, Dr. Sterling," or "Hi, Bryce." No. It was "Hey, Bryce." I emailed him back: "Steve, don't ever address me as 'Hey.' Furthermore, I cannot, and will not, give you any more money. Now is there any other reason you contacted me?"

I then laid it all out and recited all the ways they had been lying to me. They had visited me only to plead for more money and then turned right around the next day claiming Steve had a new Computer Assisted Design (CAD) project he had to go work on, which was complete BS. They suddenly left because Sherri was having severe morning sickness. We learned a few days later she was pregnant again and that was probably why they had to suddenly leave.

Sherri and Steve never gave me a word of thanks. I never heard back from either of them again. I later learned from the court notices and my wife Vangie who talked briefly with Sean on Facebook, that Sherri had later been arrested for felony embezzlement at her job.

I had contact with Steve's stepdad and mom who later got custody of their two children. He reported Steve had gotten off the drugs. The second baby had been born with some drug residual, so Sherri apparently was a druggie too. Sherri was also reportedly getting counseling, which in my opinion, is a complete waste of time and money. It is politically correct but not medically correct, not even an effective band aid. She was also collecting tattoos. "God will not lead me *to* what he will not lead me *through*" was inked onto her spine.

I had not seen Sherri or pictures since her adoption. I saw the first pictures of Sherri as a senior in high school on the soccer team. I could not recognize her because she was so obese. She had inherited Mindy's "fat gene" (Mindy's description). But she also inherited things far worse: Mindy's self-centeredness, lying, treachery, manipulation, and sense of entitlement.

Sherri claims she maintained a solid B+/A- average in high school, but not straight A's like Sean. Sherri, despite her weight, made the all-state soccer team her senior year, which I confirmed from online sports reports. So, what went wrong despite the problem with her weight, which no doubt socially and psychologically hampered her? My guess is that, unlike Sean, Sherri was definitely not a trophy daughter, so neither Ben nor Mindy gave her much, if any, attention or love. Sherri quickly remarked that there was no love between Mindy and Ben. In fact, Sherri claimed they had an open marriage, which would not be surprising, as Mindy was seen openly and flagrantly carrying on with her runner friend, Jerry Jacobs, which initiated my decision to file for divorce.

It was very interesting that Sherri produced that information without knowing the specifics of my divorce. She also confirmed that Mindy was a full-fledged hoarder, with barely enough room to walk around in the house due to the piles and boxes of clothes sitting around the house. It was interesting to hear her first unprompted remark when she entered my and Vangie's house: "Wow! There is actually room to walk around here." She said there was even a bat's nest in one stack of Mindy's clothes.

I am sure Mindy had arranged to spend the money she earned on things she wanted. Just like during our marriage, it was a what's-yours-is-ours-and-what's-mine-is-mine arrangement.

Sherri claimed she was even imprisoned while she had been pregnant with her second child, again out of wedlock by Steve, after I had given them over $60,000 to bail Steve out, and got Sherri started back into nursing school where she stated she had planned on becoming a certified registered nurse anesthetist (CRNA). Of course, this never happened.

I didn't believe the bail had been set at $60,000. For stealing and pawning a few pieces of jewelry? I called the police and the prison to verify that Steve was incarcerated, and the officer or clerk said, "Yes, bail was set at $60,000." I don't know if that guy at the prison or the bail office knew what he was talking about or if Mindy and Ben had influence with the DA. I don't trust any of them: law enforcement, judges, lawyers. Not one bit. But I was caught between conflicting emotions. I wanted to help Sherri and give her a second chance that I'd never had.

I figured that there was a good chance she and Steve were lying, especially after having seen some of these drug-user losers first hand at the funny farm. They were magnificent liars. Finally, I have to admit that I got a little satisfaction out of thwarting Mindy, who was furious that this little slime ball Steve had been snitching her jewelry.

The lesson I learned was that Mindy, her family, Sean, and Sherri are toxic. Sean was clearly obeying Mindy and keeping me at distance, even though he must have had some idea of the type of person his mother was. Mindy was so treacherous because you only realized it after was too late. So, in my opinion, Sean made the choice for our estrangement, not I. I do not trust him. I don't like him. After his last email, I vowed never to contact him again, and I think it is a good decision. The farther I get away from that clan, the better off I am.

Even if the two grandchildren tried to contact me, I would refuse to have any communication with them, as I could never be certain that Sherri was not using them. The problem, especially with Sherri, is that she is a liar and manipulator like her mother. Sherri indeed had a lot of insight about Mindy. Sherri is smart, had an IQ of 131, which was one point higher than Sean's. (He was shocked when I told him that. Their IQ tests were done as part of the custody evaluation.)

So, whom do you believe? Mindy or Sherri? Liar number one or liar number two? I think back again to the 1962 movie *Mutiny on the Bounty*. Fletcher Christian was listening to two sailors on the loading dock, accusing each other of having stolen one of the cheeses. (In the movie, it was later learned that Captain Bligh had taken it.) Fletcher Christian (Marlon Brando) listened patiently and inquisitively as the accusations flew back and forth. Then Captain Bligh (Trevor Howard) approached and asked what was the problem. After Christian explained, Bligh admonished his first officer: "Mr. Christian, taking one man's word against another's is a fool's errand. Simply cut the rations until the deficiency is made up." Classic. I was the fool. I had taken both Mindy's and Sherri's word at the outset. The solution was simply to have nothing to do with either of them. Ever. The latest I heard via Facebook rumor was that Sherri and Steve had broken up.

My Start of Travel

After breaking up with Tessie in 1999, I went scuba diving in the Philippines. I had been to the Barrier Reef and Fiji. Vangie and I met in Cebu on a scuba diving boat. She was along for a ride to see the sights with her cousins. This German and I were the only people diving. After the dives, I took Vangie and her cousins out for lunch and was presented a bill for four hundred. At first, I said, "What? Four hundred dollars for four people?"

"No, Bryce, that's four hundred pesos, sir. The exchange is fifty pesos to the dollar. That's only eight dollars, sir."

"Oh. Okay!" I said with delight (like Jon McEnroe's car rental ad when he found out he could seriously choose any rental car he wanted in the car rental lot). Vangie, her cousins, and I crammed into the back seat of a taxi to go shopping. They were jabbering away in one of the dialects, either Ilongo, where they grew up, Cebuano, where they were currently living, or Tagalog, the unified national Philippine language.

"What are you all talking about?" I asked Vangie. She chatted a few seconds, and then they all burst out laughing. She said, "They think you are very handsome." Damn! No one had ever said that to me before. Some cynics would say they say that to all the foreigners because they have money. I didn't care, because for once, I really didn't care—about anything.

I realized, hey, you know, when I am here, I forget all about my troubles back home. They don't worry about anything here. And they even think I am handsome, even though I am twenty-two years older than they are. In fact, when I went to the Super Mall (SM) in Cebu, my fourteen-year-old niece-in-law accompanied me to the optical shop to get me a few pairs of reading glasses.

The saleslady asked me where I was from, where I was staying, for how long, and what part of the States, and so on. When I replied, she gave a response to indicate she knew where that was and, to keep the conversation going, matter-of-factly asked, "And this is your wife?"

Whoa! Bem-Bem was only fourteen, four ten, and very pretty, but in the Philippines, no one batted an eye at such an obscene age discrepancy.

Years later, I told an anesthesiologist at my third practice who had never been married that it would be impossible to stay married if you went to the Philippines to retire. There was so much temptation at every turn. I could not even go into the record store without getting approached by three or four very young uniformed sales girls showing me various CDs.

"Man, talk about the hard sell," I later told Vangie.

"No, dear, they were not trying to sell you a CD."

Wow.

I returned to Philippines two more times in 1999, and I was convinced that I wanted to retire there. Vangie, of course, wanted to go to the United States. Either way, we stuck together: Vangie having grown up in a hut with ten brothers and sisters with three of them now dead because of lack of money and medical care, and essentially no education, now struggling in the big city like so many who leave the rice or sugar farms to search out the lure of the big city, and me, a washed-up doctor, trying to find refuge in some corner of the earth, having been burned by American women, my lawyers, my professional peers, the courts, and resolving never to have nothing to do with any of them if I could help it.

I explained from the outset to Vangie that I had had a vasectomy in 1992 and that I could not give her children. A few years later, Dr. Marvin Mace, that urologist who spearheaded my three probations later told me that since I was near fifty and had the vasectomy years ago (right after my divorce), my chances for reversal were poor.

Vangie came over on a fiancée visa, which placed a ninety-day deadline on marriage; otherwise she would have to return to the Philippines. Talk about rushing things. We got married by the magistrate and signed some legal documents. No formal wedding but Vangie was absolutely ecstatic with the rings I gave her, in contrast to Mindy's disappointment.

About three years into our marriage, Vangie pleaded for a child. To show her good faith, I agreed to get a reversal, knowing in my mind that, based on Dr. Mace's opinion, it would be probably have been unsuccessful and therefore a waste of money and more heartbreak. I saw a urologist at a big institution, and had the reversal (vasovasostomy).

While I was in the surgical holding room, an Indian urology resident came up and introduced himself and said he was going to assist. His quiet presence had a spiritual quality about it. I have never gotten over it. It was as if he already knew that I would father the daughter of my dreams. I still have his unfilled pain med prescription he wrote for me.

Sure enough, even before the follow-up office visit, Vangie was pregnant. I called the urologist's office and told the secretary to cancel the appointment. She asked if there was a problem or if I wanted to reschedule.

"Don't need to. My wife is already pregnant." The medical system has been so good to me-as a patient. I later had bilateral total hip replacements for advanced arthritis. Again, another godsend. Here medicine has done so much for me, but not for Arthur Smith or some of my patients who did not have good outcomes. It lays a guilt trip on me, and I try not to think about it.

I now get anxious thinking about what my life would have been like had my daughter not been born. She is generous, kind, ethical, giving, obeys her parents, and so on, the exact opposite of Mindy and Sherri. I only wish that Vangie and I could have had more kids, but time was closing in. I was fifty, and my situation very uncertain. I am also anxious that under my constant duress, I could still screw up the raising of my daughter. She is not being brought up in a happy family.

More Doldrums and Anxiety

Closing my second practice in 2011 reintroduced those old familiar anx-ieties of life as a medical refugee. This time, I was finally able to get an employed position in the South in July 2012. One year had elapsed since I'd performed my last surgery. I interviewed in March 2012 and applied for a state license. The location was the classic, tired old river town. I got all my ham radio ratings and would sit and watch the barges ply up and down the river, while I worked contacts from all over the country and even a few overseas.

My first impressions were, of course, that the town could not support two hospitals. It was a dying town. Industry had moved out, and the tax base was drying up. The middle school was ninety years old and badly in need of refurbishing.

Still, I took a liking to the place, especially the auditorium where my daughter performed ballet and the yearly production of *The Nutcracker*. The instructor was great. I get goose bumps when I hear the Arabian Dance and was able to watch my daughter dance to it. She was able to perform the dance as required: slowly, deliberately, and controlled. Great flexibility and balance were required.

We liked that location more than we ever thought we would, and here I had told recruiters that the area I least liked would be the Deep South. How wrong I was. The doctors and administration treated me much better than at my previous locations. There was one big problem: I had been promised, or at least reassured, that I would be the only orthopedist. I was concerned already that there were two hospitals with one orthopedist at the more popular, it seemed, private hospital. I was concerned, as before, that there was not enough work for two orthopedists at this second county owned hospital. I, therefore, asked everyone the question three ways: (1) I will be the only orthopedist here? "Yes," (2) Dr. Higgins is leaving? "Yes," (3) and Dr. Danneker, the *locums tenum* (the temporary doctor), who recently left after finishing his contract, is not coming back? "Correct."

At the time, I thought I had a chance at the VA hospital where I'd grown up and, therefore, thought I might have a choice, but I did not have time to wait to find out. The Veterans Administration hospital, in usual form, was very slow in getting its act together.

It was academic. I had to take in this position in the South because I might not get another chance. It was the only other position willing to consider me after hundreds of contacts and endless excuses and explanations to recruiters who usually said they would get back to me, but never did. If the recruiter was an in-house recruiter, that is, one employed by that hospital, then he or she might take more time with you because they were not paid on commission rather an hourly wage or salary and would be more likely to consider all candidates.

The commission-only boiler room recruiters from recruiting firms understandably had a different incentive. They were paid by their client hospital only when that doctor was successfully recruited. It would not take long for the experienced commission-based recruiters to determine how much time to invest on a doctor who had as much baggage as I, because it was unlikely that the hospital would accept me. They would usually say they'd get back to me, but of course it never happened.

We didn't sell our home because I really didn't have a good feeling about this new position. How long would we be able to stay? If the practice didn't stabilize, we would have to return home, where it might take a long time to find another job, if ever again. This new job was different in that it was paying me a salary guarantee with a production bonus. No more solo private practice. I too had been finally forced to follow increasing numbers of doctors, now a majority, who have thrown their hands up trying to run a private practice with all the regulations and insurance billing hassles. But a guarantee is good for only so long. In the end, you have to produce. You have to justify your salary. Much of my job with was data input into the computer. Peck, peck, peck. I had finally evolved into a full-fledged computer data-entry clerk.

Most doctors can't appreciate my predicament with relocating. Usually, while they are working their current job, they can plan, research, visit, and choose another position. They can make a controlled exit from their current job after they have secured a license, malpractice insurance, and hospital privileges. Sometimes they already have a buyer for their house. The transition is smooth and relatively low anxiety. After all, you in theory are leaving a bad place and relocating to a better position.

My situation was always high anxiety. I was always trying to leave my second practice where I had been struggling from day one due to administrators' beliefs that I was inadequate or that the town should support at least three orthopedists and thus the need to recruit additional orthopedists. Orthopedic surgeons bring a ton of money for the hospitals, so administrators were always trying to add orthopedists to their staff.

The problem is, if they have too many, those in private practice get hurt first because they have to cover their overhead, and if they can't, they may be forced to leave. To attract and keep employed orthopedists on staff in the smaller towns, the hospitals often had to subsidize them. However, if the physicians didn't produce by the second or third year, the hospital started losing money, as my hospital did, especially if those physicians left. My third and final orthopedic practice location ran into the same problem. It lost money on the orthopedists individually and collectively.

While waiting for my state license, the hospital's medical foundation director, Diane Givens, called me at home asking when I was getting my license as they had all these total joints waiting and Dr. Danneker didn't do total joints.

"Wait. Stop! Dr. Danneker is there? I thought he had left. I was told flat out by multiple sources that he was *not* returning." I asked anxiously, "Diane, are you *sure* that this hospital can support two orthopedic surgeons?"

"Definitely" was her one-word response.

This really distressed me. It looked like that I was about to get caught up in the same old problem all over again. Why do administrators always try to pile on the recruitment? Why don't they let one physician get established first before adding a second, and only when there is a demonstrated need for the second physician, or the first needs relief from call, or if the one they have hired is a dud and needs to be let go, and so on? The rumor was that this administrator got a bonus for every physician he recruited, so that certainly may have been an incentive.

I was then informed that this hospital had just emerged from bankruptcy. It certainly showed the signs of financial distress. The equipment was broken, worn out, missing. The building was old, and it was generally acknowledged that it was beyond renovation and a new hospital was needed. Emergency portable air condition units had to be brought in. The units were placed outside with huge white snake tubes connecting to the second floor. Operating rooms frequently had to be closed because of excess heat or humidity. The billing department was totally mismanaged and the hospital was hemorrhaging uncollected money. The news was relentless about all the financial problems and mismanagement, and how the hospital lawyer was accused of keeping the hospital mired in financial distress ("fleecing") so that his services would remain in perpetual need.

The hospital soon foundered again and entered a second bankruptcy, and was finally acquired by a hospital chain that had also purchased the neighboring private hospital earlier. This private hospital had been run by another chain who had been investigated for billing fraud. My county owned hospital successfully sued its management company for mismanagement. An undisclosed amount, rumored to be $13–18 million, was reached, which was just enough to pay off the debt.

Against this background, I was just waiting for the clock to run out. I hoped that I could make it at least three years. I almost made it for four, and I covered more ground there financially than I would have in fourteen years had I stayed at my second practice. I certainly didn't buy a house, and several people asked why I continued to rent such a modest apartment. My urology colleague there could certainly vouch for my concerns. He had worked there for six years, and had been let go a few months earlier. He had difficulty selling his house, still unsold after dropping the price, and reportedly was considering mailing the keys back to the bank.

Even after the merger/buyout, the patient numbers continued to decline. The corporation pumped a lot of money into refurbishing the hospital, but I think all the bad publicity continued to drive the numbers down. Total joint replacements are the flagship procedure for a hospital's orthopedic surgery program. It is elective, often times heavily advertised, but it is difficult to keep the patients from seeking out the big city "Mecca" for joint replacement surgery. I had been recruited to do total joints, but since my specialty was one of the most susceptible, I was hit very hard, and the hospital had to let me go. My replacement is a doctor from a neighboring town who comes in twice a month to do a few joints.

It did not matter that I had tried to do everything that the hospital asked. My partner would not use the EMR or computer-dictation system. He had someone else do traditional transcription and another to do data entry. He refused to take the rehab medical director position, which I took. (No one else would take it.) That rehab unit also was in trouble and had to deal with ongoing Medicare overpayment claw backs.

While I was there, I steadied it through two different management companies, and it finally received a full three-year Commission on Accreditation of Rehab Facilities (CARF) accreditation. I spent a lot of time and effort with it. It did not matter. No consideration was given for that. I was given three months' notice.

I was desperately trying to get a new job during this time, and the only one that came thorough was in rural New England. The in-house physician recruiter, a semiretired OB-GYN, was able to look through my history and realize that I had been put through the ringer, but he didn't first screen me with the state mutual insurance company, the exclusive insurer for the hospital, or the physicians on the credentialing committee. I took time out to interview and was called back for a second site visit and house hunting with my wife and daughter. I spent many hours and hundreds of dollars applying for medical-malpractice insurance, a state license, and hospital privileges. This time I had to also apply through the Federation Credentialing Verification Service (FCVS), a new national unified credentialing service that would benefit young doctors who might have to apply multiple times during their careers, but was of absolutely no use to me on my final stop. I also had to fill out a supplemental individual application for the state. A new agency seemed to pop out of the woodwork at every corner to capitalize on the application process. I would have to call hospitals and state medical boards and request verification of my stay at each facility and my licenses. Most of these were at additional cost.

The problem was also that I had accumulated a lot of baggage during my career that made each application an enormous burden. Each application had a new twist and required new information, whether for the VA, the Army, Indian Health Service or a regular civilian position. The key points for any doctor stepping out into practice today:

1. Get out of debt as quickly as possible. It adds another source of anxiety you don't need. It limits your ability to be flexible.

2. Do not buy a house, or if you do, buy a very inexpensive one that you can resell very quickly. If you are employed by a hospital, you can almost count on the hospital administrator knowing your banker from the weekly rotary club meetings. Nothing is more reassuring to a hospital administrator than hearing a new doctor has three kids, $250,000 in outstanding school debt, and has a $400,000 mortgage on his house. You, the freshly minted doctor, are stuck. The hospital can squeeze you by adding extra duties, meetings you have to attend, extra numbers of patients to see, and so on. Doctors' only defense these days is to be mobile. Don't waste energy and lawyer fees fighting. A doctor versus a hospital is almost as juicy a case for a lawyer as a divorce. Doctors are no longer the lions; we are now wildebeests who will not stand up for members of our herd who are attacked, and whose only defense now is to flee. It is ironic: if you work a minimum-wage job at McDonalds, you don't have to leave the area if you lose your job. You can quickly pick up another one locally. But if you are an executive or a doctor and you have to quit your job, unless you are in a very large metropolitan area, it can often be very difficult to stay in town and find an equivalent high-paying job. Noncompete clauses in the event of a physician's termination are no longer necessary or enforced, since a lot of hospitals own the referral market. If you are not with them as part of the herd, you are the solitary wildebeest and cannot survive. In contrast, a lawyer can screw up all day long and stay in the area. He is unlikely to get reprimanded by or censured by his bar association. He can move

to another firm or office in the same town without missing a step. His incompetence or negligence never reaches public awareness. Try going to a lawyer's website. You won't see descriptive consumer-satisfaction ratings or scores. Now go to a doctor's website or Google his name. You are immediately directed to sites like Health Grades, which allow patients to rate and comment on their doctors like me: "I wouldn't send my cat to him," a "buffoon," "misdiagnosed my fibromyalgia." Usually, these sample sizes are small, and more likely these ratings are weighted with dissatisfied patients. Some, in contrast, are clearly fudged with unanimous 4 1/2 or 5 star ratings for each and every physician at the hospital. Yeah, right!

3. Keep meticulous records of everything in your career with emphasis on quick recovery and production. Your board scores and ID number, your licenses, medical school transcripts, even from high school and college, any lawsuits and so on. You will have to be able to dig them up on short notice and for multiple applications, whether for licenses or provider insurances—or at least until health care becomes single payer. I was not organized, which is why my applications were such a hassle, the sheer volume of my baggage notwithstanding, and also, because some of my records were old and existed before the age of computerized recordkeeping/scanning and email.

4. Consider keeping a continuous, low-key lookout for two or three job opportunities and, to that end, applying for and keeping one or maybe two additional state licenses (which admittedly costs money in annual renewal fees) but which will allow you to act more quickly in case you need to bail on your current job. On the other hand, it is definitely a hassle having too many licenses. Probably three is about ideal. The downside is, of course, if you decide to let a license lapse; then you need to notify other licensure boards who might assume that you have done something wrong and are surrendering your license.

5. Don't own or collect a lot of crap. If you have to move, it really slows you down. Trust me on this one. My junk owns me. Travel more instead. My various travel experiences throughout the world have left me with a far greater sense of fulfillment than any fancy house, boat,

or car. Learn skills instead: flying, scuba diving, ham radio, musical instrument. Make sure they're portable. I got heavily into reef aquariums with thousand-gallon setup, ozone generator, huge protein skimmer, calcium reactor, four-hundred-watt metal halide and actinic lamps, forty-five kW backup generator to run all the Iwaki 70RLT pumps and lights, computer, Carlson surge device/wavemaker, and so. Really got into it. But no sooner did I get it all set up than I had to leave it all behind. Can't take that amount of junk with you as a refugee.

Another Dead End

The New England hospital recruiter suddenly informed me July 17, 2016, that my contract had been rescinded. The malpractice carrier was also about to (unofficially) reject me despite the recruiter personally having met with the CEO of the malpractice company to plead my case, but to no avail. The hospital credentialing committee, probably following the lead of the insurance company, was set to reject me as well. Why hadn't he checked this out before offering me a contract, having me make two visits and go through an exhaustive application process? What a dumb twit. Unbelievable. Well, I guess my wife and daughter at least got to see the maple sugar harvest in full swing that spring with all the blue tubing lines, buckets and the stills running full blast.

But now, this rescind meant more emergency damage control. I scrambled to call the state medical board and insurance company to withdraw my applications before I got official denials that would then be added onto the data bank. Certainly, no need for the license now as there were no other offers in the state, or even in the most remote places you have never heard of, like Caribou, Maine, or Truth or Consequences, New Mexico.

I guess the only good thing that came out of the New England position was that it made the departure from my third practice more psychologically tolerable. Imagine having to load a twenty-six-foot U-Haul, drive it back half-way across the country, unload, fly back and make two more trips if you didn't think you had a job waiting for you. It would have been a seemingly endless "Trail of Tears". Thinking that I had the job in New England sure relieved a lot of anxiety- but not all. Medical boards just don't realize the devastation they can wreck upon a physician's life. They simply don't care.

I also had an interview in two other small hospitals in New England the week following my initial interview with this rescinded position. This was a combined interview in which two small hospitals would employ me. It would involve an hour of traveling from a central area, which was close to a major college town.

This was definitely worth a look, especially if I could live near the college. The problem was that the administrator at the first hospital immediately lost interest when my medical license suspension and malpractice baggage came up. He started yawning and looking at his watch, and he was very relieved at the sight of me recognizing his sudden loss of interest and my abruptly concluding the interview. It was an even more swift exit from the second hospital interview. After about five minutes, even before I mentioned my baggage, she was already looking to stop. I figured the administrator at the first hospital had already called her and told her I was a no-go. Why hadn't they vetted me a little more thoroughly before inviting me for an interview?

We had been all set to make the move to New England. Everything had been lined up and waiting. Even the rental truck had been scheduled. This time we were not going to take as much junk. Only one truckload, max. And then, *wham*! The call came from the hospital recruiter, and suddenly everything crashed. People don't understand the disruptions that follow you through your life, how relentless they are, and how negatively they impact your family and career as a medical refugee.

I had wasted over three months on this New England dead end, and then had to suddenly start yet another application for another VA position, which, in retrospect, I should have been doing concurrently, but it was in a very un-desirable part of the country. I would not have to apply for any new license because to work in the VA hospital system—a license from any state is suffi-cient. Furthermore, insurance is already provided.

I applied to various VA hospitals. I got one phone interview at a very desirable position that I knew I would never get. I would have given my eye-teeth to have been accepted there, but it was for director of the department. I did not realize at that time how remote my chances were for any opportunity with the government. They were courteous as they phone interviewed me conference-call style with several people, including a nurse and physician's assistant who asked politically correct questions like "How many disagreements have you gotten into during your medical career, and how did you resolve them, and were you successful?"

They sent me a post interview email notifying me of their decision to go with another candidate, and wished me continued success with my *professional life*. Actually, they disguised their decision stating that it came down to two candidates. Quite cynically, they didn't mention how many other candidates there were. Of the other ten or so that may have applied, I was probably dead last.

I finally applied to this VA position in a small hospital near the Mexican border. The chief of staff and in charge of the orthopedic surgery recruitment was an anesthesiologist. She understood thoroughly what had happened with my license suspension and said emphatically she had no problem with it. I suspect they were very hard up for an orthopedist. She and I emailed each other back and forth, and she called me several times. She informed me via email that I "was getting excellent references." Within a few weeks, I received an acceptance letter for the position with instructions to get paperwork, medical exam, blood tests, fingerprints, urine drug screen and so on at a VA close to my home—the one where I had been rejected five years earlier.

In the meantime, I had also applied to the Indian Health Service (IHS). Again, quite a bit of paperwork. It was similar to the VA, which had a universal national application, plus a hospital-specific application that required me to go to the courthouse to get some additional court records copied from one of my malpractice cases. The application process never ended. Each position it seemed had a new wrinkle, for example, who was the plaintiff's attorney and what was his address on the each of the malpractice claims, even those that were dropped. I had to submit the copy of the actual complaint or claim, not just the case number, court address, title of the case, when it was filed, when it was closed or settled, and so on, for the IHS application.

I waited and waited for the IHS decision. I spoke with the director of the human resources at the IHS several times concerning the application. The other orthopedist there wouldn't return my call, and I wound up accidentally calling his wife who was temporarily carrying her husband's phone that day. She knew nothing about any recruitment. After about a month, I called the recruiter a final time and asked her point blank whether I was even being considered. I had expended a lot of time and effort with that application. Only then did she inform me that I had already been rejected because of my record. She hadn't even bothered to inform me of my rejection. I had to pry it out of her. Wow, after all the talk I have heard about the desperate need for providers in under-served areas like the Indian reservations, for them to reject me like that was the ultimate indignation. I still remembered a pediatrician's very kind words to me from my third position: "Gee, Bryce, a small town like that (the one in New England) would be very lucky to have you."

It was down to this VA to determine whether I would ever work in orthopedics again. Too old for the military at sixty-one with the cut-off age fifty-eight, too old to work overseas with the cut off at age sixty. No offers from hundreds of small hospitals throughout places like Truth or Consequences, New Mexico; Glendive, Montana; Arkansas City, Kansas; and various other places no one has ever heard of.

To exhaust my search, I even contacted hospitals in Appalachia. They rejected me, quite coldly. The administrators and secretaries were all giddy at first at the prospect of a white, American-trained, board-certified orthopedist. They promised they would keep in close contact with me and so on. But after two weeks, I got the run around from the secretary that the administrator was still working on my application. I never heard from them again, even after my third and final follow-up call to them. Not even a "thanks, but we were unable to consider you."

I knew that I was in serious trouble by that time.

And Then, the End

Rescind of Tentative Job Offer read the email:

Dear Dr. Sterling,

I regret to inform you that I have to rescind the tentative job offer for the Orthopedic Physician at the HCS.

Based on the VHA 1100.19 P. 19, paragraph (d), which states that … those healthcare professionals who have a current, full and unrestricted license in one or more States, but who currently have or have ever had a license, registration, or certification restricted, suspended, limited, issued and/or places on probation status, or denied upon application, must not be appointed without a thorough documented review. The credentials file must be reviewed with Regional Counsel, or designee, to determine if the practitioner meets appointment requirement.

Regretfully, the Regional Counsel has determined that your Credentials File does not meet the appointment requirements.

Thank you for your interest in working at the Department of Veterans Affairs.

For some reason, I immediately recalled how Forest Gump took it so calmly when Jenny, his childhood sweetheart, returned home to Alabama as an adult and visited him, only to suddenly leave him cold, again, for the life of a hippy. "And just like that, she was gone."

And just like that, my orthopedic career was over. Metaphorically, I had now been cast in a lifeboat drifting farther and farther from the orthopedic coastline. I would never see it again. Any sporadic recruiter calls I would receive in the future would be like passing ships way off on the horizon that would never see me. For a few months, I had been taking walks around the middle school walking path to think things over and ruminate. That day, I road my bicycle over to the middle school soccer fields. No mercy. The sheriff intercepted me and asked me for identification. As an adult, I was not permitted to ride my bicycle though the school parking lot on my way to the walking path during school hours. Forget about all the property taxes I had been paying since 1995.

I received the usual dead-on-arrival recommendations from my friends. They suggested working in the Indian Health Service, becoming an instructor at a medical school, or working from home as a case reviewer doing reviews of insurance forms or peer-to-peer reviews for insurance companies. These reviews would involve assessing whether a patient could be admitted to a rehab hospital instead of a skilled nursing facility (SNF). This latter job would be turning the tables on my colleagues. In the past, I had always been annoyed when some doctor, not even in my specialty and who had never seen the patient, would decide over the phone whether certain care could be authorized (paid for) by his insurance company.

With my licensure-board and malpractice record, I could not qualify for even this type of job. My opinion would not stand up to thorough scrutiny/challenge. I would not, could not, be recognized as an expert. These agencies required applicants have a clean record in order to get the required multiple state licenses. I talked to my trusted orthopedic sales rep about getting into sales, but he didn't advise it at my age, and again with my record. I certainly will not work for law firms screening medical-malpractice cases.

I then realized how lucky I was to have not waited on my initial hometown VA opportunity five years earlier and instead gone to my third and final position in the South. That hometown VA position would have been rescinded as well. I was recently contacted by two other VA hospitals in West Virginia and Kansas. I forwarded the rescind letter from the VA to both of these positions

(I finally learned do my own prescreening—quite a far cry from fluffing your resume as applicants are advised by these resume builder companies) and they immediately confirmed that I could not be considered at their locations either. At least those rejections were mercifully quick, courteous, and anticipated.

My abysmal failure to secure any orthopedic position naturally begs the question, and one that any reader would be left hanging if I did not answer: What else am I not telling about my history? What about all these malpractice cases in addition to the medical-board suspension that make me such a medical leper? There are fourteen claims over twenty-nine years. Yes, *fourteen*!

It gets worse. Three of those years I was inactive, so over one claim every two years working twenty-six years in the trenches. Remember: claims are allegations of malpractice, not actual trial verdicts or settlements. On the other hand, the disclaimer "settlement is not an admission of wrongdoing" is complete bullshit if you are the doctor applying for hospital privileges, medical-malpractice insurance, licensure, or commercial-insurance-provider participation. If you have a record of a settlement reported on the NPDB it is treated exactly as if you were found liable, as if it were a judgment reached at trial. The only question is, how much did your insurance company pay?

Nevertheless, all claims, even the ones that were thrown out, have to be entered on every application whether for a state license, insurance provider application, malpractice-insurance company, or when applying for hospital privileges. The public, however, does not see the number of *claims*, rather, only many *settlements* or *verdicts* on the NPDB. The threshold amount for reporting a claim to the NPDB, I think, is $10,000.

What is the average number of claims for an orthopedist over a thirty-year career? I don't know. I know my partner in my first practice had over six claims in four years. Another orthopedist at my third practice was rumored to have accumulated about nine in three years before he was terminated. In contrast, when I go online to physician forums, I see doctors quite righteously claim (with false modesty?) that they may have had only one claim in their entire career that they successfully defended. I remember visiting my senior orthopedic resident just before staring my career. He expressed his amazement that his senior partner had never been sued in his ongoing career of over twenty years. My mother, who worked for over thirty-five years from 1954 to 1991 and performed thousands of anesthesia cases, was never sued to my knowledge.

The Malpractice List

I had to recite all these claims for the last plaintiff's attorney in my deposition in 2016, so here we go again.

1. The wrong knee scoped on twelve-year-old girl in 1989, mentioned earlier on the TV tabloid show. When I arrived at the surgical center after being detained at the hospital emergency room that morning, she had already been checked through by several staff members, put to sleep, but the wrong knee still had been prepped and draped. I discovered the error immediately and scoped the correct knee. The amount of damages was small and therefore not worth naming the surgical center. She had full recovery from the one quarter inch arthroscopy incision. I was the easiest target. **$3,000.**
2. The twenty-one-year-old man who died on the operating table so tragically and needlessly. **$200,000 r**eported on the NPDB.
3. A thirty-seven-year-old man who presented with advanced multiple myeloma mentioned earlier. Again, the case was not "worth" that much, as unfortunately, he already had one foot in the grave from this very unusual form of cancer for someone his age. He had previously sustained a pathologic fracture of his spine from the cancer by the time he presented to my office. I immediately was suspicious and ordered a bone scan, which was not brought to my attention on follow-up a week later. None of the doctors, including those radiologists who actually missed the diagnosis, both at the city hospital a few months earlier and the radiologist at my local hospital, who could not grasp the significance of the whole scan lighting up like a Christmas tree, and did not call me,

were sued. It would have cost the plaintiff attorney too much to depose everyone. It would have cost my insurance company extra to depose all the other defendants. Pay if you are the insurance company, and take, if you are the plaintiff's attorney, the **$175,000** and run.

4. A fifty-year-old man, heavy smoker, who jammed his ring finger in a car accident, refused full exam on his initial office visit. He left my office in a huff, but then returned one month later with a fracture that had not been apparent on initial x-ray, even retrospectively, and then sued me. The case went to trial and was immediately thrown out on directed verdict. He had no expert to testify on his behalf.

5. A two-week-old girl victim of child abuse who was killed by her mother about three to four days after discharge from the hospital with a broken arm. Pediatrician and I had admitted her for child-abuse protection, notified social services, but they failed to follow up after discharge. I was dismissed.

6. A middle-aged female who had a broken retractor prong (like a prong on a comb) inadvertently left in her subcutaneous skin after a shoulder operation. It took five minutes to retrieve it under a second procedure, for which she was not charged. It was totally asymptomatic, picked up only on routine x-ray. Still, she filed a demand note, but no formal law suit. My insurance carrier denied her demand note. The matter was dropped.

7. A fifty-year-old lady who claimed I had failed to diagnose and treat her jammed index finger properly. It developed a delayed Boutonniere deformity (droop of her index finger) even though clinical exam and x-rays initially showed no disruption, dislocation, or fracture had occurred. After three lawyers, the case was dropped. (But she dropped in uninvited to my office workers' party.)

8. Forty-eight-year-old female who had a failed corrective knee surgery (an osteotomy) done by my colleague to realign her joint in order to hold off on knee replacement for arthritis in view of her age. I later replaced her knee. She did fine on postop follow-up for three months, continued to improve, and was discharged. She was later incarcerated for dealing drugs and from prison decided to sue me for something I

had done to her knee. No medical records of anything wrong with her knee or any surgery or hospitalization and so on. Claimed in her *pro se* complaint that I had "assaulted her knee" and caused irrevocable damage and pain and suffering and demanded $650,000 or something like that. The case was thrown out by the court.

9. An eighty-three-year-old woman with advanced Alzheimer's who sustained a severe, shattered femur fracture above her old total knee replacement. I operated on it and wired the huge fragment back in addition to plates and screws. Because she was so demented, no specific complaints or complications could be identified postoperatively in the hospital. Her circulation had appeared intact. She was discharged to a nursing home routinely after two days but then returned almost a month later with overt signs of loss of circulation, full thickness sores, and skin breakdown. I probably entrapped the artery by the fixation loop, and the vascular surgeon who performed the arteriogram advised me that I had "better settle this one." The amputation specimen was never examined by the pathologist to see if the artery had indeed been entrapped or instead been blocked or torn due to the original injury. Even my orthopedic colleague Dr. Thompson, when I showed him the x-ray, said immediately, "Oh wow, send it out." Settled for **$385,000.**

10. Fifty-year-old motorcyclist broke and dislocated his ankle which I treated immediately in the x-ray department with provisional cast to expedite the rest of his work up. (Difficult to get x-rays and CT scan when your foot was dislocated and rotated ninety degrees and flopping around, even when it is "splinted".) A blood clot in the vena cava was missed on CT by the radiologist. The patient was admitted by the general surgeon for a liver laceration and discharged a day or two later. The patient had been scheduled to return to me for later surgery but suddenly died from the undiagnosed embolus that dislodged from his vena cava. I was deposed and then dropped from the suit.

11. Fifty-four-year-old man with bipolar disorder fell after reportedly being given nitroglycerin by EMS while he had been standing. He suffered a dislocation of his shoulder which was reportedly put back in place

by the emergency room physician at the outlying hospital. He was re-ferred to my hospital for cardiology evaluation, but none of his records, x-rays, reports and were sent with him to confirm the exact injury, just hearsay that that his shoulder had been put back in place. On exam, I had confirmed that his shoulder, although sore and swollen, was no longer dislocated. I was unable to find the x-rays. He was discharged by the cardiologist before I could locate them. I had indicated physical therapy would be needed and to follow up in six weeks. Later, it was discovered he had sustained a nondisplaced hairline fracture in the ball of the shoulder joint, for which he never received any surgery (not sure if it was actually needed or refused). He sued for failure to diagnose. The case was thrown out on some technicality before full discovery. I was never deposed.

12. Mentioned earlier, a forty-nine-year-old black female sustained a grossly unstable leg fracture when she fell while intoxicated. I treated her with an intramedullary rod and used a tourniquet to cut down on bleeding. The tourniquet would allow better visibility to get the exact entry point of the rod at the knee incision. Because she had poor skin quality, was diabetic and a smoker, I treated the ankle part of the frac-ture with a cast. The plaintiff claimed I caused thermal necrosis (death of the skin from heat) because I used a tourniquet which caused a loss of cooling blood flow during reaming of the canal of the tibia of the leg. I claimed the skin had been damaged from the injury caused by the fracture itself. The leg was flopping all over when I initially saw her in the emergency room. There had already been a place in the skin where the bone had punctured through.

Either way, seven weeks after the surgery, the one-inch scab was crusted dry, adherent, and intact and had no signs of infection. I removed the cast and referred her to a plastic surgeon for removal of the scab (eschar) and immediate coverage of the site with a vascularized muscle/skin graft to be done in a one-stage operation before it could become infected. He saw her in his office and scheduled her for elective surgery, but for some reason, he only lifted the scab off thereby exposing the fracture site. He then referred her to another plastic surgeon days later for the muscle/skin graft.

By then, it was too late. The now exposed site had become infected, and she later required a below-knee amputation. I never saw any of the experts' opinions. The first plastic surgeon was not named in the suit. I suspect the plaintiff's attorney was not going to waste the time, effort, and money dragging in other defendants when it would not increase the award, and my insurance company wasn't going to spend money trying to defend me by filing a cross claim (suing the plastic surgeon as partly responsible). It was cheaper just to pay a settlement of **$485,000** and be done with it. The company settled against my wishes. I suspect since my patient was black, the judge was black, the judge had a history of being very plaintiff friendly, the judge's husband was a plaintiff's attorney, and that I was a lame duck physician who was leaving town, the insurance company realized I would never get justice.

The female plaintiff attorney who took my deposition in this case had a cold, sociopathic personality: very arrogant and cruel. Very cruel. But this was not unusual for members of the legal profession. I remarked to my attorney that I sure would have hated to be her husband or partner. She spent the first hour and a half going through my entire medical-malpractice and licensure-board history. Then she produced three comments I had made in a medical legal blog site and asked me to read them into the record and repeatedly asked me what specifically did the abbreviation "POS" stood for, as if she really didn't know. She tried to get me to admit that I hated lawyers and that I had done a lot of legal research. I didn't fall for it. All of this was designed to get me angry or poison the judge's mind. Remember, this case was scheduled as a bench trial. No jury. Only the judge decided. If the judge read the deposition and saw all the claims I've had, she would assume that I must be a terrible doctor and, therefore, probably liable in this case. In my opinion, once you have had several lawsuits or a history of licensure-board action(s), you are more vulnerable as a defendant in future actions.

I responded, "Sure, I'll read them. I stand by these comments," essentially referring to the fact the medical system was in trouble because there was not enough money to keep funding health care as we have come to enjoy it, and that "POS" was in reference to my EMR software program.

She then tried to summarize, or rather, antagonize: "So over your career, you have been responsible for three deaths and payouts of $788,000 dollars," to which I immediately called her on the fact that the pulmonary embolus death of the motorcyclist and the child-abuse death had had nothing to do with my care. But this was typical of how lawyers lie and deceive. Then she wanted me to confirm that this licensure-board action had cost me millions over my career. She really enjoyed taunting me with this and visibly delighted in my misfortune. And you wonder why lawyers are so despised. This kind of blatantly false misleading statement should have resulted in disciplinary action and not be simply disregarded as "legal tactics" that can be addressed by counsel simply saying, "Objection." Surprisingly, my attorney made no objections during the entire deposition, the fact that wide leeway is given in depositions as opposed to what is allowed at trial as evidence notwithstanding.

When it came time to actually discussing the case, her deposition prep work, in contrast, was absolutely abysmal: little more than having clipped a Walmart coupon. She introduced only one review paper from an institution that had summarized two studies. Both squarely supported me. It took me less than thirty seconds to scan through each to totally refute their relevance and use them as supporting for my handling of the case. One study had showed that surgically opening a fracture and putting a plate and screws had a higher rate of infection than an intramedullary rod introduced from the knee and advanced down the leg across the fracture site without having to open it. Not only had I used the intramedullary rod, but the leg had not gotten acutely infected from the rod. Therefore, this study was totally nonapplicable. The other study from Switzerland involved a series of patients operated over years. It noted that the problem of thermal necrosis (heat-induced injury to the skin from reaming) had occurred in only three patients: all young men ages eighteen to thirty with extremely hard bone and very small canals that had required prolonged, extensive heat generating reaming to pass the rod. Tourniquets had been used in all of the patients comprising the study and thus established a long-established standard of care: using a tourniquet when performing an intramedullary rodding of a tibia fracture. My patient did not fit this profile of the three young men with hard bone and narrow canals. My patient was female and forty-nine. She had softer bone, a wider canal, and had not required prolonged reaming. The plaintiff argued that because I had used a tourniquet, the lack of cooling blood flow had caused the thermal necrosis (burn injury and skin breakdown). I informed her that there had been absolutely no evidence that a tourniquet alone was sufficient to cause the thermal burn/skin breakdown during routine reaming of tibia fractures. Rather, according to these authors, it was the prolonged reaming of very hard bone in a small canal that had caused it. The relative contribution of use the tourniquet against these other glaring risk factors was purely speculative and coincidental in this series. Junk science. She was a lousy attorney who came unprepared, and yet whose firm still "won" the case.

13. Patella foreign body. Kind of like claim #6. Then there is the ungrateful and greedy patient. This case too, was settled against my wishes. A sixty-four year- old who black male ruptured his quadriceps tendon (connects his thigh muscle to his kneecap). Once ruptured, when you try to stand, your knee collapses. You can't straighten your knee against gravity. During the repair, a drill bit broke off in the kneecap. I decided to leave it in and remove it after the repair had healed rather than risk compromising the repair trying to find the proverbial needle in the hay-stack. Once the repair had healed, it took all of ten minutes to get the drill bit out in a second operation as an outpatient. No special physical therapy was required after this second minor outpatient procedure. It was much easier and less risky since the repair had healed and there was no worry about accidentally cutting the sutures or compromising the suture anchors. The drill bit had never entered the joint or tendon.

It caused no harm. He would never have even known it was even there had I not told him. After the original operation, the physical therapist reported he had a typical post op recovery and was not complaining of any unusual pain. His family doctor also reported no specific complaints of any knee pain. Then about a year later, the patient suddenly claimed that his knee was killing him and wanted the drill bit out and $500,000. I am sure his knee suddenly felt a whole lot better when he literally walked away with **$200,000.** Well, actually, his lawyer got at least a third ($75,000) of that. Still, he walked away with $125,000. And you don't we need think tort reform?

14. Still in litigation. Fifty-year-old extreme alcoholic and heavy smoker (three-plus packs per day) who fell and broke her hip, which was fixed by my colleague. She was admitted to the rehab center where I had been medical director. She was noncompliant, agitated, and would not participate in therapy. She only wanted to drink and smoke. By the rehab/insurance guidelines, she, therefore, had to be discharged. At the nursing home, a few weeks later she developed loss of circulation from long-standing, progressive peripheral artery disease that later required amputations. Lawsuit claimed all the doctors caring for her, including an orthopedist who saw her weeks later after discharge failed to recognize her circulation problem and was the cause of her amputations.

Wound Care

The wound company contacted me after I had responded to a bulk email recruitment. It was interested in hiring me to provide wound care in a rural part of the state. The recruiter was very persistent. I stalled him for a few weeks as the VA position hung in balance. I fully disclosed all my baggage to avoid another false hire. When I got the rescind notice from the VA, my choice was academic. It was wound care or nothing. Even if I retrained as a family practitioner, I could still have difficulty getting a license and/or malpractice insurance, and no guarantee of a job. It would also take time and expense to retrain adequately. I would face a tail coverage malpractice premium upon retirement if I had to go independent. Wound care was near the lowest risk of all specialties as far as getting sued. The retraining time, especially since I was already familiar with wounds, was minimal. At my age, wound care was probably the most logical choice.

Just like my other positions, this one had problems. Two of the companies' previous physicians had left—one allegedly because he had declined participation in Medicare, so he could not get his services billed. The other had left to for the East Coast where his wife's family lived. The city had already been saturated by a competing wound-care company.

It was told through secondhand information by a wound-care sales rep that this physician's assistant (not even an MD) from the competing company wasn't taking any more facilities. He was full. My one and only facility in town had only one or two patients. I would not be surprised if he had been offered this facility but refused, simply because it did not have enough patients to make it worth his while. When I expressed initial concern that the company could only provide me with only one facility in town and two in in a small town about thirty miles away, it responded with a mutual-understanding agreement. This was not a contract but was meant to "reassure" me that the practice would build quickly.

This company proudly stood by its claim of "under promising and over delivering." I would see thirty patients a week the first month, then sixty the next, and then up to ninety per week by the end of the third month. Then they pulled out a new contract concept of paying me a fixed salary on the assumption, or trying to give me the impression, that I would be seeing sixty patients a week in short order. In turn, I agreed to drive up to forty miles to a facility for which I would be reimbursed $0.40 a mile.

The wound company otherwise appeared to have a good program of training, organization, and support of its physicians. I even had to go back for an extra week of training because my progress, well, was slower than most. Most of this was due to my inability to adapt to computerized recordkeeping and logistics as quickly as the (younger) doctors, a surprising number of which were general surgeons only three years out of fellowships.

But the patient numbers never materialized. True, other facilities were found, but one that was signed on after I arrived lasted for only about six weeks before it became obvious to me that the facility had never really wanted a wound physician, a sort of recruitment remorse. This facility had already terminated another doctor from a competing company. My company had spent a long time reportedly trying to negotiate for this facility. The second time I visited the facility, the wound nurse, who was a real pill, announced she was moving to the position of assistant administrator, and that there were no plans to find a new wound nurse. Generally, nurses do not like wound care. This one sure didn't.

The census numbers dropped off my third and fourth week at this facility. The fifth week, I was told not to come because state inspectors were there. (Not a reason to cancel wound care.) I think I visited one more week, then on the seventh week, I was told again not to come because there was "flu going around." (Again, not a reason to cancel wound care.) I confronted the nurse on the phone and asked her point blank if the facility was really interested in having a wound-care physician. The next day, the contract was canceled. Of course, I got all the blame by my company. But that is supposed to be my nature, correct? Blame everyone else for all my failures.

Wound care epitomizes the adversity confronting doctors. Whether I get hired or remain at facility is essentially determined by the director of nursing or the wound nurse herself. After all, I am only a doctor. Some wound nurses were pleasures to work with. Then there were others, like the facility from which I was most recently let go, where the wound nurse thought she knew more than I did, and, therefore, would flagrantly ignore my orders or became upset because my wound measurements didn't "agree" with hers which made it look like she was not healing them. Some of her rogue treatments were contraindicated, but I sensed that if I didn't let her have her way, I would lose the facility. It was a pretty helpless feeling especially when you are a board-certified physician with a hell of a lot more training, experience, and knowledge. How the times have changed.

Bryce Sterling

The last day, she and a wound dressing sales rep basically took off on wound rounds themselves and ignored me. I realized that it was the end at that facility. Even when I explained to both of them that you don't pack collagen powder into a wound that is grossly necrotic and needs surgical excision of the dead tissue first, they ignored me. This was a very frustrating situation for a traveling physician. I always at the mercy of the wound-care nurse or director of nursing. The retention of nursing home facilities was also far more problematic than the wound care company had let on to. After about three months at another facility and five different wound nurses, I finally cleaned up all but one wound. It boiled down to the fact that there was simply no reason for me to make the trip. Another facility needed primary care to handle the wounds because wound care was available only once a week. Another facility was so chaotic, with administration turn over, director of nursing turnover, so rampant and care so disorganized that I had to quit. It was a lawsuit in the making. It was one star program. At one point I spent an hour in a meeting with the state inspectors to rescue the facility. The director of nursing was begging me. The wound care sales reps were amazed that I was able to work at this facility. The worst they had ever seen. Overall, the patient and facility numbers never increased. I started out with three facilities and 25 patients, and one year later, that's where I ended.

My plan had been to relocate the family for four years so my daughter could have four uninterrupted years of high school. In theory, I would have a job, and my daughter would get a better education. These were two solid reasons to leave my permanent residence yet again. As stated before, and as always was the case, I could not sell the house because I didn't know if this new job would work out. It was like the old behavioral science experiment where the rat is placed in the cage and never knows when a shock is going to be delivered until the light flashes, but in my situation, I didn't even have the "courtesy" of a warning light.

It had only taken about three or four weeks for me to realize that this wound-care job would not financially support placing my daughter into a private school and I'd have to place her in public school, which was still better than the one back home.

I was making less than a third of what I'd been led to believe, and there would be no paid vacation, no health-care benefits. I was making less than one-tenth the amount I'd made at my last orthopedic job, and now, less than a nurse.

My family had to go on vacation without me. I extended my range to fifty-one miles, even as the company reduced mileage allowance by twenty-five percent starting in 2017. It then asked if I would be interested in driving ninety-three miles to three new facilities in the middle of the state for a combined daily total triangular drive of 220 miles and see twenty-five patients.

In view of what I had already experienced, the likely scenario would devolve into me driving two hundred miles to two places for a combined total of only twelve to sixteen patients, as one facility would likely drop out within three months and the number of patients in each facility decreased as more wounds healed than new ones occurred. I was being used like a pizza delivery boy. I recently got a phone call from the company informing me they were going to lock my computer and prevent me from visiting my facilities (denial of access) while they "reviewed my records," and then in one month they would get back to me. One month later, they informed me that I was being terminated without cause. It was a blatant summary termination and breach of contract which had required the company to give me sixty days' notice for termination. The company had used the one-month records review period to allow another physician, who also was concerned about not having enough patients, to take over my facilities and see if this new arrangement would be satisfactory. Incredible treachery. More legal action. I wonder if this time, I'll finally get justice?

Thoughts on Medicine Today

A young doctor is better off being more specialized rather than being a generalist. Do the exact opposite of what the government wants you to do. It is all about protecting the need for your unique skill and preserving your ability to relocate. You can go from the big city to a small town. It is more difficult as time goes by to do the reverse. Rural hospitals are struggling financially, as medical care, like government, becomes increasingly centralized. Doctors in rural hospitals have increasingly become generalists while at the same time their jobs are being steadily encroached upon by nurses, physician's assistants, nurse practitioners, also known as "noctors" (nurse + doctor). To make it worse, the salary differential may be narrowing, but doctors are still being held to higher standards, longer training, higher education costs, greater malpractice exposure, more stringent recertification and continuing medical education requirements, and so on. It has become a farce. These "noctors" don't even correct a patient when he calls them "doctor." Everyone wants to practice medicine, no one wants to go to medical school, or face all the hassles a real doctor encounters.

The small-town surgeon or "interventionalist" doesn't see the number of patients or the complexity of cases to maintain proficiency. For example, a patient may have a broken femur easily fixed by a rural orthopedist, but because that patient has a head injury or congestive heart failure, that patient has to go to the big city trauma center because the small rural hospital has no neurosurgeon or cardiologist.

If a doctor tries to return to the big city after several years in a small town, he will more likely be passed over in favor of the freshly minted, fellowship-trained hotshot. Managed Care Organizations (MCOs) entice a young doctor with a too-good-to-be-true initial-salary guarantee, but he too has to look down the road. Eventually (three to four years) he has to produce or he will be let go, or be forced to go on production.

Then there are doctors, whom I call the carpetbaggers, who are like the ones I encountered in my second position. They are job-hoppers. They practice in small towns until their guarantees run out and then leave for another two-to three-year stint elsewhere. Moving is not so problematic for them if they have clean records and their kids are grown. The small-town rural hospitals with their naïve, sophomoric administrators and hospital boards only see the dollars an orthopedic surgeon brings to the hospital (among the highest of all specialties) and are all too willing to hire them. Frequently in these smaller towns, there really has been no demonstrated need for more than one of them. The need is based only on statistical projections.

Orthopedics is a glutted specialty in my opinion and based on my extensive searches. Believe me, there are very few doctors who have searched as long and hard and faced as many rejections as I have looking for a position. Orthopedic surgeons are now everywhere. When it came to assessing how acute was the need for a second orthopedic surgeon at every position for which I applied, it became clear that it was not.

More than ever, hospital corporations hire only "credentially correct candidates." This is driven in large part by their medical malpractice insurance carrier, who insures all the employed physician and ancillary medical extenders. If a doctor is not employed by the hospital, of course he shops for his own medical malpractice insurance. But at my age, I was not about to set up a private practice again.

My 1991 event, listed in 1994 on the data bank, is as if it happened yesterday. I had to start out every conversation with a recruiter by advising him to forget about finding me a five-star position in the big city. I would never be considered. Only a small, rural, one-star position having extreme difficulty recruiting or retaining an orthopedist would consider me. I would inform the recruiter over the phone to feel free to end the call when he had heard enough, or, if he was still interested, he could read my summary by email attachment and not having to listen to me rehash it over the phone. The calls always ended with that familiar recruiter refrain "I'll get back to you." Maybe a few out of hundreds ever did.

After a long, heartbreaking fruitless search lasting six months, I would have to resign myself to toughing it out in in my second position as long as I could. Every three or four years, I would launch a new job search. It seemed that the same places were still trying to hire. I didn't know if they had been unable to hire anyone in the first place, or if they had, the doctor had already come and left. I was very lucky to have landed the third and final position in the South. My two rescinded positions promptly recruited other orthopedists. I am well satisfied, even to the point that I would stake my life on it, that I can never work in medicine, and most certainly, orthopedics again.

Most of the recruitments are, therefore, what I call "soft" recruitments, meaning they don't really urgently need an orthopedist. They can often get a *locums tenum* (temporary) doctor in a real crunch. Instead, maybe one of the existing orthopedists wants to slow down, or not have to take call, or wants a buyer for his practice if he has been solo, or is part of a group looking to transition someone in to keep the overhead down. It simply will not be a bona fide opportunity if you are a marginal candidate. But then, there is the ambitious administrator who thinks more doctors mean more income for the hospital.

Two big problems with that short-sightedness:

One, if there is already a solo private practitioner, bringing in hospital-employed doctors may force the solo practitioner to have to leave. He can cannot compete with doctors who are subsidized, have their office, billing, and so on already set up for them and then have no hassle closing the office when they decide to leave. Even worse, referrals are redirected away from that private physician to the hospital-employed group.

Two, if the doctors simply leave after their contract guarantees end, the hospital often loses. In my opinion, federal government programs like Medicare and Medicaid, even if they traditionally have never paid as much as commercial insurers like Blue Cross/Blue Shield, nevertheless provide an artificial financial backstop for hospitals that enables them to pursue more reckless and financially unsound business models which include subsidizing doctors. Some of the rural hospitals have razor-thin profit margins or are at best break even. Seventy percent or more of their patients are Medicare/Medicaid. These hospitals are, therefore, dependent on Medicare/Medicaid payments. If the government cuts back reimbursement, these hospitals are suddenly under water. Whenever the government starts paying for anything, it causes distortions in the markets. It now has a say in how the system is going to operate, and ultimately whether it survives. It usually jacks up the cost. Government guaranteed home loans? The cost of housing goes up. Government education assistance/loans? The cost of college tuition goes up. Interestingly, many medical websites claim that physician salaries are on the rise. Is this just click bait to get a physician to sign up on a website that sponsors such claims when in fact most physicians' incomes, especially when one factors in the afterhours computer EMR record "catch-up" time, hours spent in administrative tasks, and billing hassles, are declining? There is simply too much disinformation out there to verify these seemingly contradicting claims.

If a new grad starts out in private practice with a group, it too could be a long time before becoming a partner. Solo? Forget about it now days. I did that for sixteen years as a refugee after my suspension. When I was asked how much it cost to start up a private solo practice by my anesthesiologist colleague in my last job, I replied cynically, "Hal, you're asking the wrong question. How much does it cost to *close* a practice—especially if you have no buyer?"

Start with malpractice tail payments. Then you have to keep patient records for up to ten years. Then you have to try to sell or rent your home, office, or equipment if you own them or, even worse, get stuck with a lease contract on the building or your computer software. I had used my EMR for only a few months before I had to close the practice, but I had to continue payments on the $60,000 contract for five years. I couldn't transfer it to another doctor. I was fortunate, however, to be able to lease the building for five years, but just recently my renter suddenly left. No advance notice was given as required by the contract. The building is now up for sale.

Does organized medicine make sense? Not really. It costs the hospitals, especially the more rural hospitals, a *lot* of money to recruit a new physician, especially those in surgical specialties. Not just the bonus and salary guarantee, but also the recruiter's fee $20,000–$30,000, the airline tickets, hotel and car rental costs. Then the redundant equipment (a recruiting hospital has to match other hospitals' equipment and services) in order for the doctor to come. (Remember the $90,000 behemoth fracture table one of my competitors requested and received? A medical arm's race.) I think Medicare and Medicaid are quiet enablers of this kind of waste, even if for some items, especially hospital expansion, there is a certificate of need (CON) requirement. In my second hospital, it was clearly shown that there was no need for the new operating room expansion, even though CON was approved. Nothing like good old bureaucracy at work. All the money is being spent on everything but actual patient care.

Don't forget the shareholders and these CEOs who divert money from actual health care. We won't talk about all the computer software, practice management, coding classes, seminars, recertification, maintenance of certification, recertification prep courses, and so on. Procedures that could be performed in doctors' offices for less cost are now performed in the corporate owned hospitals who tack on additional "facility fees" to the bloated price of the procedure. The stream of opportunistic cockroaches crawling out of the woodwork looking to capitalize off doctors is endless. Realtors and bankers salivate when a new doctor comes to town—and leaves. Doctors are probably the last of the high-income dumb money: juicy commissions for the real estate agents, assuming the doctor is dumb enough to buy a big house, and a big mortgage by the bank, translating into debt slavery for him and bank profits for years. Remember: you are not buying a house. The bank is selling you a mortgage, as much debt as it can, on top of your school loans. Make sure you really, really need that house, or better yet, rent at least for the first year. Be prepared to move, as medicine is increasingly becoming a nomadic existence. It wasn't bad when the real estate market was appreciating ten years ago. Even if a doctor left, he could usually easily sell his house, even at a profit. Now, such a prospect is not as certain unless in the usual select cities. As the baby boomer generation ages, they are looking to downsize. More houses are on the market, maybe not overtly posted for sale, but rather in a shadow market: people who would like to sell their homes but can't, so they don't bother listing them. Interest rates have remained as low as they can go and any increase will make mortgages increasingly unaffordable. Millennials can't afford to, or don't want to, buy new houses. They have too much school debt and their jobs don't pay like the breadwinner jobs boomers enjoyed decades ago when the wife could stay at home with the kids and only one paycheck was needed to live the American Dream. We are now a renter society, with traditional home ownership numbers declining. Remember the Federal Reserve Bank? It loaned out free money at no interest to big corporations, including hedge funds who bought up the homes in niche cities, causing prices to increase to the point that they are unaffordable to traditional homebuyers who could not get those same low interest loans. The corporations and banks increasingly own and rent the houses and apartment complexes. Rents are going up as thwarted homebuyers crowd into the rental market.

The entire health-care industry business model has incorporated huge distortions because of reliance on substantial government funding. When

Medicare was established back in the '60s, there were plenty of people working high-paying jobs, and life expectancy was less. The whole thing was the front end of a Ponzi. Remember: when you get in on a Ponzi scheme early, you do well. Everything is great and you get a great return on your money. But eventually, it runs out of cash input from new "investors." Like a Ponzi scheme that is running out of new investors, the government is now broke. The health-care system will have to go through some gut-wrenching changes. Big corporate health care providers will eventually suffer severe downdrafts in their bottom lines once the government is unable to maintain the artificial level of Medicare and Medicaid payments and people can no longer afford traditional health insurance premiums, especially those that are exploding under the Affordable Care Act.

Health care is putting a stranglehold on an already-struggling economy that has become overburdened with debt. You cannot have people who make $20,000–$30,000 a year affording $100,000 bypasses, $100,000 total knee replacements, or $100,000 ICU stays. People can't even afford the co-pays or the deductibles. Their savings are being ravaged and funneled to shareholders, CEOs, and elites in part by this health care behemoth which constitutes 20 percent of the economy and a major conduit for wealth transfer from the middle class to the elites. There is the military industrial complex, and now there is the medical industrial complex. Doctors' salaries are a small percentage of this, but draw all the criticism. It's because they are on the front line.

It is true that insurance companies are ripping off many consumers with outrageous premiums and hospitals patients with outrageous bills, but health insurance companies are going to start losing money. Under Obamacare, they are being forced to be medical-care payers, not insurers. You can't buy house insurance after your house burns down or automobile-collision insurance after you've had a wreck. You have to buy it before the event. That is why it is called *insurance*. The Affordable Care Act (ACA) requires insurance companies write you a policy *after* you become sick. Madness! So once the private health insurance milk and honey stops flowing and the government Medicare and Medicaid programs start getting strapped for money, the hospitals and other health care providers will start to get squeezed as well. The ACA is just the tip of the spear of non-affordability.

New advances in medicine are not labor-saving devices. They create need for more labor and money, more technicians to run and repair them, more sales people to market them, more needless duplication in a medical arms race. Two $100,000 da Vinci robots in a tired, old river town? Yep, until the one hospital was closed. One might think that it is a good thing because more jobs are being created, taxes paid, and so on, but the reality is these are not value-added jobs that increase society's overall net wealth. Acutely ill patients now live *six months longer* and *double their health-care costs* as a result of these advances, and for what?

Health care in my opinion will have to eventually transition from the current system to the false promise of a single provider, which in turn will lead to more acute rationing when the government can no longer afford it. Only then will the old-fashioned fee-for-service and openly priced competition gradually reemerge, as it has in a certain Oklahoma clinic, or via medical tourism in other countries like Thailand or Mexico. I paid $1,800 for my wife's cousin's back surgery for disc herniation (L4-5 lumbar laminectomy and discectomy) in the Philippines five years ago. That included the MRI (which I reviewed to confirm diagnosis and surgical indication), a three-day hospital stay, and the radiologist's, surgeon's, and anesthesiologist's fees. $1,800 doesn't even cover a one-month insurance premium payment for a family here in the US.

Some doctors are transitioning to boutique medicine. They accept cash only at the desk, do not participate in Medicare, and for a yearly fee will offer to follow you medically in their office or at the hospital. But, if you require hospitalization or surgery then that is extra. But eventually, providers, including doctors, will have to work for less. Many, including insurance companies, medical equipment manufacturers, and so on, will eventually go out of business, but, and I am being quite cynical here, not before their CEOs have cashed out their stock options.

Recapitulation

So there you have it. What started out as a promising medical career and storybook family crashed and burned, and a young man needlessly lost his life because I was stuck doing my wife's job in violation of the most fundamental statutes concerning dissolution of marriage. At age sixty-three, I am too old to retrain in primary care because of my inability to get a second residency position, probably even license or insurance, yet too young to retire, and too qualified for Walmart or Lowe's to seriously consider me. But in the meantime, I am a perfectly capable orthopedic surgeon who must sit on the sidelines and watch as my skills evaporate.

I remember a hand therapist's simple admonition to marriage: "Choose wisely." I had chosen disastrously, but the divorce statutes in my state should have protected me and my children, especially in a case as straightforward as this, and for which the court did not have to worry whether the children would be provided for under any scenario. I really, really, really needed a good lawyer but instead was sold out, at best by incompetent lawyers whose knowledge of the statutes was at best "that's the way it is done here" or at worst, by ones who were looking after their own financial interests to the point of fraud by needlessly throwing my divorce case into an all-out protracted conflict resulting in increased billable hours, and then at the end, sacrificing me through an ill-advised settlement which would get them off the hook. I still to this day cannot believe Salazar walked into my *pendente lite* hearing cold and served me up to be slaughtered by a commissioner and judge whom he knew were absolutely, totally, and utterly incompetent and whose rulings later confirmed this. His act could only be compared to an emergency room doctor who rendered emergency medical treatment to a 65-year ashen colored old man clutching his chest, gasping for breath with all the signs of a heart attack, by the medieval practice of bloodletting. He left me to bleed out in that court room that morning. All my divorce lawyers were telling me I had to pay this support as they billed me for tens of thousands of dollars. (In today's dollars, they ripped me for a quarter million.) So much for a second opinion that winds up billing you double and messes up the case even more. And then there was this second commissioner, Selig, reciting the purpose of divorce laws: to mitigate the harmful consequences of dissolution of marriage, and so on. The lawyers and judges always recite the statutes before they screw you. They want you to think that the statutes are being applied to your case. They aren't.

What infuriates me even more is that these lawyers, commissioner, judge, and the state bar to *deny to this day* their responsibility and incompetence. Instead, they claim I am unreasonable and vitriolic, a verifiable nut job who thinks he knows the law, who simply blames everyone else simply because I don't agree with them, who refuses to accept responsibility for his actions, and therefore, cannot be correct in my accusations.

Arthur Smith arrived at 3:00 that fateful afternoon at which time I normally would have been certainly been finished with my elective cases and would have had an anesthesiologist who would not have had to beg off the case because "he had to go home and get some rest." Never in my entire career had an anesthesiologist begged off a case in which the patient had already arrived in the operating room like that.

Yes, I have a bad temper, but that was not the cause of these events. They only served to exacerbate it. Salazar had a duty to act to mitigate this through reasonable representation of my interests, especially after my having explicitly warned him of Mindy's sociopathic treachery. I was the epitome of a vulnerable target in a divorce under these unique circumstances. None of these lawyers ever talked about any of these issues specifically, only in vague and general terms:

- I got a good settlement.
- The property has been evenly divided.
- The facts are not in dispute.
- I am ignoble to blame the nurse.
- I am a "disgruntled orthopedic surgeon."
- I am "mad at the world."
- I am dissatisfied with my lawyers and the courts.
- The agreement is not one-sided.

- I fail to take responsibility for my actions.
- I show no remorse

In fact, most readers fire off the old standby admonishment: "Dr. Sterling, these events happened twenty-five years ago. Get over it." I can't. This licensure board suspension cuts me down as if it happened only yesterday. The final blow was the VA Hospital position.

I wrote in my appeals that the divorce laws were written with some degree of predictability and consistency so that parties would have a foundation upon which to contemplate equitable settlement, the very path the courts encourage the parties to pursue in the first place. The courts should be ruling on cases like my mine to ensure that these statutes uniformly apply whether one is *settling* a case, *trying* a case, or *suing attorneys* for legal malpractice. No informed client would have settled my divorce as I did. No competent attorney would have ever recommended it to his client. In all other plaintiff civil actions, intangibles of pain and suffering and emotional distress leave the door wide open for recovery of these losses, but not for lawsuits against attorneys. Everything becomes automatically speculative and evidence will never be permitted to see the light of day.

Wearing Captain Bligh's hat, I would have simply admonished Judge Hubbell in the way Captain Bligh had done to Fletcher Christian over the cheese dispute in the movie Mutiny on the Bounty mentioned earlier:

> Mr. Hubbell. Taking Skyler's word against Sterling's is a fool's errand. Simply tally up the marital assets each side received through this settlement and see if the amount Dr. Mindy received exceeds the highest amount Dr. Sterling could have paid.

Such an exercise should have been no burden at all for Skyler. After all, she had all the numbers of all the marital property valuations, both disputed and undisputed, and the tax basis for those where taxes would be applicable already tabulated. (sarcasm). Well, Skyler and Salazar, you had these tax numbers, didn't you? You had a CPA review these numbers before trial, didn't you (even more sarcasm)? For the sake of argument, even if the amount I paid had been a little less than the highest amount I could have paid, would this have made it a *good* settlement? Most people I know don't make decisions based on some unlikely worst-case scenario. They make them based on the most probable or typical scenario. That the court would smile on this settlement reached in such a fashion sends a direct message to litigating parties: Never settle! And we haven't even factored in that no provisions whatsoever had been made for my known medical-malpractice suit or my impending medical license suspension. These losses were imminent and would ultimately dwarf the entire marital estate.

I now have to wonder if Skyler's strategy in all of her divorces was to deliberately withhold the numbers and their tabulations from her clients. That way, they would arrive at trial uniformed and could be more easily blindsided into a settlement-- for Skyler's benefit, not theirs. There would be no "evidence trail" if her client later tried to sue her for legal malpractice. If the settlement number was a single "winged it" grand total like mine, it would be even more difficult to go back and reconstruct. Skyler had now covered up her tracks. She could just claim that she had been "ready," the "facts were not in dispute," and "she had taken everything into account," (including taxes,) when she recommended a last-minute settlement. The Courts, of course, love these tactics: Anything that will allow them not to have to hear a case. That is the ultimate Catch-22. The Courts want you to settle your case, even if your attorneys have botched it and settling will result in a bad outcome for their client. In other words, the Judicial system actually enables and encourages legal malpractice. It is like a health insurer quietly encouraging the death of a covered patient so it will no longer have to pay for their medical care. A case that is settled is a case that is done. A patient that dies is a future bill that will no longer be due.

It would be very interesting to go back over some of Skyler's previous clients and see if they had actually been presented, via hard copy, and at least several days prior to trial, a "high -medium-low" settlement scenario range of valuations that had gone into making a settlement proposal, and if a careful retrospective calculation showed that a fair and equitable settlement had been reached.

Even my own appeals attorney informed me of the wrong deadline for appeals. The incompetence and malpractice never ended. I could not sue him for legal malpractice, because the case upon which my new claim would be based had already been disposed of by the appeals court. It would be heaping inference upon inference, speculation upon speculation, so I didn't bother suing him. He would now be arguing against the very case for which I had hired him to advocate for me. It would have been the court/legal system of the absurd. The attorney representing these defendant divorce attorneys wrote a memorandum in support of the state supreme court's decision to deny me enlargement of time for my belated filing of my *pro se* appeal. They argued that I had been instructed by my former counsel to get counsel, citing this advice on the same page where he had instructed me that I had thirty days instead of the actual twenty days to file my appeal. That was the problem. I kept getting counsel, but they kept giving me not just *bad advice*, but *dead-wrong advice*— the whole goddamned lot of them!

The legal incompetence and dishonesty did not end with my divorce, as a new version was played out in front of the medical board. My defense attorney, who died in 2009, received glowing praise of his legal prowess, yet he fumbled a simple but critical communication with the medical board as it fired off the lawsuit against my license before even knowing all the facts in blatant violation of the statutes. He was making too much money to be bothered with this simple but critical task. His motivation was very easy to understand compared to Skyler's and Salazar's; Goerbing just didn't give a shit. He argued only at the most basic level- that I was held to the wrong standard of care, but not elaborating why, and that other orthopedists were doing Bier Blocks.

He then tried to deceive me into thinking that it was *my fault* for not appearing before the board in 1991 when the board realized their error and wanted to clarify the facts. All he had to do was inform the board that the board's original counsel had filed the suit prematurely in violation of the medical-practice act because the board was completely unaware of the fact that I had asked for the correct drug and dose.

Every time I wrote an *ex parte* communication to the board or commissioner they informed my attorneys that I was a loose cannon, and I should communicate through my attorneys. My medical-board defense attorney, Goerbing, was too busy ogling my girlfriend, Tessie, chasing after my officer manager's skirt, lying to me about not being able to sever my case with the codefendant anesthesiologist, bragging about how many doctors he had gotten off, playing Perry Mason with his last-minute "gotcha" antics of delayed revelation of the nurse's error, last-minute "gotcha" production of the exoneration by the board's own orthopedic expert opinion and most of all, downplaying the nurse's act as simply a mistake, when it was much more than that. It was a premeditated act: directing an unauthorized and untrained tech to do the most critical part of an RN's job. The facts outlining the ruling by the medical board, my appeal, my lawsuit against my divorce lawyers all speak for themselves. My attorney Goerbing's advice to me was "relax." Relax? When my whole career is on the line and the board clearly has an agenda? Fuck you in your grave, Goerbing! Here you were rolling in the dough from the malpractice-insurance company for your so-called defense of me while you enjoyed the gladiatorial spectacle from your cozy corner office and my career was about to get destroyed by a righteous medical board that clearly had a public relations problem whose solution required sacrificing a doctor, and you were telling me to "relax"?

As a medical refugee, I could never get a stable position after the suspension, and was continuously placed under situational anxiety, above and beyond what doctors normally experience. The two positions I did get were clearly ones that no other candidate would take and for which the hospitals could neither recruit nor keep candidates for long. I was harassed, sued, and persecuted at my second location by patients, the hospital and that state's medical board. I was indeed very grateful for my four years at my third and final practice but as I had correctly predicted, it could not last, and got tagged with three more lawsuits.

Wound care was a dead end, and in my opinion, is a bullshit "specialty" desperately trying to cling to relevance-and to the government Medicare payments. Medicare has stepped up enforcement of nursing home prevention of pressure associated wounds by docking the facilities for the expense of their treatment. I think there are therefore fewer pressure related wounds. But the older data these wound care companies claim to justify their existence may need to be revised in view of these new trends. Facilities may be more carefully selecting their patients to avoid those who may be potential wound care problems. Increasingly, it is the hospitals where wounds originate, as they try to cut costs for providing acute care. Nursing home facilities are cancelling their relationships with wound care physicians more frequently I suspect as they train their own nurses to do these tasks, ninety-five percent which do not require a physician level of training. There are more competing wound care companies. I suspect I was terminated in part because of the company's need to accommodate a newer physician nearby who was complaining or threatening to quit if she didn't get more patients. She was facing the same issue as I: insufficient patient volume.

In retrospect, I now wish I had gone into the military. I probably could have made it there. After college, I took the USAF airman qualifying exam and scored all perfect "9"s, but my eyes weren't good enough.

Even worse, and I hate to admit it, I may have even been a better attorney than a competent, compassionate doctor, although that is not saying much, as most attorneys are absolutely useless at best, at least from what I have seen.

I certainly never had a chance to develop as an orthopedist, and therefore, I never had the confidence that I was ever competent. I was always distracted by my marital, malpractice, licensure and job insecurity problems. How did I rate myself as an orthopedist? Somewhere (hopefully) in the middle, maybe. Or, more evasively, "better than some but not as good as others." I wonder how successful I could have been had my ex-wife not lured me to her hometown? I really don't know, because my poor residency training coupled with this early career derailment render it all guesswork.

I know I sacrificed a better orthopedic residency in my hometown for a marginal one out of my ex-wife's insistence that she needed a good anesthesiology program—implying she was going to work as an anesthesiologist. "Bryce, I need anesthesia" were her exact words as I looked at my hometown residency, whose anesthesia program was definitely subpar. I remember the chairman of anesthesiology at her residency telling her, "Don't go to there." What did she wind up doing? Next to nothing. She took an academic position in her state, which would allow her to duck out of as much work as possible. She published a few papers early during her return to the university anesthesia department on a trajectory toward full professor with tenure, but I'll bet she hasn't done squat in the last twenty years, just milk the system. Mindy was quite the hypocrite and opportunist.

Mindy never needed a good training program. She was able to take off five years and still got a job at the university because the department was in such shambles under the chairmanship of Dr. Stockli.

Of course, there were better places for me to have started a practice, but I think the critical mistake was not having done a fellowship, especially since my residency was so poor. I wish I had done a fellowship in total joints, which was my main interest. However, after the licensure-board action, any accredited fellowship path, a possible road to career rehabilitation, was essentially closed forever.

Even retraining and switching to family practice/primary care would be problematic, because I could never be sure if I would be insurable, even in this new specialty, or if I could even get a license in another state if a position did not open up in my two currently licensed states. But it is more problematic than that. Simple retraining and reentry programs do not result in board certification. If a doctor is not board certified or eligible, that is a huge strike against him for ever getting a position. A history of license suspension is the second. Most medical corporations now require board eligibility/certification for insurability with their own malpractice insurance company. Few residencies, if any, will offer me a residency position, even if they are one of those less desirable programs that does not fill, since I have already completed a five-year residency. The government will therefore only fund them half the reimbursement rate. My residency spot would actually cost the program to sponsor me. Residencies that do not fill their first-year spots with medical school graduates now require a prolonged convoluted match program for the second-round positions. If one is not in the loop, he can wind up being idle for a whole year. Many programs require a candidate to have graduated from medical school within 5 years. At 63, obviously, it is a dead end for me.

Rescinds from the VA Hospital and New England wasted six months of time in dead-end searches. Rejection anxiety and uncertainty really suck, especially when you have invested so much of your time and life into a narrowly defined profession like medicine, are close to the end of your career, and alternative careers are few and far between because of the job market, advancing age, and the time it takes to retrain.

I would not mind being an aeronautical engineer, but it would not make sense for me to go to school for two to four years and then come out at age sixty-five and expect to get hired. It looks increasingly like some menial type minimum wage work may wind up being my only option. I am a fish out of water.

Incredibly, my daughter thinks she may want to be a doctor. My first reaction was to say *hell no!* Don't even think about it. Haven't you seen enough with all the mental anguish your father has gone through, how I suddenly start cursing in the car or home for seemingly no reason at all, even at Christmas parties? It is a form of posttraumatic stress and it is quite pathological. Nothing I can do about it, especially in view of all the useless evaluations and in-house therapy I received during my exile at the funny farm. These only poured gasoline on the fire. I still hope I can talk her out of it.

Fortunately, my daughter is more tolerant, patient, understanding, and giving. I try to rationalize everything that has transpired in terms of "if this is the course I had to take to have my daughter enter the world, then it was worth it." Even now, as I am typing this, she is playing Mozart's K 37 Concerto No. 1 in F major 1st movement on the piano. I never get tired of hearing it. My fondest memories were sitting in on her piano lessons with a great teacher when she was only about seven. So yes, she would be a good, compassionate doctor, and I will support her in whatever career she chooses. I just pray that she has a less stormy career than mine and that I don't screw up as a parent. But at least she is aware of the treachery of lawyers, hospital administrators, doctors, medical boards, and the government.

Here's hoping that writing this book gives me some badly needed closure, but I doubt it. It has been a very long, bitter, and frustrating endeavor. I have hated it and rushed through it, even though I have had plenty of time to write it while I was "working" doing wound care and spending the other days rather aimlessly.

Every time I try to proofread this, I just get even more angry, more frustrated, and want to add more events to the point that now it has become overly long and repetitive. I am fed up with it and just want to submit this as is and be done with it.

I still wake up very early in the mornings in disbelief and despair that my orthopedic profession is gone forever. I still go to bed at night praying that some random thought does not emerge and trigger a rage to the point that I get up and start screaming, cursing, and threatening to torture and kill my ex-wife, my lawyers, the judges, the medical board, certain doctors, my estranged daughter, her ex-boyfriend, and the former administrator.

I even recently wrote the medical board a rant accusing them of using me as a scapegoat, but of course, it will be to no avail. It will always be conveniently argued that I was represented by counsel, had the opportunity to argue my defense at a hearing, exercised my rights through two appeals, and therefore, no grounds exist for my dissatisfaction. I am just a disgruntled doctor who blames everyone else for his troubles.

On long drives back home every month, it is difficult for these thoughts not to erupt. I am having to make these drives because of my career disruption. It is not only about the huge loss in income, or that I may eventually have to work a menial job long into what should have been good retirement years, or that I may be looking at living in a double wide. Rather, it is the indescribable constant, gnawing anxiety that I do not have a job, nor do I have the prospects of ever getting a real job. I now spend most of my days sitting around the apartment waiting for sale of my office building and possibly my house—at steep losses before I can make further plans.

But then, I step back, rethink, and tell my daughter that it would be my duty to explain the good and the bad about her aspiration(s) to the best of my ability. I don't have to explain the bad. She has seen that in spades, so I would not be failing her in that regard. I think she is beginning to see the decline in my emotional state as I continue to struggle with the realization that I can't get my life back. I have stopped playing my drums, stopped my ham radio, or camping trips. Worried about the cut-off from any income steam, I have stopped travel. I guess I am lucky to have seen a good part of the world, especially under the circumstances. After having promised her that we would stay at the place I had relocated for my wound care job until she finished high school, I realize this will not happen. We will be joining her mother back home on the other side of the state after this school year.

Getting up and going to work as a doctor, from my perspective, obviously was like playing Russian roulette. There was a live round waiting to go off, and it did. I got up and went to work one day and returned home with my life and career forever thrown into chaos. There was no consistent or predictable rule of law affording me recourse. I could never get justice. My medical colleagues, with very few exceptions, were not "nice" people either. One physician on a medical blog site opined this book was an obsession, not about seeking vindication. Another accused me of refusing to accept responsibility for my actions. Yes, I should admit responsibility for my mistakes and not blame others, but I think my focus here has been more on the *degree* to which I have punished for my mistakes, and the double standards which have been applied to me compared to others. My three hospital suspensions and medical license suspension were unprecedented in their harshness and verifiable quantum leaps in severity, to the point that I doubt such punitive standards have ever been applied to another doctor before or since. Instead of recognizing that it was bad enough that one man's life had already been lost, the medical board decided that my career and life needed to be ruined too for public relations. Meanwhile, my former divorce lawyers still practice today, not having missed a step. They screwed up, they made a lot money off me, they lied, and they left me. Having said all this, furiously, and certainly not hopefully, these are my back pages. I can finally say that I have said my piece and move on.

My Back Pages

About the front cover picture: The idea took me less than ten seconds.
I haven't done a drawing since my self-image sketch required for my custody psychological evaluation years ago.

I drew this sketch in less than ten minutes. I was going to send it off to an artist to draw a more "artistic" version. In a split second, I asked myself, what good would that do? The message is clear.

It is simply a smashed gavel reflecting my opinion of the broken legal system and the collateral damage done to the stethoscope, obviously representative of the medical profession, or more precisely, my medical career. Torn apart and useless, as if the gavel had pounded the stethoscope until both were completely broken. Together they lie in a heap.

It is a seemingly violent picture, and is consistent with my underlying rage with the medical and legal systems. After reading the book, I am sure most readers will agree.

Printed in the United States
By Bookmasters